WAR

— 81474

KU-792-368

FOR
REFERENCE
ONLY

THIS BOOK

belongs

to

....

....

THE KINGFISHER
CHILDREN'S
*B*IBLE

Retold by

TREVOR BARNES

KING*f*ISHER

10-1-02

WARRINGTON
BOROUGH
COUNCIL

In this book, CE stands for
Common Era and BCE stands for
Before Common Era, with the
Common Era beginning in the year 0

The publisher would like to thank the following consultants for their help:
Dr Catherine Dooley, OP, Associate Professor in the Department of Religion and Religious
Education, The Catholic University of America, Washington, DC
The Reverend Dr Timothy A Friedrichsen, Assistant Professor of New Testament in the Department
of Religion and Religious Education, The Catholic University of America, Washington, DC
Rabbi Judd Kruger Levingston, Principal at Solomon Schechter High School of New York
Father Gerard Mulligan, CSSR, STL, LSS, Team Minister at the John Paul Centre, Middlesborough
Rabbi Dr Jonathan Romain, Rabbi at Maidenhead Synagogue
Right Reverend John B Taylor, KCVO, former Bishop of St Albans

The publisher would also like to thank the following consultants:
Annette Reynolds, Cathi Thacker and Derek Williams at AD Publishing Services Ltd

EDITORS Jonathan Stroud, Emma Wild, Laura Marshall
SENIOR DESIGNER Jane Tassie
ADDITIONAL DESIGN Jane Buckley, Rebecca Johns
DTP MANAGER Nicky Studdart
PRODUCTION CONTROLLER Debbie Otter
ARTWORK ARCHIVISTS Wendy Allison, Steve Robinson
PICTURE RESEARCH MANAGER Jane Lambert
INDEXER AD Publishing Services Ltd
PROOFREADER Julie Ferris

KINGFISHER

Kingfisher Publications Plc
New Penderel House, 283–288 High Holborn, London WC1V 7HZ
www.kingfisherpub.com

First published by Kingfisher Publications Plc in 2001
2 4 6 8 10 9 7 5 3 1
ITR/0601/C&C/MAR(MAR)/128KMA
Copyright © Kingfisher Publications Plc 2001

All rights reserved. No part of this publication may be reproduced, stored
in a retrieval system or transmitted by any means, electronic, mechanical,
photocopying or otherwise, without the prior permission of the publisher.

A CIP catalogue record for this book is available from the British Library.

ISBN 0 7534 0573 3

Printed in Hong Kong

CONTENTS

INTRODUCTION

There is no other book like the Bible. It is one of the most important books ever written. It has a huge influence on the way in which people understand the world and make sense of their lives.

Strictly speaking, the Bible is not a book at all, but a whole library of books containing history, poetry, laws, prayers, family trees, songs, stories, wise sayings and more, written down over a period of about a thousand years, and completed towards the end of the First Century CE. The writers (many of them unknown) tell a series of stories about a world brought into being by God. They describe God's continuing relationship with creation, whose crowning glory is humanity — men and women, boys and girls. You and me.

At the heart of that relationship is a so-called covenant — a binding agreement between God and human beings, who have the freedom to say, 'Yes, I accept' or 'No, I refuse'. The nature of the cosmic bargain is this: God promises to bless humanity in exchange for humanity's obedience to God. Obedience will be rewarded, while disobedience will be punished. The writers tell of a world which said 'yes' to God's offer, an offer which comes with responsibilities on both sides.

After describing the events of Creation, the writers turn their attention to their shared history. The first major figure is Abraham, *the father of the great nation of Israel, whose acceptance of the covenant ultimately leads his descendants into the Promised Land. But the story does not end there. At times the Israelites obey God, at times they rebel against God. The ups and downs of their fortunes are recorded in the Hebrew Bible, the holy book of the Jewish people.*

Christians refer to this as the Old Testament and look to another collection of Scripture, the New Testament, to complete their understanding of God's purpose for humanity. The New Testament describes the life and message of Jesus Christ, whom Christians believe to be the Messiah, the Son of God and Saviour of the world.

What both sets of Scriptures do is to provide answers to some of the big questions in life like 'Why were we born? How should we behave while we are alive? What happens when we die?' More than that, however, they describe a world in which God is a reality. The Bible's task is to explain why that matters. And how better to explain than by using stories?

The stories you are about to read are only a fraction of those told in the actual Bible. They have been told to children and adults for thousands of years. But they are as meaningful today as they were all those centuries ago. They have changed people's lives. Perhaps they will change yours.

T r e v o r   B a r n e s

THE
Old
TESTAMENT

CREATION

Genesis 1:1 – 2:3

**I**n the beginning, God created the universe. All was chaos and darkness. Deep, raging waters swirled around and covered everything, until the power of God gave the world a shape. God said, "Let there be light!" And there was light.

And the light was good. On the first day of creation, God separated the light from the darkness and called the light Day and the darkness Night.

On the second day, God said, "Let there be a dome above the waters and let it be called Heaven." And so the sky appeared.

On the third day, God said, "Let the waters come together in one place to form the sea and let the dry land appear to make the earth." And so, on the third day of creation, the earth and oceans were formed beneath the sky.

Then God commanded the earth to produce grasses and herbs and seeds and plants of every kind – those bearing fruit and those bearing grain. The plants grew up and covered the earth, and God saw

that they were good.

On the fourth day of creation, God commanded lights to appear in the sky – the Sun to rule over the day, and the Moon and Stars to rule over the night. By these lights, the days, the years and the seasons could now be calculated.

On the fifth day, God commanded the seas and skies to be filled with countless living creatures. Great whales and tiny fish swam in the oceans, while flocks of birds of every size, colour and shape flew joyfully above. God blessed them all and told them to reproduce so that the sea and sky would be full of marvellous living things.

On the sixth day, God ordered the earth to produce every kind of animal – from the largest elephant to the smallest mouse. And when the earth was full, God looked at the result and was very pleased.

Then God said, "Now it is time to make human beings. They will be like me and have something of me in them." And so humanity was created in God's image. God made some humans male and some humans female, and all of them were blessed. "Be fruitful and multiply," God said, "so that your children and your children's children will inhabit every part of the earth and take good care of it. I am putting you in charge of the fish, the birds and the animals. And the plants shall be yours for food."

On the sixth day, the universe was complete. On the seventh day, God rested. For ever more, the seventh day would be set aside as a day of rest. It would be blessed and treated as a holy day, marking the creation of the world.

ADAM AND EVE

Genesis 2:4 – 3:24

When God first made the earth, nothing grew there. Seeds did not sprout, because there was no one to cultivate them. But then a mist appeared, forming droplets of rain that watered the land. And God made man from a handful of dust, breathing the breath of life into his nostrils until he became a living soul.

In the east, in Eden, God planted a garden watered by a cool river. God made trees and beautiful things grow in the garden – flowers that were pretty to look at and fruit that was good to eat. In the middle of the garden stood the Tree of Life and the Tree of Knowledge of Good and Evil.

God took the man – Adam was his name – and placed him in the Garden of Eden, with instructions to eat

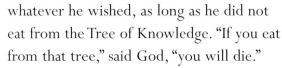

whatever he wished, as long as he did not eat from the Tree of Knowledge. "If you eat from that tree," said God, "you will die."

Adam looked after the garden as he had been told, but after a while he became very lonely. "It is not good for man to be alone," said God, who had made many animals and birds to keep Adam company. Adam gave each one of them a name, but still he felt alone. He needed a true companion.

So God sent Adam into a deep sleep and, as he slept, removed one of his ribs, closed up the wound in his side, and made the rib into a woman. Her name was Eve. When Adam awoke and saw her, he said, "Here is a creature of my own kind, a woman, who is made of flesh and blood and bone like me. Together we shall be one." Adam and Eve walked in the garden together. Although both of them were naked, neither of them felt any shame or embarrassment.

Now, of all the animals that God had made, the snake was the slyest. It slid up to Eve and asked, "Did God really tell you not to eat from certain trees?"

"We can eat from all of them… except from the tree in the middle of the garden," Eve replied. "God has said that if we do that we will certainly die."

"No, no, you will not die," said the snake, "because God knows that as soon as you eat from it, you will be given tremendous power. You will understand Good and Evil and be like God."

The woman saw how beautiful the tree was and how tasty the fruit looked, and she thought to herself how marvellous it would be to be like God and to know everything. So she reached for the fruit and ate it. Then she offered it to her husband, who ate it too. No sooner had they eaten, than something changed. For the first time they saw, to their shame and embarrassment, that they were naked, and they quickly sewed fig leaves together to cover themselves.

At that moment, they heard the sound of God walking in the garden. Adam and Eve hid among the trees, but God called out to Adam and asked, "Where are you?"

"I am here," Adam replied. "I heard your voice and I was afraid because I was naked. So I hid."

And God said, "Who told you that you were naked? Have you eaten from the tree that I told you not to touch?"

Adam replied, "The woman you put here with me offered me some of its fruit and I ate it."

God turned to Eve and asked, "Why did you do such a thing?"

"The snake tricked me into it," she replied.

Then God turned to the snake and said,

"You will be punished for this. You will crawl on your belly for ever more and eat dust for as long as you live."

To Adam and his wife, Eve, God said, "Because you ate the forbidden fruit, the ground beneath your feet will be cursed. It will produce thorns and thistles so that, from now on, working the land will be hard, back-breaking toil. And this work will not be over until you die and return to the earth from which you came. For you are dust, and to dust you will return."

Then God said, "Now that you have knowledge of Good and Evil, you cannot remain in Eden, in case you eat from the Tree of Life and live forever."

So God made coats out of animal skins and clothed them both, before sending them out of the beautiful Garden of Eden into the world beyond.

CAIN AND ABEL

Genesis 4:1-16

A dam and Eve had two sons – Cain, who grew up to be a farmer and Abel, who became a shepherd. One day, Cain gathered up part of his crop and gave it to God as an offering. His brother Abel gave the Lord a lamb.

God valued Abel's offering far more than Cain's. This made Cain angry and upset, and the disappointment showed on his face.

"Why are you looking like that?" God asked. "If you do good, I will treat you well. If you do evil, then your sinful nature will never set you free."

Cain suggested to Abel that they go out together into the fields, but when they got there Cain turned on Abel and killed him.

"Where is your brother?" God asked.

"I do not know," replied Cain. "Am I my brother's keeper?"

Then God said, "Abel's blood is crying out to me from the ground. For committing this terrible crime you are cursed. From this day on, your crops will be diseased and you will roam the earth like an outcast."

Cain pleaded with God. "You are too harsh," he said. "You have driven me off the land and pushed me away from you. Everyone who comes near me now will want to kill me."

But God put a mark on Cain so that people would recognize him and leave him alone. Then Cain fled from God and went to live in the Land of Nod, east of Eden.

NOAH AND THE FLOOD

Genesis 6 – 7

Many years passed and the number of people on earth increased. But their behaviour grew worse and worse. Evil was all they cared about. In fact, people were now so wicked that God began to regret having created them in the first place.

So God said, "I have created the world. Now I will destroy it. I will destroy everything – men, women, animals, birds and insects. I am sorry I created them at all."

But God made one exception, and his name was Noah. Unlike everybody else, Noah was a truly good man who did everything the Lord commanded.

And God said to Noah, "I have decided to destroy everything I have created, but you and your family will be spared. I will make a covenant – a firm agreement – with you. Keep your side of it and I will keep mine.

"Build a huge wooden boat three storeys high with many rooms in it. Be sure to make the boat watertight, with plenty of tar to seal up any cracks. When you have finished, gather together two of every kind of animal, bird and insect and load them into the boat. Then climb aboard with your wife and sons and their wives. Make sure

you have food for them and for the animals because in a short while I will send rain from the skies. For forty days and forty nights, it will pour down onto the earth and flood it. Everything will be destroyed except for you, your family and the animals. When the flood subsides, this life will repopulate the world."

Noah did as he was told. The animals went into the boat two by two, male and female, side by side. Soon, just as God had promised, the rain began to fall in torrents. As the waters rose and the ground was submerged, Noah's boat began to float.

The rain fell and the water deepened, until it covered the tops of even the highest mountains. Every living thing that moved on the earth died, drowned beneath the waves. Everything was destroyed except the boat – Noah's ark – which, with its precious cargo, floated on the surface of an endless sea.

GOD'S PROMISE

Genesis 8:1 — 9:17

God did not forget Noah during the great flood. He and his family and all the animals were kept safe inside the ark. Eventually, the rain stopped falling. A wind was sent to blow away the water, and when the flood started to go down, the ark came to rest on the top of Mount Ararat.

Noah opened a window and sent out a raven to see if the water had gone down enough to let everybody out. But the raven just flew back and forth above the waters. Then Noah sent out a dove, but it could not find a dry spot on which to land.

Noah sent the dove out again and this time, when it came back, it had an olive branch in its beak. Noah knew then that the waters had finally subsided. Soon God told him to leave the ark, and to take his family and the animals with him, so that they could start to repopulate the earth.

The first thing Noah did was to build an altar and give thanks to the Lord. God was very pleased and blessed Noah and his family, saying to them, "Be fruitful and multiply and fill the earth again. The animals will be food for you, but take care of them according to my laws."

Then God said, "Never again will I destroy the earth. And this promise is not only for you, but for every future generation."

Just then, a rainbow appeared in the sky and God said, "Look! This is a sign of the covenant. Every time I see a rainbow, I shall remember my promise."

THE TOWER OF BABEL

Genesis 11:1-9

*N*oah's sons had many children, and their children had children too, so that the earth was filled with people who all spoke the same language. As they came from the east, they settled on the plains of Babylonia and there they learnt to build.

They took clay from the ground and baked it hard to make bricks, which they stuck together with mortar. With these they built towers and fortresses and looked on them with pride. But their pride soon turned to arrogance. They began to construct vast buildings – each one bigger than the last – until one day, they proposed building a city with a gigantic tower that would reach up to Heaven itself. "We shall become famous throughout the world," they said.

"This is only the beginning of their vanity," said God, who went down among them and confused their speech. No longer able to understand each other, they were forced to disperse all over the earth.

From then on, the tower – now known as the Tower of Babel – was a reminder of how content they had once been, before vanity and the 'babble' of different languages had torn them apart forever.

THE STORY OF ABRAM

Genesis 12

In the city of Haran lived a man named Abram. One day, God spoke to him and said, "Leave your country and your relatives. Leave your father's house and make your way to a country that I have set aside for you. Then I will bless you and make you the father of a great nation."

It was hard for an old man of seventy-five to leave behind his home and friends and set off into the unknown. But Abram did as he was told because he trusted in the Lord. "I shall bless all those who bless you and curse all those who curse you," said God. "And through you and your family all families and nations on earth will be blessed."

So Abram, who was a rich man, took his wife Sarai, his nephew Lot, and all their servants, sheep, cattle and other possessions, and set off for the land of Canaan far away.

When they arrived in Canaan, they stopped first at the town of Shechem, which was a place of worship for the Canaanite people. Here God appeared to Abram and renewed his promise to him, saying, "This is the land I am giving to you and your descendants." Immediately, Abram built an altar to the Lord and offered up his thanks.

After that, he moved on through Canaan, building altars to the Lord wherever he pitched his camp. But then a terrible famine settled on the land, killing people and animals alike. It became so severe that Abram and his family were forced to leave and live for a while in Egypt.

As they approached the border, Abram spoke to his wife, Sarai. "You are a very beautiful woman," he said, "and when the Egyptians see you and realize that you are my wife, they will kill me and take you for themselves. But if you tell them you are my sister, they will spare me."

Abram was right. The Egyptians saw how beautiful Sarai was and told Pharaoh. He immediately took her as his wife and installed her in his palace. In return he treated Abram very well, giving him gifts of sheep, cattle and slaves.

But God was not happy with this arrangement and sent plagues to punish Pharaoh for taking another man's wife. At last, Pharaoh called Abram and said to him, "What have you done to me? Why did you not tell me Sarai was your wife? Why did you say she was your sister and lead me to believe I could take her for my own? You must leave the country at once! Take your wife and all your belongings and go!"

So Abram left Egypt, and returned with his family to the land of Canaan.

ABRAHAM AND LOT

Genesis 13; 15 – 19

Abram made his way to the southern part of Canaan, taking with him his sheep and cattle, and his silver and gold. At first, he travelled with his nephew Lot who, like Abram, was a rich man. But the land was not fertile enough to support both families, and soon quarrels broke out among their servants.

Abram and Lot decided it would be best to separate. Abram went to live at Hebron, but Lot decided to move to the lush Plain of Jordan, where he settled near Sodom – a city full of wicked people who sinned against the Lord.

One night, Abram had a vision. God spoke to him and promised him many rewards. "But Lord, what good will they do me?" Abram asked. "I have no children, so my servant will inherit my property."

"No, he will not," said God. "Your own son will inherit what you have. Go outside the tent." When Abram had done so, God said, "Look up at the sky. You will have as many descendants as there are stars in the heavens. Trust me. I am the Lord who called you out of your homeland."

Time passed, and still Sarai had no children. One day, she suggested to Abram

that he should have a child by her Egyptian slave girl, Hagar. He agreed, and at the age of eighty-six, he had a son, Ishmael.

When Abram was ninety-nine years old, God appeared to him again, saying, "Obey me and do only what is right. I will make a covenant with you."

"I promise," said God, "that you will be the father of many nations. As a sign of this promise, your name will no longer be Abram, but Abraham, which means 'father of many'. And this covenant will last forever.

"The land of Canaan will be yours," the Lord went on. "And I alone will be your God. But you, and those who come after you, must keep your side of the covenant too.

"As a sign of this you must be circumcised. Any man who has not been circumcised will no longer be considered one of my people.

"You must not call your wife Sarai any

more. From now on, she is to be called Sarah. That, too, is a sign. I will bless her and give you a son by her. And there will be kings among her descendants."

When he heard this, Abraham began to laugh. "How can a man who is nearly one hundred have a child?" he said. "And Sarah is far too old to give birth! Why not let Ishmael inherit from me?"

"No," said God. "Sarah will give birth to your son and his name will be Isaac."

Some days later, the Lord appeared to Abraham again. In the heat of the midday sun, he saw three strangers standing by his tent. Abraham invited them to sit down and eat a meal, and the men agreed.

"Where is your wife?" asked one.

"She is inside the tent," Abraham replied.

"In nine months' time, she will have a son," the stranger said.

Inside the tent, Sarah heard this. "How can I have a child at my age?" she laughed.

"Nothing is too hard for the Lord," the stranger said, and Abraham knew that it was God and two angels who were before him.

After the meal, the two angels went on to Sodom, while God stayed with Abraham. Then the Lord told Abraham that the city of Sodom and its neighbour, Gomorrah, were so wicked that they would now be destroyed.

"Surely you would not destroy innocent people along with the guilty," said Abraham. "If there are fifty innocent people there – or even ten – would you destroy them all?"

"No," replied God. "If there were just ten innocent people found within their walls, I would spare the cities for their sake."

Lot, who was now living in Sodom, was sitting by the city gate when the two strangers approached him. Lot greeted the visitors warmly, and invited them to eat with him. But while they were eating, the men of Sodom surrounded the house and threatened the strangers with violence.

Lot went out and pleaded with the mob to respect the protection and hospitality he was offering his guests. But the men refused and began to break down the door.

Inside the house, the two strangers were listening to the commotion. They pulled Lot back inside and struck the men outside with blindness. "Leave the city immediately," they said to Lot. "Take your family and go. We have come from the Lord. All the people of the city are wicked, and we shall destroy them."

Seeing Lot hesitate, the angels took him by the hand and led him, his wife and his two daughters out of the city. "Run for your lives," they shouted. "Destruction is at hand. And whatever you do, do not look back!"

Lot and his family fled just as dawn was breaking. Suddenly, the sky was lit up with flames, as God sent fiery rain to wipe out Sodom and Gomorrah. No one there survived. Every living thing perished.

But Lot's wife ignored the instruction the angels had given and turned to watch the cities burn. "No!" cried Lot. "Do not look back!" But it was too late. The moment she looked, she was turned into a pillar of salt.

Early the next morning, Abraham, who was camped at the other edge of the valley, looked down at a scene of devastation. It was as if the whole valley was one gigantic furnace, belching out smoke from the smouldering ruins of Sodom and Gomorrah.

ABRAHAM AND ISAAC

Genesis 21:1-20; 22:1-19

G od's promise to Sarah and Abraham was fulfilled, and in her old age, Sarah became pregnant. When she realized that she was expecting a baby so late in life, she laughed and could hardly believe it. But sure enough, she was blessed with a son, Isaac, who was born when Abraham was one hundred years old.

But Abraham already had a son, Ishmael, whose mother was the Egyptian slave, Hagar. Now that she had a son of her own, Sarah became jealous of them and told Abraham to send Hagar and Ishmael away from the tribe. Abraham was greatly saddened by this because he loved Ishmael. But God said to him, "Do not worry. I will take care of them and make Ishmael's children into a great nation."

So the next day, Abraham woke up early and prepared a bag of food and a skin of water for Hagar. Then he put them on her shoulder and sent her and Ishmael away. God watched over them, and in time Ishmael married an Egyptian woman.

Many years later, God decided to test Abraham's faithfulness. "Take your son," God said, "your only son, Isaac, whom you love so much, and go to the land of Moriah. There on a mountain that I will show you, offer him up to me as a sacrifice."

Next morning, Abraham saddled his donkey and loaded it up with wood for the sacrificial fire. He called Isaac and, accompanied by two of his men, set off for

the spot that God had told him about. On the third day, Abraham saw the mountain in the distance and he took his two servants to one side. "Stay here with the donkey," he said. "The boy and I will go over there and pray a while. We will be back soon." Then he took the wood and handed it over to Isaac for him to carry. In the meantime, Abraham had been preparing hot coals, which he now took with him to start the sacrificial fire. Finally, he picked up his knife, and father and son set off together.

"Father," said Isaac, "we have the wood and the coals to start the fire, but where is the lamb for the burnt offering?"

"God will provide it," said Abraham. And the two of them walked on.

When they arrived at the spot, Abraham built an altar and carefully arranged the wood on top of it. Then he tied Isaac's hands, laid him on the altar, and raised the knife to kill his son.

Just at that moment, an angel of the Lord called out to him. "Abraham, Abraham!" it said. "Do not touch the boy. Now that I know how great your trust is in

God, you need not sacrifice your son."

Abraham looked up and saw a ram caught by its horns in a nearby bush. He walked over to it and brought it back to the altar, where he sacrificed it instead of his son. And the angel spoke again. "The Lord says: 'Because you were prepared to sacrifice your only son for my sake, I shall bless you and give you as many descendants as there are stars in the sky, or grains of sand on the seashore. Your children's children will defeat all their enemies, and through them all nations on earth will be richly rewarded.

And all this will happen because you obeyed my command.'"

So Abraham went back to his servants, and together with Isaac, returned to his home in Beersheba.

REBECCA

Genesis 24

The years passed. Sarah died, and Abraham himself grew very old. One day, he summoned his most trusted servant and said, "Before I die, choose a wife for Isaac. But do not choose her from the women of Canaan. She must come from the land of my birth, Mesopotamia, which I left so many years ago."

Abraham gave his servant ten camels and sent him off on the long journey to the land of Mesopotamia. After many weeks, the servant arrived at the edge of a town. Here he stopped by a well, where he knew that the women would come to fetch water. Then he prayed to God for a sign.

"I shall ask one of the young women for a drink," he prayed. "If she also offers me water for the camels, then – with your help – I shall know she is meant to be Isaac's wife."

Before he had finished praying, a very beautiful young woman arrived, carrying a jar on her shoulder. Her name was Rebecca. The servant asked her for a drink and when she had poured him some water, she offered to fetch him water for his camels as well.

The servant knew that God had answered him. He took out an expensive gold earring and two gold bracelets and gave them to Rebecca. Then he asked her if he could spend the night in her father's house.

Rebecca's family made the servant very welcome. They brought straw for his camels and food for him and his men. Then the servant told them about Abraham, who had

been blessed by God. He also told them why he had come.

"Now you must decide whether Rebecca should come back with me to be Isaac's wife," he said.

"How can we refuse to do God's will?" said Rebecca's father. "Take her with you."

To mark the engagement, the servant gave the family many expensive presents, and offered Rebecca gold and silver jewellery and beautiful clothes.

The next morning the family was reluctant to see Rebecca go. "Let her stay here for just a few more days," they said.

"Don't make us stay any longer," replied the servant. "I must return to Abraham."

The family called for Rebecca.

"Do you want to go with this man?" they asked her.

"I do," she replied.

Then they let her go with their blessing.

So Rebecca came to Isaac's house, and became his wife, and Isaac loved her very much. Not long after that, Abraham died, and after his death, his son Isaac was blessed by God.

JACOB AND ESAU

Genesis 25:19-34

After a time, Rebecca bore Isaac two sons. While she was expecting the twins, she could feel them moving inside her and it seemed to her that they were fighting with each other – even before they were born.

Rebecca was troubled by this, so she asked God what was happening to her.

And God said, "You will give birth to two boys, who will grow up to be the leaders of two nations at war. One of them will be stronger than the other and the older one will serve the younger."

The time came for her to give birth. The first child to be born had rough, red skin and was covered in a thick coat of hair. He was called Esau. When the second child was born, he was seen to be holding on to Esau's heel. He was called Jacob.

As the boys grew up, Esau became a skilful hunter and loved the outdoor life, while Jacob was a quiet man who preferred to spend his time at home. Isaac favoured Esau above his younger twin and was particularly fond of the tasty meats he would bring him from his hunting trips. But Rebecca had her favourite too – Jacob.

In those days, the first-born son had special rights and privileges. It was the custom for the eldest son to become the head of the household when his father died and for him to inherit a large portion of the family property. These privileges were usually carefully guarded.

However, when Jacob and Esau had grown up into young men, something important happened that changed their lives forever and turned them into the bitterest of enemies.

One day, Jacob was preparing a meal of stew, when Esau, faint with hunger, came in from the fields.

"Let me have some of that stew," said Esau. "I'm starving."

"You can have some in exchange for your rights as the first-born son," replied Jacob.

Esau did not take long deciding. "I'm so hungry I could faint away," he said to himself. "What use are my birth rights compared to a hearty meal?"

"Well?" said Jacob.

"It's a deal," said Esau.

So Jacob gave Esau some stew and a piece of bread and when Esau's strength returned he went on his way. That was how much Esau valued his birth rights! He was prepared to sell them for a bowl of stew.

Later, Esau came to regret his hasty decision, but it was too late. His birth rights had gone to his younger brother.

JACOB'S TRICK

Genesis 27

As Isaac got older his eyesight began to fail. One day, he called Esau, the elder son, and told him that, being close to death, he wanted to give him a blessing. "But before I do, take your bow and arrows and go out and hunt an animal for me," he said, "so that I can taste your delicious meat for one last time."

Rebecca was listening to this. She had always wanted her favourite son Jacob to have the blessing instead. As soon as Esau had left, she said to Jacob, "Go out and fetch me two fat young goats so that I can prepare the meat your father likes. Then take it to him and receive his blessing yourself."

"But, Mother," said Jacob, "Esau has hairy skin and my skin is smooth. When my father touches me, he will know I am playing a trick on him and he will curse me instead."

"Just do as I say," she said.

When Jacob returned, Rebecca made him change into Esau's clothes. She cooked the food, then placed the goatskins over his arm and across his shoulders.

Jacob went to Isaac and said, "Here I am."

His father, by now almost blind, said, "Who are you?"

"I am Esau," said Jacob. "Esau, your first-born son. I have prepared you this meat. Please give me your blessing."

"But how did you manage to come back so quickly?" asked his father.

"With God's help," said Jacob.

"Come nearer," Isaac said, "and let me touch you." So Jacob held out the arm covered in goatskin for his father to hold.

"How strange," said Isaac. "The voice sounds like Jacob's, but the rough arm feels like Esau's. Come a little closer and kiss me." As Jacob did so, Isaac could smell Esau's clothes and he was convinced it was his first-born son in front of him. And so he blessed him – "May your fields be fertile. May you have plenty of corn and wine. And may people serve you."

After Jacob left, Esau came back from his hunting trip and brought food to his father.

"But I have eaten," said Isaac, "and given my final blessing. Who are you?"

"Your elder son, Esau," he said.

Isaac began to tremble and said, "In that case, your brother has tricked me!"

"Give me your blessing, Father," said Esau.

"I cannot," Isaac replied. "Your brother has taken your blessing. I have made him master over you. Now I cannot help you."

"Once again, Jacob has cheated me out of something that was mine," cried Esau. "After my father dies, I shall kill him!" But Rebecca learnt of this and warned Jacob to run away.

Jacob's Dream

Genesis 28

 **J**acob set out for Mesopotamia, where his father had told him to find a wife. All day he travelled. At sunset, he stopped, and using a stone as a pillow, lay down to rest. That night, he had a strange dream.

He dreamt he saw a stairway stretching from earth to Heaven and on it were angels going up and down. At the top he saw the figure of the Lord God who said, "I am the God of Abraham and of Isaac. The land on which you sleep will be yours. I am giving it to you, and you will have as many descendants as there are grains of sand on the seashore. I shall look after you wherever you go and one day bring you back to this land."

Then Jacob awoke and was afraid. He felt the presence of God all around him and thought he was at the gate of Heaven.

The next morning, he rose early, took the stone he had used as a pillow, and poured oil on it. He called the spot Bethel and dedicated it to God with this promise: "If you stay with me and protect me, then you will be my God."

JACOB'S EXILE AND RETURN

Genesis 29 – 32

Jacob headed eastwards, making for the home of his uncle, Laban. When he was almost there, he stopped by a well, and soon afterwards he saw Laban's daughter, Rachel, approaching with her sheep. Jacob immediately introduced himself.

Rachel was overjoyed to discover that Jacob was her cousin. She rushed home to tell her father the good news. Laban too was delighted and he welcomed Jacob as part of the family. Jacob stayed with Laban for a month, working on his land. One day, Laban said, "You should be paid for all the work you are doing. How much do you want?"

Laban had two daughters – Leah, the elder, and Rachel, who was very beautiful. By now Jacob was in love with Rachel, so he answered, "I will work for you for seven years, if you

will let me marry Rachel."

Laban agreed. For seven years, Jacob worked for his uncle, but to him they seemed like seven days because he was so completely in love.

At the end of that time, however, Laban changed his mind. He gave Jacob his elder daughter, Leah, instead. Jacob was furious. "I have served you faithfully for Rachel!" he said. "Why have you deceived me?"

"We always give our elder daughter in marriage first," Laban replied smoothly. "But I will give you Rachel now too, providing you work for me for another seven years." Jacob could only agree.

So Jacob now had two wives. He worked hard for Laban for seven more years, and helped to make his uncle rich. Although he loved Rachel more than Leah, she was unable to bear him any children. But Leah bore him six sons – Reuben, Simeon, Levi, Judah, Issachar and Zebulun. In desperation Rachel said, "Here is my slave girl, Bilhah. Sleep with her and let her have

a child for me. That way I can at least be a mother through her." Twice Bilhah became pregnant and presented Jacob with two sons, Dan and Naphtali. When Leah realized she would have no more children of her own, she offered Jacob her slave girl, Zilpah, who gave birth to two more boys, Gad and Asher.

At last, God remembered Rachel and answered her prayer with a son, Joseph.

After the birth of Rachel's son, Jacob asked Laban to let him leave and return to his homeland. But Laban refused – after all, Jacob had helped him to grow rich. The atmosphere between the two families got worse and finally Jacob decided to leave without telling anyone. When Laban was away, he loaded his wives and children on camels, and driving his livestock in front of him, set off for his father's home.

As they drew near to his homeland, Jacob began to grow fearful. He was sure his brother Esau would hear of his arrival, and come seeking revenge. To prevent this, Jacob sent messengers on ahead with a peace offering, but they soon came back with the news that Esau had gathered four hundred men and was hurrying to find Jacob. In terror, Jacob prayed to God for help.

That night a strange thing happened. Jacob had sent his wives and children off ahead to leave him time to think alone. Suddenly, a man appeared before him and began to wrestle with him. All night they fought, until dawn broke. They seemed to be evenly matched until the stranger touched Jacob on the hip, making him limp, but still Jacob held on. At last the stranger

asked Jacob to let him go, but Jacob refused. "Not unless you bless me," he said.

The stranger said, "What is your name?"

"Jacob," came the reply.

"From now on you will be called Israel – 'he who struggles with God' – because you have struggled with God and men and won."

"What is your name?" asked Jacob.

"Why do you need to know?" the stranger said, and blessing Jacob, vanished from his sight.

"I have seen God face to face, yet I am still alive," said Jacob.

But now the time for his meeting with Esau was at hand. When Jacob saw his brother and the four hundred men approaching he feared the worst. He walked towards his brother and bowed down to him seven times. But Esau threw his arms around Jacob and, with tears streaming down his cheeks, hugged him tightly. Now Jacob too was crying and he offered his brother gifts saying, "Please accept them. To see your face is like seeing the face of God. You have been so kind and forgiving." And so it was that the brothers were reunited at last.

JOSEPH AND HIS BROTHERS

Genesis 37

Jacob settled back in the land of Canaan. He now had twelve sons, for Rachel had given birth to his youngest, Benjamin. Of all his sons, Joseph was Jacob's favourite. To show his love, Jacob made him a fine coat woven with threads of many colours. But the special attention Joseph received made his brothers hate him.

One night, Joseph had a dream. When he told it to his brothers, it made them hate him even more.

"We were all in the field tying up sheaves of wheat," he said, "when my sheaf suddenly stood up straight. Then your sheaves formed a circle around it and bowed down to it."

"So you think that means you can lord it over us, do you?" they sneered.

A while later, Joseph had another dream in which he saw the sun, the moon and the stars bowing down to him. This time he told it to his father as well as to his brothers. Jacob was furious. "What is this dream of yours supposed to mean?" he asked. "Do you expect all the family to bow down before you?" All the same, Jacob could not get the dream out of his mind. Joseph's brothers despised him more than ever.

One day, Jacob asked Joseph to join his brothers in the fields. "Check that your brothers are safe and well and that the flock is being properly looked after," he said. "Then come back and tell me."

But as soon as the brothers saw Joseph approaching, their anger and resentment got the better of them. There and then, they decided to murder him.

"Here comes the dreamer," they said. "Let's kill him and drop his body into a pit. We can say that he was eaten by a wild animal and nobody will be any the wiser. Let's see what his dreaming makes of that!"

Then Reuben spoke up. He did not have the courage to disagree, but he thought their plan was going too far. "No, let's not kill him," he said. "Let's just leave him in a pit in the desert." Reuben hoped to be able to rescue Joseph later and take him back home to his father. And with that he went off to tend the sheep.

When Joseph came up to his brothers, the rest of them pounced on him. Despite his frantic pleas, they stripped him of his colourful coat and threw him into one of the nearby dry wells. No sooner had they done this, than they saw a group of Ishmaelite merchants coming towards them. The merchants were on their way from Gilead to Egypt, and were loaded up with spices and precious resins. This gave one of the brothers an idea.

"What good will it do us," said Judah, "if we kill our brother and cover up the murder? Why not simply sell him to these Ishmaelites? That way we will be spared getting our hands dirty with violence. He is our flesh and blood after all."

The brothers readily agreed, and when the traders came by on their camels, they pulled Joseph out of the well and sold him for twenty pieces of silver. Then the Ishmaelites carried Joseph off to Egypt.

A little later, Reuben, who was unaware of what had happened, went back to the well and found to his great distress that Joseph was not there. He rushed to his brothers and said, "He's gone! What am I going to do?"

Meanwhile his brothers had killed a goat and dipped Joseph's coat in the blood. They took it to their father and said, "We have found this in the fields. Does it belong to Joseph?"

To his horror, Jacob recognized it immediately. "Yes, it is his," he cried in grief. "A wild animal must have attacked him and eaten him alive."

Jacob was inconsolable. He mourned his son for many days. His children tried to comfort him, but they could not.

"I shall be full of sorrow for as long as I live," he said, weeping. "And I shall go to my grave mourning my son."

But what he did not know was that Joseph was still alive. By now the traders had arrived in Egypt and had sold him as a slave to one of Pharaoh's men.

— 33 —

JOSEPH IN EGYPT

Genesis 39 — 40

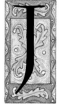**J**oseph the slave was sold to Potiphar, one of Pharaoh's senior officers and captain of the Palace Guard. He was put straight to work, but God took care of Joseph and helped him to become successful at everything he turned his hand to.

Potiphar noticed this and was so pleased with Joseph that he put him in charge of all his household business. As a result, the Egyptian's house was blessed and everything in it flourished.

Joseph was a strong, handsome young man, and after a while Potiphar's wife began to feel very attracted to him. She asked him to come to her bedchamber and lie with her, but he refused.

"Look," he said, "my master has put me in charge of the household because he trusts me. He lets me have everything I need, but that does not include you. How could I do such a sinful thing? It would be a crime against God."

But still she pleaded and pleaded. And still Joseph said no. All this was very difficult for him because he did not want to upset his master's wife, but neither did he want to break God's Law by committing a sin. He decided that it would be better for him to stay out of the way.

But this did not work. Potiphar's wife took every opportunity to follow Joseph about the house, asking the same question.

One day, when Joseph was alone, she grabbed hold of him by his robe. "Joseph, come to my chamber and lie down with me," she begged.

At this, Joseph ran away from her, leaving his robe in her hand. As he did so, Potiphar's wife let out a bloodcurdling scream, and when her servants rushed in, she told them that Joseph had tried to attack her. "See how the Israelite has insulted our hospitality," she said. "He came to attack me and ran off when I screamed."

She kept the robe with her as evidence and showed it to her husband when he returned. Potiphar was beside himself with rage and immediately had Joseph thrown into prison.

But even now God took care of Joseph. He became very popular with the head jailer who soon put him in charge of the day-to-day running of the jail. He also had responsibility for some of the prisoners – in particular the new arrivals. In time, these included Pharaoh's personal wine taster and his chief baker, who had both annoyed their master. Joseph was told to keep an eye on them.

One night, both of them had disturbing

dreams and were very upset when they woke up the next morning. Joseph noticed this and asked them why they were so distressed. "Our dreams trouble us," said one, "and no one can tell us what they mean."

"Only God can show us the meaning of dreams," said Joseph. "Tell me exactly what you dreamt."

The wine taster spoke first. "I dreamt I saw a grapevine," he said, "and the vine had three branches. All of a sudden it sprouted leaves and then, just as quickly, ripe bunches of grapes appeared. I was holding Pharaoh's cup at the time, so I picked the grapes and squeezed their juice into it. Then I handed the cup to Pharaoh."

"This is what your dream means," said Joseph promptly. "The three branches stand for three days. In three days' time, Pharaoh will pardon you, set you free and give you your old job back."

The wine taster listened carefully as

Joseph continued. "But when you are free, please make a point of telling Pharaoh all the good things I have been doing in this prison so that he will let me out, too. After all, I have done nothing to deserve being here in the first place. I was kidnapped from my homeland and brought to Egypt as a captive."

When the chief baker heard all this and realized Joseph's interpretation was favourable, he turned to Joseph and described his own dream to him. "In my dream," the chief baker began, "I was carrying three bread baskets on my head. The top one was full of cakes and pastries for Pharaoh, but a flock of birds was eating them."

Joseph immediately told him what the dream meant. "The three baskets stand for three days and within three days Pharaoh will have you executed. He will chop off your head and hang your body on a pole, where the birds will peck at it."

Three days later, Pharaoh held a splendid banquet for all his staff to celebrate his birthday. When it was over, he brought out his wine taster and his baker and stood them in front of everyone. He released the wine taster and gave him back his old job, but the baker he had executed – exactly as Joseph had foretold.

As for the happy wine taster, he completely forgot about Joseph and never once gave him another thought.

JOSEPH AND PHARAOH

Genesis 41

or two whole years, Joseph remained in prison. Then, one day, Pharaoh had a dream. He dreamt that he was standing by the River Nile, when seven well-fed cows emerged from the water and began to graze in the field nearby.

They had not been grazing long when seven more cows – this time horribly thin and bony – came up out of the river. Then a strange thing happened – the thin cows fell upon the fat ones and ate them up, and Pharaoh woke up with a start.

He went back to sleep again, but was troubled by a similar dream. This time he saw seven ripe ears of corn sprouting on a single stalk. Then seven withered ears of corn, parched by the wind, grew out from the stalk, and swallowed up the seven ripe ones. Once again, Pharaoh woke up in a sweat, puzzled and disturbed.

In the morning, Pharaoh sent for his advisors and court magicians and described his dreams to them. But no one could tell him what they meant. Then the wine taster spoke up. "I must confess that I have forgotten to tell you something very important," he said. "I forgot to mention the Hebrew slave who was in charge of the prison a couple of years ago when the baker and I had offended you, Your Majesty. We too had strange dreams which he interpreted for us. And things turned out just as he had said."

Immediately Joseph was sent for. He was taken out of jail and smartened up, then brought before Pharaoh.

"I have heard that you can interpret dreams," Pharaoh said. "Is that the truth?"

"No," answered Joseph. "Only God can do that."

"Well, listen to my dreams," said Pharaoh. "No one else can make sense of them. First I dreamt of seven thin cows eating up seven fat cows – not that you could tell they had eaten them, because the thin cows were just as scrawny afterwards as they were before. Then I had a dream about seven parched ears of corn gobbling up seven ripe ones. How do you explain that? None of my advisors can."

Joseph said to Pharaoh, "The two dreams mean the same thing. They are God's way of telling you something. The cows and the corn represent years. The plump cows and the ripe corn mean good harvests, and the thin cows and parched corn mean famine. There will be seven years of record crops in the land of Egypt, followed by seven years of famine. And when the famine strikes, all the good years will be forgotten. The fact that you had the same kind of dream twice means this is what God has in store for you very shortly.

"Now, Your Majesty," Joseph continued, "you should appoint a wise man to take charge of the country, and you should choose other officials to set aside food from the good years to feed the people during the bad times. That way Egypt will not starve."

Pharaoh listened and said, "You are that man, Joseph. Since God has shown you all this, it is clear that there is nobody with greater wisdom than you. I now appoint you Governor of Egypt. Your authority will be second only to mine and I shall instruct the people to do as you say."

With that Pharaoh took off his ring and put it on Joseph's finger. He dressed him in

fine clothes and put a gold chain of office round his neck. Then he gave him a royal chariot to ride in. As Joseph toured the city all the people bowed down to him, hailing him as their Governor. Joseph was only thirty years old.

Sure enough, for the next seven years, the land produced record harvests. Joseph measured out large quantities of food and stored it all in the cities. Soon there was so much corn that he gave up measuring it.

But the years of plenty came to an end, just as Joseph had foretold. The crops failed and famine began to take hold. There was starvation in every country – except for Egypt, where Joseph's grain stores were crammed to bursting.

As the famine worsened, Joseph ordered all the stores to be opened and the corn distributed. Soon people were travelling from many lands to buy corn from Joseph, the Governor of Egypt.

Joseph's Brothers in Egypt

Genesis 42 – 49

There was famine in the land of Canaan, and Joseph's family was suffering as much as everyone else. Then Jacob learnt that there was corn to be had in Egypt, and he instructed ten of his sons to go there to buy food. However, his youngest son Benjamin was ordered to stay at home, in case harm came to him.

When the ten brothers arrived in Egypt, they paid their respects to Joseph, the Governor of the land, not recognizing who he was. Joseph recognized them immediately – but pretended not to.

"Where are you from?" he asked gruffly.

"From Canaan," they replied. "We have come to buy food."

"You are spies," said Joseph. "You have come to see where our country's defences are weak."

"No, sir," they said. "We are just ordinary men from Canaan. There were twelve of us, but one of our brothers is dead and the other is at home with our father."

"I still say you are spies," said Joseph, "and I will not believe you until I see this brother for myself. But for now I am putting you under lock and key." And with that he put them in jail for three days.

On the third day, Joseph had his brothers brought before him again. "I shall keep one of you here as hostage," he told them. "The rest of you may go home. But if you do not

bring your youngest brother back here to me, the hostage will die." Then he had Simeon taken aside and tied up.

All the brothers blamed themselves for the trouble they were in. "I told you not to harm Joseph," shouted Reuben. "But you wouldn't listen. This is our punishment!" What the brothers did not know was that Joseph understood everything they were saying, even though he pretended not to by using the services of an interpreter. In the end he could listen no longer and had to walk away, so that they would not see how upset he was. At last, he composed himself, and told his men to send the brothers on their way with full sacks of corn.

When they got home, the brothers told their father what had happened. Jacob was terrified. "Am I to lose all my sons?" he cried. "Joseph is dead. Simeon is a prisoner. And now you want to take Benjamin from me!"

Then Reuben said, "Put Benjamin in my care and I promise, on my own sons' lives, to bring him back safe and sound."

At first Jacob refused to let them go. But the famine grew still worse, and finally Jacob was forced to send the brothers back to Egypt to buy more food. This time, Benjamin went with them.

When the brothers came before Joseph again, he brought Simeon out to them, and ordered his servants to prepare a meal for them all. The brothers were confused and afraid, suspecting an elaborate trick. But Joseph had been moved to tears at the sight of his younger brother, and at the feast that evening, Benjamin was given five times as much as anyone else.

When the time came for the brothers to depart, Joseph devised a plan. As their sacks were being filled with grain, he ordered his men to hide his silver drinking cup in Benjamin's saddlebag.

The brothers set off, but they had not ridden far when Joseph's steward caught up with them. "Stop, thieves!" he shouted. "You have stolen my master's precious cup! Is this how you repay his kindness?"

When the panic-stricken brothers swore they were innocent, the steward replied, "Very well. But if I find that one of you has the cup, he shall become my master's slave."

Sure enough, when the packs were searched, the cup was found in Benjamin's bag. At this, the brothers tore their clothes in grief. Then they were led back in shame to Joseph's house, where they flung themselves at his feet.

"Do not arrest Benjamin!" Judah cried. "We promised our father that we would return him safely. Take me instead!"

By now Joseph could see that his brothers were changed men, and they believed that what they had done all those years ago had led to this punishment from God. He could not keep up the pretence any longer and burst into tears. "I am Joseph your brother," he said. "Is my father still alive?"

His brothers were speechless with astonishment. "I am Joseph, the brother you sold into slavery all those years ago," he went on. "But do not be sad or angry with yourselves. God sent me here so that I could keep our family alive. The famine will last another five years, so hurry back home and bring our father here."

Then Joseph put his arms round Benjamin and the two of them wept. A moment later all the brothers were weeping and hugging one another. When Pharaoh heard the glad news he said to Joseph, "Tell your brothers to bring all your family here."

This they did, and Joseph was joyfully reunited with his father Jacob. Then the people of Israel settled in Goshen, the best and most fertile part of Egypt.

When Jacob felt his death approaching, he called his sons and said, "Do not bury me in Egypt, but lay me to rest in Canaan, the land of my fathers." Then Jacob died.

Joseph's brothers were very worried that he might still hate them for the wrong they had done to him. But Joseph reassured them. "You were planning to do evil, but God turned it into good," he said. "So do not be afraid. I will take care of your families."

Joseph was true to his word. The Israelites prospered in Goshen and they and their children grew into a strong people.

SLAVERY IN EGYPT

Genesis 50:15-26; Exodus 1

Joseph lived to a very old age. When his death drew near, he called his brothers and said, "In time, God will lead you out of Egypt into the land that has been promised to us. When that happens, take my body with you." When his brothers had sworn that they would do so, Joseph died content.

For many years afterwards, the Israelites flourished in Egypt, growing in wealth and number. But then a new Pharaoh came to power and things changed forever.

"There are now too many Israelites in Egypt," he said. "They are becoming stronger than we are and a threat to the country. We shall have to control their numbers in case they join forces with our enemies to overcome us."

The Egyptians acted swiftly. The Israelites were enslaved and their wealth taken from them. They were forced to make bricks and grind mortar for Pharaoh's buildings, and their lives were made hard by constant persecution. Slave drivers were set over them to crush their spirits with hard labour. But despite this oppression, their numbers still grew, and at last Pharaoh decided to take drastic action.

He gave instructions to two midwives who worked with the Israelites. "When you deliver their children," he said, "be sure to kill the baby boys."

But the midwives were obedient to God and they let the boys live. When Pharaoh heard about this, he summoned the midwives to him and demanded an explanation.

The midwives made up an excuse. "The Israelite women are not like the Egyptians," they said. "They give birth easily and their children are born before we have time to get there." Pharaoh believed this story and the baby boys were spared for a time. As for the midwives, God rewarded them with healthy families of their own.

Yet still the Israelites grew stronger, until in desperation Pharaoh issued one last terrible command: "Every newborn Israelite boy is to be thrown into the Nile and drowned at birth."

MOSES IN THE REEDS

Exodus 2:1-10

An Israelite couple had two children, Aaron and Miriam. Early in the reign of the new Pharaoh, they had a third child — a boy. This made them very frightened, for Pharaoh had decreed that all Israelite boys should be put to death.

For three months, the mother hid her baby, but when she could hide him no longer she made a little basket out of reeds, sealed it with tar to make it waterproof and placed the baby inside. Then she went to the River Nile, put the basket among the reeds at the water's edge and told Miriam to keep watch.

After a while, Pharaoh's daughter came down to the river with her maids to bathe. Seeing the little basket, she sent a maid to fetch it. They carefully lifted the lid and saw a tiny baby crying. Immediately, their hearts melted. "This is one of the Israelite children," said Pharaoh's daughter.

Suddenly she heard a voice. It was Miriam.

"Shall I fetch an Israelite nursemaid to look after him for you?" she asked.

"Yes," said Pharaoh's daughter, who had no children of her own. So Miriam went away and returned with her mother.

"Take this child away," said Pharaoh's daughter to the mother, "and look after him for me. I will pay you to be his nurse."

So the child was brought up in the royal palace as an Egyptian prince. And Pharaoh's daughter named him Moses.

THE BURNING BUSH

Exodus 2:11 — 4:17

Moses was brought up as an Egyptian, but he knew he was an Israelite. It pained him to see his people being treated cruelly. One day, seeing an Egyptian slave driver beating an Israelite slave, Moses attacked the man's tormentor and killed him.

When Pharaoh heard of this, he wanted Moses dead, but Moses fled far away to the land of Midian. He stayed there for many years and married Zipporah, the daughter of Jethro, the Midianite priest. Meanwhile, the suffering of the Israelites grew worse, and they cried out to God, who remembered the covenant with Abraham, Isaac and Jacob.

One day, while Moses was looking after Jethro's flocks on Mount Sinai, he saw a flame coming from the middle of a bush. "This is very strange," he thought. "The bush is on fire, but it is not burning up."

As Moses moved closer, the voice of God called out to him from the middle of the burning bush. "Moses!" it said. "Do not come any nearer. Take off your sandals, for you are on holy ground. I am the Lord, your God."

At this Moses covered his eyes, for how could he see the face of God and live?

God spoke again. "I have seen how cruelly my people are being treated in Egypt and I have come to set them free. I shall bring them out of Egypt and into Canaan, a land flowing with milk and honey. Now go to Pharaoh and tell him that you will lead my people into freedom."

"But how can I do that?" Moses asked. "Who am I to confront Pharaoh?"

God answered, "I will be with you at all times."

"But when I go to the Israelites, who shall I say sent me?" asked Moses.

"The God of Abraham, Isaac and Jacob! Pharaoh will not willingly let my people leave, but I will use my power to force him. And I will punish the Egyptians with terrible plagues."

"But what if the Israelites do not believe that I have been sent by God?" asked Moses.

"Take your rod and throw it on the ground!" ordered the Lord.

Moses did so and instantly the rod turned into a snake. Moses fled in terror.

"Pick up the snake by the tail," God said. As Moses did so, it turned back into a rod.

God gave Moses the power to perform two more miracles, but still he was reluctant to face Pharaoh. "Please send someone else, Lord," he pleaded. "I am not good at speaking in public."

"No!" said God angrily. "Your brother Aaron will talk. And I will tell you what to do. Trust me and I will give you the strength."

MOSES AND AARON AT COURT

Exodus 4:18 – 7:13

After his encounter with God, Moses returned to Jethro, his father-in-law, and asked to be allowed to go back to his people in Egypt. Jethro agreed and wished him well. So Moses set off, taking with him his wife and sons and the miraculous rod that God had given him.

And again God spoke to Moses. "Do not be afraid of going to Egypt," God said. "The people who wanted to kill you are dead, and there is a new Pharaoh. When you get there, go to Pharaoh's court and be sure to carry out the miracle that I have shown you. I will harden his heart and make him so stubborn that at first he will refuse to let the people go. But tell him that Israel is as precious to me as my first-born son. And that if he refuses to let my son go, then I shall kill his own first-born son in return."

Meanwhile, God had spoken to Aaron and told him to go into the desert to meet Moses on Mount Sinai. When the brothers met, they embraced each other. Then they set off for Egypt, where they gathered together all the leaders of the Israelites. Aaron told them everything that God had said, and Moses, to convince them of the truth, performed the miracles he had been shown. The leaders were amazed and worshipped God.

Now Moses and Aaron went to the court of Pharaoh and spoke with him. "This is what the Lord God commands," they said.

"You must let the Israelites go, so they can travel for three days into the desert and worship God. If not, plague and death will surely follow."

Pharaoh was unmoved. "What do you mean by keeping your people from their duties?" he said. "Get them back to work immediately!" Then he turned to his slave drivers and said, "From now on, stop giving the Israelites straw to make bricks. Let them gather their own straw. But don't let their quota of bricks drop. They obviously haven't enough work or they wouldn't be bothering me with this nonsense about going into the desert to worship their god. Get them to work harder."

This harsh ruling made some Israelites angry with Moses and Aaron. "Just look at what you two have done!" they said. "You've made the Egyptians hate us even more!"

Moses could see their point. When he was alone, he cried out to God, saying, "Oh, Lord, why did you send me to Pharaoh? It has only made things worse. He has made our lives unbearable now and you have done nothing to help us gain our freedom."

But God said to Moses, "It is time for you to see what I shall do to Pharaoh. I shall force him to let my people go. For I am the Lord your God, who appeared to Abraham and Isaac and Jacob and promised them the land of Canaan. I have heard the groaning of the Israelites kept in slavery in Egypt, and I have not forgotten my covenant with them. Tell them that I will stretch out my arm to deliver them from captivity. They are my people and I am their God."

Moses reported this to the Israelites, but their spirit had been so crushed by the Egyptians' cruelty that they did not listen.

"If even the Israelites will not listen to me," said Moses, "why should Pharaoh?"

"Go to Pharaoh again," God said. "At first he will not listen, but I shall bring such punishments upon him that he will be forced to recognize that I am the Almighty."

Back at the court, Moses and Aaron presented their demand again. Moses knew he was not a good speaker so, as God had instructed, he let Aaron speak for them.

Pharaoh was not persuaded, and he challenged the two of them to prove their power. So Aaron took the rod and threw it down to the floor. Instantly, it became a writhing snake. Then Pharaoh summoned his own magicians, and they did the same in their turn. Yet no sooner had their rods turned into snakes than Aaron's rod slithered over to them and swallowed them up.

Even after this demonstration, Pharaoh refused to listen. He sent Moses and Aaron away, little realizing that there were far more terrible things to come.

THE PLAGUES OF EGYPT

Exodus 7:14 – 10:29

Seeing that Pharaoh refused to let the Israelites go, God said to Moses, "Go down to the River Nile tomorrow and arrange to meet Pharaoh there. Tell him that because he has not freed my people, you will strike the water with your rod and turn the river into blood.

"Tell him also that the fish will die, the river will stink and the Egyptians will not be able to drink from it. And tell Aaron to take the rod and wave it over every stretch of water in the land, so that rivers, streams and ponds – and even the contents of the barrels and stone jars – turn to blood."

Moses and Aaron did as the Lord commanded and there was blood throughout the land of Egypt. But the Egyptians dug holes along the Nile to get fresh drinking water and Pharaoh's resolve did not weaken.

So the Lord said to Moses, "Go back to Pharaoh and tell him that if he does not free the Israelites, I shall unleash a plague of frogs. They will be everywhere. The river will be choked with them, the palace will be full of them, and even his bed will be crawling with them! Tell him that the frogs will get into people's clothes and into their hair and into their food and wine."

But Pharaoh made light of this threat too. So Aaron stretched out his rod – and suddenly, the frogs were everywhere. People found them hopping through their houses, and even sitting in their cooking pots.

Pharaoh begged Moses and Aaron to remove the frogs, but no sooner had they done so than he dug his heels in again and refused to let the Israelites go.

Then Moses told Aaron to stretch out his

rod and to strike the earth, turning the dust into filthy lice that infested men, women, children and animals throughout the whole of Egypt. But still Pharaoh did not budge.

So God commanded Moses to send a swarm of flies, which descended over Egypt and blackened the skies, sparing only Goshen where the Israelites lived. The flies crawled over everything and everybody, driving people mad with their constant buzzing.

"Send the flies away," pleaded Pharaoh. "Then you can go into the desert to worship your God." The next day the flies had gone, but Pharaoh was as stubborn as ever.

God then told Moses to tell Pharaoh that, if he did not relent, a terrible disease would strike every animal in the country and that only the Israelites' herds would survive. The next day, the Egyptians awoke to find all their animals dead. Cattle, sheep and goats littered the fields; donkeys and camels lay dead in the streets. But even this did not persuade Pharaoh to let the people go.

Neither did a plague of boils, which erupted in open sores on the hands and bodies and faces of the Egyptians. Pharaoh was horrified to see his wives and daughters scarred by ugly, festering sores, but still he did not give in. Even when a plague of hailstones devastated the Egyptians' crops, and when a plague of millions of locusts stripped bare the trees and plants, his heart remained hard.

So God told Moses to stretch out his hand towards Heaven and bring darkness to cover the land of Egypt. For three days, the country was plunged into a darkness no one had ever experienced before. Candles would not light, fires would not burn, no one could see a thing – except for the Israelites, whose homes were filled with light.

Finally, Pharaoh called for Moses and said that the Israelites could go on one condition – they had to leave their animals behind. But this was unacceptable to Moses. "Without our animals," he told Pharaoh, "we will not be able to make our sacrifices to God. The beasts must come too."

"Then you shall stay!" said Pharaoh to Moses in fury. "Get out of my sight. If I ever see you again, you will die!"

Moses went. But God had one last plague to inflict on Egypt – the most terrible of all.

PASSOVER

Exodus 11 – 13

At last the Lord said to Moses, "I shall bring one more plague upon the land of Egypt and then Pharaoh will surely let you go. One day soon, at midnight, I shall move over the country and then the first-born son of every Egyptian family will die."

Moses went to Pharaoh and told him God's words. "If you do not let my people go," he said, "every first-born Egyptian boy will perish – from your own son to the son of the lowliest servant girl who grinds your corn. Then there will be a cry of sorrow in Egypt such as no one has ever heard before. But the sons of the Israelites will all be spared, and your servants will come on their knees to me and beg me to take my people out of Egypt. This is what the Lord has said." And with that, in great anger, Moses strode away.

But still Pharaoh refused to let the Israelites leave his land.

Again God spoke, giving Moses and Aaron precise instructions to prepare for that terrible night. "On the tenth day of the month every Israelite household is to get a lamb. Then, on the evening of the fourteenth day of the month, the lambs are to be killed and the blood smeared on the doorposts and above the door of every house. The lambs must be roasted and eaten with bitter herbs and bread made without yeast. Eat the meal quickly and be dressed, ready to travel at a moment's notice.

"This will be the first Festival of Passover. For on that night I shall pass through the land of Egypt and strike dead every Egyptian first-born male – both human and animal. But the blood on your houses will be a sign to me, so that I pass over your houses and spare your children.

"Ever afterwards, you must keep this day as a solemn religious festival. For seven days, you must eat bread made without yeast. And be sure there is no trace of yeast in your house, because if anyone eats bread made with yeast at this time then he or she will no longer be considered one of my people."

Moses passed on God's instructions to his people and told them to celebrate the Festival of Passover every year, in memory of the night on which the Lord would spare the Israelites.

On the fourteenth day of the month, the Israelites did exactly as God had commanded. They slaughtered the lambs and smeared the doorways with blood. Then they waited. Midnight came, and the Lord moved across Egypt and struck down every first-born son. From the highest to the lowest no family was spared – not even the cattle in the fields. And Pharaoh awoke in the middle of the night to hear a great cry of sorrow resounding across the land, for there was not one Egyptian household that had not lost a son.

Immediately, he summoned Moses and Aaron and told them to take the Israelites. "Be gone!" he cried. "Take your people and your flocks and your cattle and go!"

The Egyptians were anxious to get rid of the Israelites as soon as they could, because they feared they would bring down further misfortune upon them. "Go quickly," they shouted, "or we shall all be dead!"

So the Israelites left Egypt in great haste. They had just enough time to grab their unrisen bread before they set off – over six hundred thousand of them, with their sheep, goats and cattle. The Israelites had lived in Egypt for more than four hundred years – since the

time of Joseph – but now, at last, they had their freedom.

The Lord said to Moses, "Dedicate your first-born sons to me and remember this day for all time – the day the Lord your God brought you out of slavery in Egypt. And when your sons ask you why you are celebrating the festival, tell them the story of your captivity and release."

Moses took the body of Joseph with him so that it could finally be laid to rest in Canaan according to Joseph's last request. Then the Israelites set off towards the Red Sea, the first stage of their long journey to their homeland. All the while God went with them, sending a pillar of cloud to guide them by day and a pillar of fire to light the way at night.

THE EXODUS

Exodus 14:5 — 15:22

 he Israelites had not long set off on their journey when Pharaoh and his officials had second thoughts. "Why ever did we let them go?" they exclaimed. "The Israelites were our slaves – they did everything for us. And now they have gone!"

Pharaoh immediately assembled his army. Then, with six hundred charioteers, and countless horsemen and troops, he set off in pursuit of Moses' people.

The Egyptians moved at great speed, and soon drew near the Israelites, who were camped beside the Red Sea.

When they saw the army approaching, the Israelites trembled with fear. "Were there not enough graves for us in Egypt?" they said to Moses bitterly. "Did you have to bring us out here into the desert to die? Better to be slaves than dead!"

But Moses stood firm. "Do not be afraid," he said. "The Lord will save you."

And God spoke to Moses and said, "Take your rod and stretch it out over the sea. Watch as the waters part, then lead my people across the dry ground to the other side. When Pharaoh pursues you, he will soon see that I am the Almighty!"

Then God became a pillar of cloud and separated the Israelites from the Egyptians. As night fell, the cloud cast darkness onto the Egyptians and light onto the Israelites, so that the two groups were kept safely apart.

Moses stretched out his hand towards the sea. The Lord commanded a strong east wind to part the waters, and drive them back, revealing dry land. The Israelites stepped onto it and made their way across the seabed, overshadowed by walls of water rising on either side.

As they reached the far shore, Pharaoh saw them, and gave orders to his horsemen and charioteers to charge. But as they began to cross the seabed, God loosened the chariot wheels, so that the axles stuck fast in the soft mud. Panic-stricken, the Egyptians tried to retreat – but it was too late.

Again Moses stretched out his hand over the sea, and as dawn broke, the waters came back together with an enormous crash, swallowing the Egyptian army. The Israelites looked on as all Pharaoh's soldiers, his charioteers, his horsemen and his horses went beneath the waves and were drowned.

Then Moses and the people sang a song of thanksgiving while Miriam, Moses' sister, took a tambourine and led the women in a dance of joy.

THE YEARS OF WANDERING

Exodus 15:22 – 17:7; 18

Moses led the people of Israel from the Red Sea into the desert. It was clear from the start that there were going to be great changes in their lives. All the things they had taken for granted – such as regular supplies of food and water – had vanished.

For the first three days, they had nothing at all to drink. The people began to get desperate and complained endlessly to Moses. The only water they came across was a stagnant pool with a foul, bitter taste. "What are we going to do?" the Israelites demanded. "How can we drink this?"

Moses prayed to the Lord for help, and God showed him a piece of wood, which Moses threw into the water. No sooner had he done so than the water became clear and pure. In an instant, the Israelites forgot their woes and sat down by the pool, refreshing themselves with the sweet, cool water.

But not long after, the Israelites began to complain again, saying that they did not have enough food to eat and that they had no meat at all. Moses told Aaron to assemble the people, and as he did so, a dazzling light appeared from the clouds. It was the glory of the Lord.

God said to Moses, "I have heard the complaints of the Israelites and I shall cause food to rain down from the sky – bread in the morning and meat in the evening. But the people must take only what they need to last them for one day. However tempting it is to take more, they must resist – they have to trust me. I shall provide more each day. Only on the sixth day should they collect twice the amount they need, so that they can rest on the seventh day and keep it holy."

That evening a huge flock of quails descended on the camp, and the Israelites were able to walk among them, taking only as many birds as they needed to provide their families with the day's meat.

In the morning, a dew formed on

the ground. When it evaporated, the Israelites saw a strange, white powder underneath, which looked like frost, but tasted of biscuit made with honey.

"What is it?" they asked.

"It is manna from Heaven," said Moses. "It is the food that the Lord has promised you. Go and collect it, but take only what you need for today. The Lord will provide for tomorrow."

Some people disobeyed Moses and took more than they needed, only to find that the next day it was smelly and full of maggots. But on the sixth day, when everyone gathered twice their daily ration, the food did not go off. Instead it lasted throughout the seventh day, while the people rested.

But again some disobedient Israelites went out on the seventh day to collect more food. By now God, who had clearly said there would be no food that day, was growing angry. "Just how long are you all going to refuse to do as I say?" God said to Moses.

At the spot where the Israelites next pitched camp, there was no water. Again the people became angry. "Did you bring us out of Egypt so we could slowly die of thirst?" they asked Moses mockingly, looking as if they were ready to attack him. Moses was concerned and turned to God for help.

"Take some of your leaders and go on ahead of the people," said God. "And take your rod with you. When you reach the rock at Horeb, strike it with the rod. I promise you water will appear for the people to drink." This Moses did and, miraculously, a new spring appeared.

Time went by and the Israelites had to endure many hardships, including an attack by a hostile tribe, which was beaten back by Moses and his most experienced general, Joshua. All this time they were pressing on towards the land of Canaan, the land that God had promised them as a home. It was a long, hard road to travel. Though they did not know it then, it would be forty years before their wandering in the desert was at an end and their homeland was in sight.

One day, Moses received a visit from his father-in-law, Jethro, the priest of the Midianites. When Moses had told him about all the things that the Lord had done, the two of them began to praise God. But there was something troubling Jethro. He had seen that Moses was spending all his time settling disputes among the people. All day, lines of people formed in front of Moses waiting for a ruling on this matter or that.

"You will wear yourself out," said Jethro. "This is not something that one man can do on his own. Let me give you some advice. First teach the people what God's laws are so that they can follow them and avoid disputes in the first place. Secondly, appoint God-fearing and righteous men to act as judges over the people. They can deal with the everyday matters of law, but if they come across a particularly difficult case, then they can pass it on to you. That way you will not be overburdened with work."

Then Jethro took his leave and set off home – but not before Moses had taken his advice and appointed a number of judges to interpret God's law. The precise details of that law would be revealed very soon – in the most dramatic way.

THE TEN COMMANDMENTS

Exodus 19 – 20

**T**hree months after they left Egypt, the Israelites came to the desolate Sinai Desert, where they pitched camp at the foot of Mount Sinai. Leaving the people below, Moses climbed the mountain, and there he heard the voice of God speaking to him.

"Remind the Israelites," God said, "of how I brought them here safely. Remind them of my covenant with them and tell them that, if they obey me in everything, they will continue to be my special people and grow into a holy nation."

Moses assembled the leaders and told them faithfully what the Lord had told him. When this was passed on to the people, they all agreed to do as God commanded.

And God said to Moses, "I shall come to you in a thick cloud. The people will hear me speaking to you and they will believe you for ever more. Go to them straightaway and tell them to purify themselves over the next two days, because on the third day I will descend before their very eyes."

So Moses told the Israelites to prepare themselves, and on the third day, he led them out of the camp to meet God. Thunder and lightning filled the sky and a great cloud settled on the summit of the mountain. Fire and smoke raged and the ground trembled.

Then God called Moses up the mountain and gave him ten commandments.

God said, "I am the Lord, who brought you out of slavery. Worship no other god but me.

"Do not bow down to false idols.

"Do not use my name lightly. Treat it with respect.

"Remember the seventh day, the Sabbath, and keep it holy. Work for six days and rest on the seventh – as I rested after the creation.

"Respect your father and mother.

"Do not commit murder.

"Do not commit adultery.

"Do not steal.

"Do not tell lies.

"Do not envy your neighbour's things."

Meanwhile, the Israelites saw the smoke and lightning on the mountain, and were filled with fear. When Moses returned, they cried, "Do not let God speak to us directly or we will die!"

Moses explained that God was testing their obedience. He told them the ten commandments, and the Israelites promised to obey them forever. But still they stood a long way off as Moses returned to the top of Mount Sinai. There the Lord explained the laws in detail, and gave Moses two tablets of stone on which the commandments had been written by the very hand of God.

THE GOLDEN CALF

Exodus 32

Moses stayed on Mount Sinai for forty days and nights, and the Israelites began to think he was never coming back. Finally they said to Aaron, "Something has happened to Moses. Who will lead us now? Make us a god to lead us again."

Aaron told the people to remove all their gold earrings and bring them to him so that he could melt them down. When he had done this, he poured the hot metal into a mould to produce a statue of a golden calf. Immediately the people said, "This is our god. This is the god who led us out of Egypt."

Then Aaron built an altar in front of the golden calf and announced that on the next day there would be a festival in its honour. Early next morning, the people brought animals to offer as sacrifices, and as the day wore on, they settled down to a feast that very soon turned into a frenzy of drinking and dancing.

Up on the mountain the Lord said to Moses, "Your people have sinned and rejected me. They have turned away from my laws and have begun to worship a pagan idol in the shape of a golden calf. They are already offering sacrifices to it and are saying that it is the god that led them out of Egypt. I know how disobedient and stubborn these people are. I am angry and I intend to destroy them. Then I will make your own descendants into a great nation."

But Moses pleaded with God and said, "Why are you so angry with the very people you rescued from slavery in Egypt? What would the Egyptians think if they saw that you had led them out of their country only to kill them in the desert? Please spare them. Remember your promise to Abraham, Isaac and Jacob. Remember that you promised to give their descendants a land of their own. Do not bring disaster on them now."

The Lord listened and decided to spare the Israelites. Moses acted swiftly to re-establish God's Law. With the two stone tablets in his hands, he set off to confront the people.

ORDER RESTORED

Exodus 32:17-35; 33:12 – 34:27

When Moses came down from Mount Sinai, he was boiling with rage. At the foot of the mountain he met Joshua, who had been waiting there for him all this time. Joshua told him that he could hear the people shouting. It sounded like a fight.

"No," said Moses grimly. "That is not the sound of fighting. It is the sound of singing and dancing." They approached the camp, and when Moses saw the frenzy in front of the golden calf, his anger exploded.

He threw down the tablets of stone, breaking them into small pieces. Then he melted the golden calf and ground it into a powder, which he scattered on the water for the people to drink as a punishment for their sin. "Aaron!" he cried. "How could you have allowed such wicked behaviour to take place?"

"Don't be angry," pleaded Aaron. "You know how our people can behave. With you gone, they begged me to make a god to lead them."

The next day, Moses stood before the people. "You have committed a terrible sin," he said. "But I will go back up the mountain to try to gain forgiveness for you."

When Moses stood before God again, he was perplexed. "You told me I was to lead the people to the Promised Land," he said, "but I need someone to go with me and help me."

"I will go with you always," said the Lord. "I know you very well, and I am pleased with you."

Then Moses said, "Lord, let me see you."

"I will let my splendour pass before you," said the Lord. "But I will not let you see my face – for no one can see my face and live. When the dazzling light of my presence approaches, I will place you by a rock and cover you with my hand. When I have passed by, I will take my hand away and you will see my back but not my face."

Then God instructed Moses to cut two more stone tablets to replace the ones he had broken and to carry them up to the top of Mount Sinai the next morning. There Moses wrote down God's laws once more and the covenant with Israel was renewed. And when Moses came back down the mountain, his face was shining because he had been in the presence of the Lord.

THE ARK OF THE COVENANT

Exodus 25 – 30

Again God spoke to Moses and said, "Tell the Israelites to make offerings of gold, silver and bronze, of precious wood, fine linen, leather and jewels. With these, they are to make a sanctuary – a sacred place – for me to live among them."

The Lord gave them precise instructions. First they were to build a ceremonial box, or ark, to house the tablets of stone on which the Law had been written. It was to be made of acacia wood, covered with gold inside and out, and have four gold carrying rings attached. The lid was to have two golden angels whose wings would intertwine over the box's precious contents.

When the Ark of the Covenant was made, God said, "Now make a table out of acacia wood. Cover it with pure gold and place it in front of the Ark. Make a candlestick with seven branches and cover it with decorative flowers, ensuring that the lampstand, the branches and the flowers are made of one single piece of gold."

Then the Israelites were told precisely how to build the special tent, the Tabernacle, that would contain the Lord's presence. It was to be made with the finest blue, purple and scarlet linen and then embroidered with patterns of angels. A curtain was to be stretched across it, screening off an inner chamber, and here they were to put the Ark of the Covenant. The tent was itself a holy place, but where the Ark stood was the Holy of Holies, the place containing the tablets of the Law, accessible only to the high priests.

"Summon your brother, Aaron, and his sons," said God to Moses. "They are to serve me as priests." And God taught them how to prepare for worship, what ritual clothes to wear, what festivals to celebrate, and what sacrifices to make to have their sins forgiven.

When the Tent of the Lord's Presence was finished, a cloud settled over it and a dazzling light showed the Israelites that the Lord was present among them. And from that time onwards, wherever the Israelites went, the sacred tent went with them, reminding them of the presence of God.

THE DEATH OF MOSES

Numbers 13 – 14; Deuteronomy 31 – 34

Moses continued to lead his people towards the Promised Land of Canaan, despite their frequent complaints that the journey was too hard. When they got to the border, however, a strange thing happened. The Israelites were too frightened to enter.

Spies had gone ahead to see what kind of place Canaan was, and they returned with grapes, pomegranates and figs. "It's a very fertile land, flowing with milk and honey," they said. "But the cities are well fortified and the people there are giants."

Hearing this, the Israelites lost heart. "Why did we leave Egypt?" they said. "Let's go back where we will be safe."

Then the Lord grew angry. "Why will you people not trust me?" said God. "For your lack of faith you can stay in the desert for forty years!"

And that is just what happened. For forty more years, the people remained in the desert. At last, the Lord decided to allow them into the Promised Land. But Moses was now too weak to make the final journey himself.

God said to him, "After your death, Moses, the people will become unfaithful to me and worship pagan idols. For that, they will undergo many terrible disasters. But, before you die, remind them that I alone am God and I will spare no one who fights against me."

Moses did as he was asked, then climbed alone to the top of Mount Nebo, and looked down on the Promised Land stretched out beneath him. And there he died.

There was never a prophet in Israel like Moses, for the Lord spoke to him face to face. No other prophet performed such miracles for his people.

RAHAB AND THE SPIES

Joshua 1 – 2

After the death of Moses, God spoke to Joshua and told him to lead the Israelites across the River Jordan into the Promised Land. "Be strong and courageous," said the Lord. "And know that if you keep my laws, I will not abandon you."

Joshua instructed his officers to make their way through the camp and to tell the people to prepare food for the journey ahead – for in three days' time they would be crossing the Jordan and taking possession of the land that had been promised to them by God.

But the land of Canaan, west of the Jordan, was occupied by many fierce tribes, which would have to be conquered by the Israelites. So Joshua gave these instructions. "Our wives, children and livestock will stay on this side of the river while we, armed for battle, will cross to the other side and conquer the land."

And the people replied, "We will do as you say and go wherever you send us. Just as we obeyed Moses so we will obey you. Anyone who questions your authority or challenges your orders will be put to death."

The nearest base of the Canaanites was the fortified city of Jericho. That evening, Joshua sent two spies into Jericho to check out its defences. To avoid detection, they spent the night at the house of Rahab, a prostitute, who was soon suspected by the king of Jericho of harbouring the strangers.

"The men in your house have come to spy on us," said the king's men. "Bring them out now."

"Two men did come here," replied Rahab, "but I had no idea where they were from. In any case, they have gone now. They left at sunset, just before the city gates were shut. I don't know where they are heading for, but if you set off now you will soon catch them."

In fact, Rahab had taken the two men on to her roof and hidden them under a pile of flax stalks. When the king's men had gone, she went to them and said, "I know that the Lord has given you this land. Everyone here is terrified of you. We have heard how the Lord dried up the Red Sea for you and our courage has gone. The Lord your God is the one true God.

"I beg you, repay my kindness and promise in the name of the Lord that you will spare my family. Give me some sort of sign that I can trust you. Please do not kill us."

"You have saved our lives," the men replied. "We will save yours if you promise not to tell anyone what we have been doing. When the Lord has given us this land, we will deal fairly with you and take care of you and your family."

Rahab's house was built into the city wall. When everything was quiet, she let the men down by a rope hanging from her window high up in the wall. "Go to the mountains," she whispered after them. "Stay there for three days to avoid being captured. When the king's men have returned, you can go on your way."

"We will keep our promise to you," they whispered back. "When we return with our army, tie this red rope to the window you let us down from. That will be a sign to us when we invade. Get all your family inside the house and do not let anyone leave. If they do, they will certainly be killed and their deaths will not be our responsibility. But we promise that everyone inside the house will be safe. In the meantime, do not breathe a word of this to anyone or we will take back our promise."

"I will not," Rahab said.

And with that they made their escape, while she tied the red rope to her window.

Off they went into the mountains, hiding there until the coast was clear. For three days, the king's men scoured the countryside but found no one. Eventually they returned to Jericho empty-handed.

Meanwhile, the two spies emerged from their mountain hideout and made their way back to Joshua. They told him everything that had happened to them and were convinced that God was on their side. "Now we know for sure that the Lord has given us all the country," they said. "The whole population is terrified of us."

At this, Joshua knew that the time was right to attack.

THE WALLS OF JERICHO

Joshua 3 – 6

The next morning, Joshua got up early and led the Israelites to the edge of the River Jordan, where they camped while waiting to cross. On the third day, the Ark of the Covenant was brought out and carried by the priests in front of the people.

As it was springtime, the river was in flood and quite impassable. But Joshua was unconcerned. He ordered the priests to wade into the water with the Ark and, as they did so, the water suddenly stopped flowing. The swollen river was transformed into a dry river bed, which the Israelites walked across in safety. When everyone was across, the army set up camp near Jericho and celebrated the Passover feast. The next day, for the first time, they ate food grown in the Promised Land of Canaan.

Later, while Joshua was scouting alone near the city walls, he saw a mysterious figure standing in front of him holding a sword. "Are you one of our men or an enemy?" Joshua asked.

"Neither," came the reply. "I am here as the commander of the Lord's Army."

Joshua knew that he was in the presence of God. He threw himself on the ground and said, "I am your servant. What do you want me to do?"

"Remove your sandals," said the stranger, "for you are now on holy ground."

The great gates of Jericho were shut tight against the Israelites. But God said to Joshua,

"Jericho is yours. Do as I command you.

"Every day for six days you and your men must march around the city. Seven priests carrying trumpets made of rams' horns must walk in front of the Ark of the Covenant. On the seventh day, you must walk round the city seven times and, when you hear a long blast on the horns, you must let out a great shout – then the walls of the city will come tumbling down."

Joshua and the Israelites carried out the instructions faithfully. On the seventh day, they marched round the city seven times. Then the priests sounded the horns, the people let out a great cry – and with a terrible crash, the walls of Jericho fell. Then the Israelites charged forward and stormed the city. Joshua's men went to Rahab's house and rescued her and her family, but everyone else in the city was killed.

"Jericho is to be totally destroyed," said Joshua. "Take nothing from it, or great misfortune will befall you."

And so the city was set alight, and Joshua's reputation spread throughout the whole of Canaan.

THE PROMISED LAND

Joshua 7 – 10; 24:1-29

God had commanded the people of Israel to take nothing from the city of Jericho. But that command had been broken by one of Joshua's men, Achan, who had secretly stolen a cloak and some gold and silver and buried them under his tent. For this disobedience Israel's army would pay a heavy price.

Joshua had now set his sights on the nearby city of Ai, in order to push on further into Canaan, the land promised to the Israelites by God. Scouts went on ahead and returned to tell Joshua that the town was not heavily defended. It would need only a small force – not the whole army – to capture it.

The troops set off, confident of success, but, to their horror, they were beaten back by the men of Ai and forced to retreat. The enemy chased the Israelites from the city, killing several of them. Joshua was devastated when he heard the news. He and his commanders threw themselves on the ground before the Ark of the Covenant and called out to the Lord.

"Almighty God, why did you bring us across the Jordan at all?" Joshua cried. "Now you have handed us over to our enemies, the Canaanites. We will all be killed!"

The Lord said to Joshua, "Israel has sinned against me. Did I not order you to take nothing from the condemned city of Jericho? And did you not promise to obey? Somone has broken that agreement and this defeat is the punishment."

Early next morning, Joshua gathered together the people of Israel and, tribe by tribe, family by family, conducted a thorough investigation. Eventually, Achan's guilt was discovered and he and his family were put to death.

When this was done, the Lord was no longer angry with Israel and promised Joshua that if they launched a second attack, the city of Ai would fall. Joshua came up with a plan. His men would advance on the city then, in the middle of the assault, pretend to retreat as they had before. The enemy would chase them into the surrounding countryside where Israelite forces would be hiding. The plan was for the Israelites to lure the men of Ai further and further away from the city, leaving it wide open to attack. When Ai was vulnerable, the troops who had been in hiding would rise up and take it by storm.

And that is just what happened. The first wave of Israelite troops tricked the enemy into pursuing them into the countryside, while the second wave charged up the hill into the now undefended city and set it alight. Once they had done this, they charged down the hill again and attacked the men of Ai from behind, surrounding them completely and easily defeating them.

The news soon spread, and other local rulers joined forces to fight the Israelites. One tribe, however, was more cunning.

The Gibeonites had heard of Joshua's success and decided to trick him into making a peace treaty with them. They knew that, once the treaty was agreed, the Israelites would be unable to kill them because Israel would not go back on its word.

They loaded their donkeys with old sacks and battered wineskins, put on ragged clothes and worn-out sandals, and gathered dry bread for food. Then they walked into Joshua's camp and asked to make a treaty.

"Where are you from?" asked Joshua, looking at this raggle-taggle tribe, and not entirely convinced that all was as it seemed.

"From far away," they lied. "We have heard how God led you out of Egypt. We want to put ourselves at your service."

"How do I know you do not live nearby?" asked Joshua, aware that, if they did, he would not be able to eliminate them by war.

"Look at our wineskins," they said. "They were new when we started out. And we have been reduced to eating stale bread. That is the state of our supplies after travelling so far."

At this, Joshua agreed to the treaty.

Soon, however, the Israelites discovered they had been tricked. The Gibeonites lived a mere three days' march away, as Joshua and his army found out when they moved deeper into Canaan. Joshua was annoyed,

but he knew he could not kill them.

"We have given our solemn promise," he said to his people. "God will punish us if we break it."

Then he gathered together the Gibeonites. "Why did you deceive us?" he asked.

"We feared for our lives," they said. "We knew that God had given you Canaan and that you could kill people as you made the land yours. We wanted to live."

"Very well," said Joshua, "but God has condemned you for your deception. From now on you will have to serve us, fetching our water and cutting our firewood. From now on you are our slaves."

Meanwhile, the king of Jerusalem had heard of Joshua's victory over Ai and of his peace treaty with the Gibeonites. He quickly attacked the town of Gibeon to weaken this powerful military alliance. The Gibeonites were soon surrounded and sent word to Joshua for help.

Joshua and his army set off, knowing that God had already promised them victory. They rode hard through the night and surprised the enemy with the speed of their attack. Before the battle, Joshua had spoken to the Israelites in the presence of the Lord and commanded the sun and the moon to stand still. They hung motionless in the sky until Joshua had defeated his enemies.

Even after this great triumph, the Israelites had to fight many more battles against the enemy tribes that surrounded them on every side. But God was with them, and Joshua did not rest until the Israelite people were securely established throughout the Promised Land.

DEBORAH, BARAK AND JAEL

Judges 4 – 5

After Joshua, the Israelites were ruled by a series of leaders called judges, who advised the people and interpreted God's laws. But many Israelites began to turn their backs on God's commandments, and as punishment they were conquered by Jabin, a Canaanite king who ruled with great cruelty for twenty years.

At this time, Deborah was judge of the Israelites. She was a prophet who lived in the hill country of Ephraim, where she sat beneath a palm tree dispensing advice. One day, she sent for Barak, one of the Israelite fighters, and told him that he was to take ten thousand men to Mount Tabor to prepare for battle with Sisera, the commander of Jabin's army.

"You will meet him at the River Kishon," she said. "And you will be victorious."

"I will go if you go," replied Barak.

"Very well," Deborah said. "But I must warn you that you will not get the credit for the victory. That will go to a woman."

When Sisera learnt that Deborah and Barak had gone to Mount Tabor, he gathered his troops and nine hundred chariots and set off for the River Kishon.

"Go and meet him at the river," said Deborah to Barak. "The Lord is with you."

So Barak took his army and fought Sisera. The Lord intervened. A great storm broke, and the River Kishon rose up in flood, causing chaos among the enemy. So terrified was Sisera that he got out of his chariot and fled on foot, leaving his army to be slaughtered by Barak's men.

Sisera ran for his life. At last, when he could go no further, he came to the tent of Heber, a Kenite, and his wife Jael. The Kenites had always been allies of King Jabin, so Sisera thought he was safe. But Heber and Jael had moved away from the Kenite tribe and were now friends of the Israelites.

"Come in, sir," said Jael to Sisera and she hid him behind a curtain.

"Stand at the door of the tent," said Sisera, "and if anyone asks you whether I am here, say no." And then, exhausted, he lay down on the ground and fell asleep.

This was Jael's moment. She took a hammer and a tent peg, crept quietly up to him, and drove the peg through his temple, killing him instantly.

When Barak arrived, Jael said, "Look inside." And there was Sisera, lying dead on the ground with a tent peg through his skull.

Soon afterwards, Jabin was overthrown. Then Deborah and Barak sang a song of thanksgiving to the Lord, and there was peace in the land for forty years.

GIDEON

Judges 6 – 7

Again the Israelites sinned against God and, as a punishment, the people of Midian were allowed to rule over them. Time after time, the Midianites raided the Israelites, destroying crops and stealing livestock. The Israelites were helpless.

One day, an angel of the Lord appeared to a young man named Gideon.

"The Lord is with you," said the angel. "Use your great strength to rescue Israel from the Midianites."

"But how can I?" Gideon cried. "I am just an ordinary man among many."

"The Lord will help you," the angel said.

"Please Lord," prayed Gideon, "give me a sign. I shall put a woollen fleece on the floor tonight and if, by tomorrow, the fleece is wet with dew and the floor is dry, then I will know that you will use me to save Israel."

Sure enough, by morning the fleece was wet and the floor was dry. So Gideon

brought the Israelite tribes together and set off for the Midianite camp.

God said to Gideon, "I do not want my people to think it was by their strength that they triumph today. Send some men back."

Gideon did so, but there were still too many to please God. "Take your men down to the river," said the Lord. "When they start to drink, separate those who kneel and suck up the water from those who crouch and lap the water from their cupped hands."

Three hundred men scooped up the water with their hands, looking around them as they did so. These men were chosen to fight because they had proved that they were alert to the threat of enemy attack at all times.

That night Gideon divided his men into three groups, giving each man a ram's horn and a jar with a lit torch hidden inside. Once in position by the Midianite camp, Gideon gave the signal for the men to blow their horns and shatter their jars. The sudden noise and lights utterly confused the enemy and they fled in chaos as the Israelite soldiers shouted, "For the Lord and for Gideon!"

With the Midianites routed, the land was at peace for forty years until Gideon died.

SAMSON THE STRONG

Judges 13 – 15

As time passed, the Israelites fell into their wicked ways again and, as a punishment, God allowed the Philistine people to rule over them for forty years. One day, however, the Lord sent an angel to deliver an important message to the wife of Manoah, an Israelite who lived in the town of Zorah.

"You have never been able to have children," said the angel. "But soon you will give birth to a son. Listen carefully. Do not drink wine or any other strong drink and do not eat any forbidden foods. And do not cut your son's hair, because from the day he is born, he will be dedicated to God and he will one day help rescue Israel from the Philistines."

In time, as promised, the woman gave birth to a boy and called him Samson. As the child grew into a man, the Lord blessed him and Samson became strong. One day, when Samson was in Timnah, he met a very beautiful Philistine girl and told his parents he wished to marry her. His parents pleaded with him to marry one of his own people, but they did not know that the marriage was part of God's plan. It was a way of allowing Samson to get close to the Philistines and ultimately to destroy them.

As Samson went down to Timnah ahead of his parents, he took a short cut across the vineyards. Suddenly, he came face to face with a young lion, which roared and leapt at him. The power of God made Samson strong and he tore the lion to pieces as if it were a young goat. He said nothing of this to anyone, but simply carried on to Timnah, where he asked the girl to marry him.

A few days later, Samson went back to look at the lion he had killed and noticed that a swarm of bees had settled in the carcass and filled it with honey. Samson scraped out the honey and ate it as he walked along.

In those days, it was the custom to hold a banquet to celebrate a wedding and the Philistines sent thirty of their men to eat with Samson and his new wife.

When they arrived, Samson said, "I have a riddle for you. I bet you thirty sets of the finest clothes that you will not solve it."

"Go on, then," they said. "Tell us the riddle."

"I came out of the eater as something to eat. And I came from the strong one as something sweet. What am I?"

The Philistines were completely baffled and later threatened Samson's wife with death unless she tricked her husband into telling them the solution. After seven days, she had nagged her husband so much that Samson told her the secret. Then she passed it on to the Philistines.

"Honey!" shouted the Philistines to Samson. "That's the answer to your riddle."

Samson was furious. He knew that they had made his wife betray him. Suddenly, he was filled with the strength of the Lord and he raced off to Ashkelon, where he killed thirty Philistines, stripped them, and gave their clothes to his treacherous guests.

Thinking that Samson now hated his wife, her father gave her to another man. This insult made Samson's hatred of the Philistines grow even stronger. He caught three hundred foxes and tied burning torches to their tails, before letting them loose in the Philistines' cornfields. All the crops were destroyed.

The Philistines took a terrible revenge – they trapped Samson's wife and her father and burned them to death. In response, Samson attacked the Philistines with great ferocity, killing dozens. So the Philistines set out to capture him. Samson was eventually caught and tied up with strong ropes, but when he saw his enemies, the power of the Lord made him strong and he snapped the ropes as if they were cotton thread. Then, seizing the jawbone of a donkey, he attacked his captors and killed a thousand of them.

Eventually, the Philistines trapped Samson in the city of Gaza, but once again, he outwitted them. He used his strength to take hold of the city gate – doors, doorposts, locks and all – and wrench it from the ground before making his escape.

And for twenty years, Samson led Israel against the might of the Philistines.

SAMSON AND DELILAH

Judges 16:4-31

In time, Samson fell in love with another Philistine woman, named Delilah. The Philistine leaders noticed this and offered her a bribe. "Find out the secret of Samson's strength," they said, "and we will each give you eleven hundred pieces of silver."

One evening, when Delilah was with Samson, she said, "If someone wanted to make you helpless, what would he have to do?"

"Tie me up with seven new bowstrings that have not been allowed to dry out," Samson replied. "Then I would be as weak as anybody else."

So the Philistines brought Delilah seven new bowstrings and the next night, as Samson was sleeping, she tied him up with them. Secretly, she had arranged for men to be hidden in the room, but she pretended to be surprised when they ran out and shouted, "Quick, Samson! The Philistines are here!"

Samson snapped the bowstrings like cotton threads and sent the Philistines running for their lives.

"You are making fun of me," said Delilah. "Tell me truthfully how to tie you up."

"New ropes would do it," said Samson.

So the Philistines brought new ropes and Delilah tied him up again. The same thing happened. Samson was as strong as ever.

Day after day, Delilah pleaded with him. "What is your secret?" she asked. "How can you say you love me if you will not tell me?"

Eventually, her persistence wore him down

and reluctantly Samson told her the truth.

"Ever since I was born, my hair has never been cut. I have been dedicated to God and my long hair is a sign of that. If someone were to cut it I would be as weak as anyone."

Delilah sent for the Philistines again.

That night, she lulled Samson to sleep and called a man to cut his hair. When it was cut, his strength left him and the Philistines were able to take him easily. Next they blinded him and put him in chains, setting him to work in the prison mill in Gaza.

But all the while his hair was growing.

One day, while the Philistine kings were holding a banquet in honour of their god, Dagon, they fetched Samson to entertain them. As they mocked him, Samson said to the boy who was leading him by the hand, "Guide me between the two pillars holding up the building. I need to rest against them."

As his hands touched the pillars, he prayed to God for the strength to take his revenge on the Philistines. Then, pushing both pillars with all his might, he brought the building tumbling down. Everyone died. That day, Samson killed more people with his own death than he had done in his whole life.

RUTH AND NAOMI

Ruth

Long ago, in the days before Israel had a king, a terrible famine gripped the land. A man named Elimelech, who lived in Bethlehem, decided that he and his family would have to leave to survive. So he packed his belongings and, with his wife Naomi and their two sons, went to live in the country of Moab.

After a time Elimelech died, leaving Naomi to look after the boys. They eventually married two Moabite girls, Orpah and Ruth. But about ten years later, Naomi's sons died too, and Naomi was left feeling terribly lonely, with only her daughters-in-law for company.

The years passed, and news at last reached Naomi that her people had been blessed with a good harvest, bringing the long famine to an end. It was time for her to go back to Bethlehem.

She set out with Orpah and Ruth, but before they had gone very far, Naomi stopped, turned to the young women and said, "You should not come with me. You must stay in your homeland. Go back to your families here in Moab and may God be as good to you as you have been to me. I pray that God will bless you both and that you will be happily married again soon." Then she kissed them goodbye.

Orpah and Ruth were now in tears and they refused to go back. But Naomi insisted and at last she persuaded Orpah to return.

As Orpah walked away, Naomi tried one last time. "Ruth," she pleaded, "your sister-in-law is going back home to her people and her god. Go with her, I beg you."

But Ruth stood firm. "Do not ask me to leave you," she said. "Wherever you go,

I will go. Your people will be my people and your God will be my God."

Naomi saw that Ruth was determined to stay, so she said nothing more and the two walked on together.

There was great excitement in Bethlehem when they arrived. People could not believe that Naomi had come back after all this time. But the excitement could not hide the fact that Naomi and Ruth had to find a way of surviving without husbands to support them.

Ruth had an idea. As the barley harvest was underway, she suggested to Naomi that she go out into the fields and walk behind the workers, picking up the surplus grain that they had left behind.

Now, it so happened that the field she had chosen belonged to one of Naomi's wealthy relatives, Boaz, who noticed Ruth and ask his foremen who she was.

Boaz approached her and said, "Stay in this field with my workers. You will be quite safe and if you need a drink, help yourself from the water jars."

"Thank you, sir," she replied, her eyes lowered to the ground. "But why are you being so kind to me? I was not born here. I am a foreigner."

"I have heard all about your kindness to your mother-in-law. I know how hard it must have been for you to follow her into a strange land. May the Lord God of Israel, in whom you put your trust, reward you with many blessings." And with that, he invited her to eat with him and his workers in the field.

"You are very kind, sir," she said, suddenly feeling much better.

From then on Boaz took special care of Ruth, instructing his workers to pull barley stalks from their bundles and to leave them on the ground for her to pick up.

When Ruth returned home that evening, Naomi was amazed at all the grain she had brought. "God bless the man who let you take so much from his field. What is his name?" she asked.

"Boaz," Ruth replied.

"Praise God," Naomi said. "He is one of our relatives, and is responsible for looking after us. You will be safe in his field."

So until the harvest was finished, Ruth gathered food in the fields of Boaz.

One day Naomi said to Ruth, "Daughter, you should be married. Go to Boaz. Put on clean clothes and perfume and go to his barn tonight. Wait until he has eaten and settled down to sleep, then wake him and lie at his feet. He will know what this means."

Ruth did as she was told and when Boaz woke he found her at his feet. He knew this was a request for marriage.

"Ruth," he said, "you are a fine woman. You could have asked a much younger man to marry you, but you did not. However, I am not your nearest relative. I know the man who is, and he has first responsibility to look after you. Stay here tonight and in the morning, I will ask him to marry you."

The next day Boaz met the man, but he did not wish to marry Ruth. So the matter was settled. Boaz married Ruth and in time they had a son. Naomi's friends praised God for bringing so much joy to her.

And, in the course of time, Ruth's son would become the grandfather of David, the greatest king that Israel ever had.

HANNAH'S SON

1 Samuel 1 – 3

In the hill town of Ramah, not far from Jerusalem, there lived a man whose name was Elkanah. He had two wives, one named Hannah and the other Peninnah. Peninnah had children, but to Hannah's sorrow she herself had none.

Every year, Elkanah took his family to Shiloh, where the Ark of the Covenant was kept, to worship God and offer sacrifices. On these occasions, Peninnah would deliberately torment Hannah for not having any children. Each year, she would keep up the humiliation until Hannah burst into tears and refused to eat. One day, Hannah could bear it no longer and cried out to the Lord, "Remember your humble servant, I beg you. If you give me a son, I promise I will dedicate him to your service for the whole of his life."

Eli, the priest, had been watching her odd behaviour and assumed she was drunk.

"I am not drunk," she said. "I am so very unhappy and I have been praying to God for a son. Do not think badly of me."

Immediately Eli realized his mistake. "Go in peace," he said. "And may your prayers be answered."

Nine months later, Hannah gave birth to a son, whom she named Samuel.

Hannah did not forget her promise to God. When Samuel was three years old, she took him back to Eli to be trained for God's work. "Do you remember me, sir?" she asked him. "Do you remember how I prayed for a son all those years ago? Well, here he is."

Each year, Hannah and her husband returned to Shiloh to worship and to watch Samuel's progress. He was a very dutiful boy and he served the Lord well – unlike Eli's own two sons, who were greedy and corrupt and who treated the worship of God with contempt. Samuel had to be properly dressed to perform his religious duties, so each year Hannah took him a fine robe. Eli was impressed by Hannah's devotion and said to her, "May the Lord bless you with other children to replace the one you dedicated to God's service."

And sure enough, in time, Hannah was blessed with three sons and two daughters.

By now Eli was an old man and was tired of hearing about the bad things his sons were doing. He summoned them and told them to mend their ways, but they ignored him and carried on as they had before. Samuel, by contrast, was very popular and much loved – especially by God.

One day, a man came to Eli's house. He was no ordinary man, but a prophet with a solemn warning from God that Eli's sons would be punished for their evil behaviour and that their contempt for the Lord would be rewarded by death. God, Eli was told, would strike them both dead on the same day and replace them with a faithful priest who would carry out God's duties properly.

Samuel, meanwhile, continued to serve the Lord well and one night, while he was asleep, the Lord called him by name. Samuel mistook the voice for Eli's and ran to his master's room, saying, "Here I am, sir. You called me. What do you want?"

"I did not call you," said Eli. "Go back to bed."

After a while, Samuel heard his name again and went back to Eli a second time. The same thing happened. When it happened a third time, Eli knew that it was God who was calling him, so he said to Samuel, "Go back to bed and, if you hear the voice again, say, 'Speak, Lord.

Your servant is listening.'"

As Eli had predicted, God spoke to Samuel again, saying, "The time will come when I will punish Eli's entire family for the contempt they have shown me. I warned Eli. But he did not stop his sons from dishonouring me. In future, no sacrifice or offering they make to me will take away their terrible sin."

When Samuel greeted Eli the next morning, he was afraid to reveal what the Lord had told him, but Eli insisted. "Tell me everything," he said, "or God will punish you."

When Samuel had told him, Eli said simply, "God is God. And God will do whatever is right."

Over the years, the Lord continued to bless Samuel. Everything he prophesied turned out to be true and soon his reputation spread throughout the whole land. Whenever he spoke, Israel listened.

THE PHILISTINES AND THE ARK

1 Samuel 4 – 6

Time passed and war broke out between the people of Israel and the Philistines. Two mighty armies gathered and faced each other to do battle. The Philistines attacked first and, after fierce fighting, defeated the Israelites, leaving four thousand soldiers dead or dying on the battlefield.

When the Israelite survivors returned to camp, their leaders wondered why God had allowed the Philistines to defeat them. "Quick," they shouted, "fetch the Ark of the Covenant from Shiloh and bring it here. That will protect us from our enemies."

When the Ark arrived, the Israelites let out such a cheer that the ground shook, alerting the Philistines in their camp that something important had happened.

At first the Philistines were afraid and said, "The Israelite God has come into their camp – the one who slaughtered the Egyptians in the desert. Who can save us now? We have no chance."

But their leaders rallied. "Be strong," they shouted, "and fight like men, or we will become their slaves."

The Philistines fought hard and won. Thirty thousand Israelite soldiers were slaughtered, including Eli's sons, as God had warned. The Israelites ran for their lives, hotly pursued by the Philistines, who finally captured the Ark of the Covenant and took it away in triumph.

One soldier, who fled the battle, raced back to Shiloh to break the terrible news. Everyone was horrified, especially Eli, who fell back off his chair in shock. He broke his neck and died.

Once back at home, the Philistine leaders installed the captured Ark in the temple they used for the worship of their god, Dagon. They placed it next to his statue and, the next morning, were surprised to discover the statue lying face down on the ground in front of the Ark. The Philistines picked up Dagon's statue and put it back where it belonged. The next morning, it had toppled over again – this time breaking off the head and both hands. But worse things were to come.

First, the Lord sent a plague to punish them, causing painful sores to break out all over their bodies. The Philistines were terrified and realized something had to be done. After urgent talks, the Philistine leaders decided to take the Ark to a neighbouring city. But no sooner had it arrived, than that city, too, was struck with plague and disease. In fact, the Ark brought misfortune to the Israelites' enemies everywhere it went. Panic broke out as the sickness spread until, finally, the Philistines decided to return it to the Israelites.

"Be sure to send the box back with a gift for their God," said the Philistine priests and magicians. "Then our people will be cured."

They took a new cart and hitched two cows to it. "Bring the Ark of the Covenant," said the magicians, "and load it onto the cart with the gifts you have brought."

"Where should we take it?" they asked.

"Nowhere. It will go by itself. Get the cows moving and watch where they take it. If it goes back to the Israelites, then we will know that it was their God who sent these terrible disasters. If it does not, then the plagues and diseases we have suffered were just chance misfortunes."

The Philistines were left in no doubt. The cows made their way directly to the Israelites, who were overjoyed by the return of the Ark. It was taken down from the cart and carefully placed on a large rock. After this, the cart was chopped up and burnt as an offering to God.

Even on its return to the people of Israel, the Ark of the Covenant continued to exert its terrible power. Seventy of the Israelites who were rash enough to look into the Ark were immediately struck dead. No one could stand in the presence of the Lord and live.

In time, leadership of the Israelites passed to the prophet Samuel, who had become a wise and respected man. All his life, he encouraged people to turn away from pagan gods and to worship the one true God. Only then, he said, would they be safe from the Philistine army, and only then would there be peace in the land.

SAMUEL AND SAUL

1 Samuel 8 – 15

When Samuel was an old man, he appointed his sons as judges to rule over Israel. This turned out to be a disastrous decision, because they showed no signs of following their father's devotion to God. Instead, the brothers were interested only in bribery, greed and corruption.

In desperation, the people of Israel came to Samuel and begged him to appoint a king to rule over them. Samuel was not at all happy with their request, so he prayed to God for guidance.

"You must understand that it is not your authority they are questioning – but mine!" said God. "I am their King if only they knew it. But ever since I brought them out of Egypt, they have turned away from me and worshipped other gods. Listen to the people, but make it very clear to them what they should expect this king of theirs to do."

The next day Samuel addressed them. "So you want a king," he said. "Very well. But be prepared for what this king will do. He will make soldiers out of your sons and draft them into every division of his army. They will have to work his fields, gather his crops and make weapons of war for him. As for your daughters, they will be his cooks and his bakers. Your fields, vineyards and olive groves will be taken from you and distributed among his servants. Then, of what little he allows you to keep, he will demand a tenth to give to his personal staff

at court. Your livestock will not be yours any more and you will become very bitter. But the Lord will not listen to your complaints because you were the ones who asked for a king in the first place."

The people paid no attention whatsoever. They said stubbornly, "No! We want a king, so we can be like other nations."

"Do as they wish," said God to Samuel. "Give them a king."

One day, a tall, handsome, young man from the tribe of Benjamin went out to search for some donkeys that had wandered off from his father's camp. His name was Saul and little did he know that he was to be that king. Together with his father's servant, he set off into the hills to look for the animals, but without success. Then the servant suggested visiting a local holy man who was well known as a seer – someone gifted with the power to see visions of the future. The seer was Samuel.

Samuel had been forewarned of Saul's arrival in a vision the night before and had been told by God to make him king. "Do not worry about the donkeys," he said to Saul. "They have already been found and are safe. Stay and eat with me tonight and tomorrow we will talk about more important matters. God has great things in store for you and your tribe."

Saul was puzzled because the tribe of Benjamin was not at all powerful compared to the others. In fact, it was the smallest tribe of Israel.

At dawn the next morning, as Saul got ready to leave, Samuel told Saul what God had said to him. Saul was astonished. Then Samuel took a jar of olive oil and poured it on Saul's head with these words: "The Lord anoints you as king of the people of Israel. You are to rule them and protect them from their enemies."

Some time later, Samuel called the people of Israel together and told them that he would give them the king they so desperately desired. This, he said, would be Saul, who was so reluctant that he had taken himself off and hidden behind some sacks. "Are you sure?" the people asked. "Where is he anyway? Perhaps it should be someone else?"

Just then the Lord spoke. "Saul is over there, hiding among your supplies of grain."

And with that Saul emerged, head and shoulders above any of the other men, as the people shouted in a loud voice, "Long live the king!"

At first Saul was a good king. He was a courageous man who led his people into battle and defeated Israel's enemies. But gradually he put his own desires above the wishes of God and his arrogance grew and grew. This was not what God had wanted and Samuel was told to confront Saul with his disobedience. Initially, Saul tried to wriggle out of the accusations, but it was clear that he had sinned. Eventually, Saul admitted his guilt and the two men parted forever. With a heavy heart Samuel went back to his home town as God looked on, sorry that Saul had ever been made king in the first place.

DAVID

1 Samuel 16:1 — 17:3

Samuel was still upset that he and Saul had been forced to part. God said to him, *"How long do you intend grieving over Saul? I have rejected him as the king of Israel and now someone else must take his place. Take a jar of oil and go to Bethlehem, to the house of Jesse. I have chosen one of his sons to be king."*

Samuel was worried. What if Saul got to hear of the plan? He would surely be killed for his disloyalty.

"Do it in secret," said God. "Take a calf and say you are simply offering up a sacrifice to the Lord. Invite Jesse along and await further instructions from me. I will tell you who is to be anointed king."

When Samuel arrived in Bethlehem, the elders were nervous. "Do you come

in peace?" they asked, suspiciously.

"Yes, I do," said Samuel. "I have come to offer a sacrifice to the Lord." Then he turned to Jesse and added, "Tell your sons to prepare for it."

As Jesse's sons filed in, one by one, Samuel looked at them all closely. As each one passed he thought, "He is a fine young man, so tall and handsome. Surely he is the one to be king."

But each time God said, "No! Ignore their outward appearances. Do as I do and search inside each man's heart before you judge."

When he had seen Jesse's seven sons, Samuel turned to Jesse and asked him if he had any others.

"Yes. There is still my youngest," said Jesse. "He is out in the hills taking care of the sheep."

"Send for him," said Samuel. "The sacrifice cannot begin until he is here. What is his name?"

"David," came the reply.

When the boy arrived, the Lord immediately told Samuel that David should be anointed as the future king. So Samuel took the oil and, in front of the seven brothers, poured it on David's head as a sign of his majesty.

David was never quite the same from that day on, though outwardly his life returned to normal. Each day, he went into the hills to tend the sheep and protect them from wild animals. To do this he had made himself a sling. Every day, he practised firing stones at targets until he became an expert shot – able to kill even lions and bears if

they threatened his sheep. In his spare time, he also played the harp, and he became famous for his music and songs.

Meanwhile, an evil spirit had come upon Saul, who complained to his servants that his heart was troubled. "Go and find me a man who can play sweet music to comfort me," he commanded them.

"I know just the person," said one of Saul's attendants. "Jesse's son, David. He is a fine musician, he plays the harp beautifully, and God has blessed him with courage and good looks as well."

So Saul immediately summoned David to the court. It was a great honour for Jesse's family and a cause of pride for Jesse himself, who sent David off with gifts of food and wine to offer to the king. As soon as David arrived, he made an impression on Saul with his radiant face and sparkling eyes, and was appointed Saul's personal spear carrier. The king sent Jesse a message. "I like your son, David," it read. "Let him stay here with me in my service."

From that moment, whenever Saul was troubled with evil spirits, he sent for David, who would play his harp softly to him. Immediately, the evil spirits would depart, Saul's mood would lighten, and all would be well for a time. But outside, all was far from well. Israel's sworn enemies, the Philistines, were on the march again, spoiling for a fight. This time they were preparing for a huge battle with King Saul and his people – in order to destroy them once and for all. They set up camp close to the Israelite position and waited. Then, as the battle lines were drawn, they unleashed their secret weapon.

DAVID AND GOLIATH

1 Samuel 17

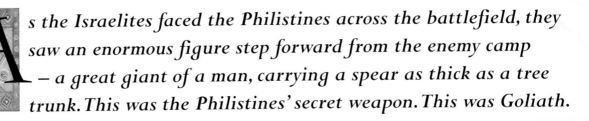

As the Israelites faced the Philistines across the battlefield, they saw an enormous figure step forward from the enemy camp — a great giant of a man, carrying a spear as thick as a tree trunk. This was the Philistines' secret weapon. This was Goliath.

Goliath faced the Israelites and challenged Saul to send one of his men to fight him. "If I die," he roared, "our army will serve yours. If not, you will be our slaves." His words struck terror into Saul and his army.

Meanwhile, David was back tending his father's sheep, as he often did when he was not with the king. His three eldest brothers had joined Saul's army and his father, Jesse, was concerned for their wellbeing. "Take some bread and cheese to the soldiers," Jesse told David, "and see how your brothers are getting on."

As David got closer to the camp, he could see the gigantic figure of Goliath.

"Who is this heathen Philistine?" he cried angrily. "Who does he think he is to take on the army of God?"

When news of David's arrival reached Saul, he sent for him. "Why let this Philistine frighten us?" asked David confidently. "I will fight him."

"You can't," said the king. "You are only a boy. Goliath has been a warrior all his life."

"I may only be a young shepherd boy," David replied, "but I have had to protect the flock from bears and lions. And if the Lord has allowed me to beat them, I'll surely be allowed to beat Goliath."

"All right," said Saul. "May the Lord be with you."

Refusing both weapons and armour, David picked five smooth pebbles from the stream then put them in his pouch. Armed only with a sling shot and a stick, he walked towards his mighty opponent.

Goliath looked at the boy and sneered, "Have you come to throw sticks at me? I will chop you up into little pieces and feed you to the birds."

"You may be armed with a sword and a shield," said David, "but, because God is on my side, I have the power to kill you. And I will."

Then David placed a pebble in his sling and sent it flying, shattering Goliath's skull with one direct hit. The giant crumpled to the ground. David ran up to his still body, took Goliath's sword, and cut off his head.

When the Philistines saw what had happened to their champion, they fled. As for the Israelites, they were overjoyed. Victory was theirs.

DAVID, SAUL AND JONATHAN

1 Samuel 18 – 20

David was invited to live permanently in the king's household. Saul's son, Jonathan, quickly took a great liking to him and swore everlasting friendship. David was successful at everything he did and rose to great prominence in the royal army, where he was very popular.

David's popularity and his astonishing defeat of Goliath had captured the people's imagination and made him a national hero. Indeed, on his return from the battlefield, David had been met by crowds of adoring women who had originally turned out to welcome Saul. They sang and danced and beat their tambourines to welcome home their victorious king, but when they caught sight of David, they sang to a different tune. "Saul has killed thousands," they chanted, "but David has killed tens of thousands!"

This angered King Saul, who began to fear that David might be a rival. From that moment on his jealousy grew and grew.

One day, David was quietly playing his harp in the king's household. He often did this, but for some reason his playing now began to annoy Saul intensely, putting him in a bad mood. He stormed through the house shouting and cursing like a madman. Suddenly, he picked up a spear and hurled it at David, who only just managed to escape with his life.

After this, Saul began to send David on more and more dangerous missions, in the hope that he would be killed in battle. But David proved to be so skilful a commander that he killed his opponents every time, which served only to increase his popularity – and the king's jealousy.

Meanwhile Saul could see that his daughter, Michal, was falling in love with this handsome and brave young man and he saw his chance to get rid of David once and for all. Yes, they could be married, but only on the condition that David proved himself by killing a hundred Philistines. But once again the plan went wrong, and the king was horrified to learn that, far from being killed in battle, David had actually slaughtered two hundred of his enemies.

By now, Saul had made it clear that he intended to rid himself of David. Jonathan passed this information on to his beloved friend, but made one last attempt to persuade his father to change his mind. For a while it was safe for David to return to the court. But it was only a matter of time before Saul's jealousy got the better of him. As before, the moment came when David was playing his harp. Saul, who had fallen

into a murderous temper, was passing by, holding a spear when he saw David. Immediately, he lunged at him, trying to pin him to the wall. But David reacted swiftly, dodged the spear, and ran away.

That same night Saul sent men to David's house to kill him. But Michal, now David's wife, had heard of the plot, and warned David to run. She laid a statue in her husband's bed, covered it with a blanket and put a pillow under its head. Saul's men stormed the house, only to be told that David was ill in bed. When they informed Saul of this, he was furious.

"Bring him to me in his bed, then, and I'll kill him myself!" he bellowed.

The men did as they were told. Once inside David's bedchamber, they pulled back the blanket and saw the statue where David should have been. The king's anger exploded. Now he had only one thing on his mind – David's murder.

Meanwhile, David had made for the only safe place he knew – Samuel's home –

where
he stayed
until he could get
a message to Jonathan
to arrange a meeting.

"Am I still in danger?" asked David.

"Yes, my friend, you are," said Jonathan, barely able to hold back his tears. "When I mentioned your name my father tried to kill me. He accused me of siding with you against him. Then he threw his spear across the room and nearly struck me. David, he wants you dead."

"Then, dear Jonathan, we must part forever."

By now both of them were weeping and they embraced each other one last time. Jonathan looked into David's eyes and said, "God be with you. Our friendship will never die."

Then the two men said goodbye for good. Jonathan went back home and David, all alone, was an outlaw in his own land.

DAVID THE OUTLAW

1 Samuel 21 – 26

avid quickly gathered around him a band of trusted men and together they lived a life on the run. They moved from place to place, sleeping and eating wherever they could, constantly in fear of attack by Saul and his army.

One day, with supplies running dangerously low, David called on a priest, named Ahimelech, and asked whether he could provide him and his men with bread.

"The only bread I have is that which has been specially blessed for the worship of God," Ahimelech said. "It can be eaten only by those who have kept themselves ritually pure."

"My men and I always purify ourselves at the start of any mission," David replied. "I can assure you that, for a mission such as this one with the king's personal backing, we are certainly purified."

"Very well," said Ahimelech and he brought David the bread.

"I need a sword, too," said David.

"Over there," said Ahimelech, pointing towards an object wrapped in cloth on the other side of the room. "This is the sword Goliath tried to use against you. Take it. It is the only weapon I have."

"Give it to me," said David. "There is no finer sword anywhere."

Then, he set off, fearing that Saul would catch up with him at any moment.

But strangely, Saul was just as afraid of

David, whom he was convinced had formed an alliance with his own son, Jonathan, to kill him. He was suspicious of everyone, even his own officers. Anyone who was discovered to have given help of any kind to the fugitive David was ruthlessly put to death.

Ahimelech was the first to pay such a price. One of the king's officials, Doeg, had seen David visit the priest. When Doeg told the king, Saul summoned Ahimelech and accused him of plotting against him. Ahimelech denied the charge of conspiracy, but admitted he had given David the bread. "Your Majesty," he said, "David is the most faithful officer you have. Everybody respects him. As for plotting against you, I would never do anything of the sort."

"Ahimelech," said the king coldly, "you have told me all I need to know. You and your family must die."

But Saul's guards refused to carry out the order. They could not bring themselves to kill one of the Lord's priests. "Very well, then," shouted Saul, turning to Doeg, "you kill him!" And so it was that Ahimelech and his fellow priests – eighty-five in all –

were put to death that day. But the killing did not stop there. All Ahimelech's family and the entire population of his home town were executed – men, women, children and babies. Even their cattle, donkeys and sheep were slaughtered where they stood. Only one of Ahimelech's sons managed to escape, joining David and telling him about the events of that terrible day.

All the time David was in hiding, the Lord watched over him and ensured that he was safe from Saul and his men, even though they were out for his blood and were hunting for him everywhere.

But one day the tables were turned and he had the upper hand over Saul.

David and his men had taken cover in a cave in the hills when, to their amazement, in walked Saul, alone and unarmed.

"Now's your chance," whispered one of David's men. "The Lord is delivering your enemy to you to deal with as you wish."

David approached Saul from behind and, with his knife, cut off a piece of the king's robe without him noticing. He did him no harm because he realized that he could not kill the man whom God had made king.

But David was anxious to let Saul know he had spared his life and, as the king left the cave, he went after him and shouted, "Your Majesty, you can see I mean you no harm. Your life was in my hands a moment ago and I spared it." With this, he waved the piece of Saul's robe as proof. Then Saul was overcome with guilt and wept, for he knew that David would one day be king.

But David's generosity did not prevent Saul from pursuing him further and several times Saul almost had him in his sights. On one occasion, Saul and three thousand of his best troops were hot on his trail. They pitched camp the night before they hoped to attack. But David had been forewarned of Saul's plans by spies and decided, once again, to turn the tables.

He and a volunteer crept into Saul's camp and found the king fast asleep lying by his spear. David's companion whispered to him, "Your enemy is in your power. Let me take his own spear and plunge it through his head. I can pin him to the ground with a single blow."

"No," David said. "The Lord will kill Saul when his time has come. I cannot kill the man God chose to be king."

Instead, he took Saul's spear and his water jar, crept out of the camp and made for the other side of the valley. Then in a loud voice which woke the entire camp, he shouted, "Fine guards you are! You should have been protecting the king – not exposing him to danger. Go and check on his spear and water jar. Where are they?"

Saul and his men looked at each other in alarm.

"You won't find them there," shouted David. "They're here. Look!" And he held them up as proof that he had been within an inch of the sleeping king.

"God bless you," shouted Saul. "You will succeed in eveything you do." David paused for a moment, realizing that Saul was sorry. But it was too late. How could David trust the king any more? David went on his way, leaving Saul sad and troubled.

DAVID BECOMES KING

2 Samuel 1 – 10

One day, important news reached David's camp. Saul and Jonathan were dead, killed in battle with the Philistines. Even though Saul had wanted him dead, David could not contain his grief and wrote a sad song to honour both Saul and his son.

"How are the mighty fallen," he sang. "Saul and Jonathan were fine men in life and now they are united in death. They were swifter than eagles; they were stronger than lions. They were brave soldiers and now they lie dead in the hills. Jonathan, my brother, how I grieve for you."

But the people of Israel were still deeply divided among themselves. After Saul's death, the northern tribes chose one of Saul's descendants to be their king, while the southern tribes chose David as theirs. For some years, the two sides were at war, before eventually burying their differences and reuniting under David, who at the age of thirty was anointed king of all Israel. And so God's promise came true. Israel would serve David and his royal line.

Their confidence restored, David's men marched north to take Jerusalem. After a swift and decisive victory, David captured the Fortress of Zion (as Jerusalem was also known) and renamed it the City of David.

Wood and stone for the royal palace were brought from Lebanon, and the city, which became the capital of the kingdom, grew stronger and stronger. But military strength alone was not enough for David.

He knew that the only true strength and power came from God.

To show his devotion, he brought the Ark of the Covenant to the city, where it was installed in a ceremonial tent. The crowds sang and danced – with King David outdancing them all. The city was now not just his capital. It was the city of God.

But one day, David's conscience began to trouble him. "Here I am living in a palace of cedar wood and stone," he said to the prophet Nathan, "when God's Ark is kept in a tent."

"In that case, Your Majesty," Nathan replied, "you should do something about it."

But that night, the Lord spoke to Nathan and told him that on no account should David construct anything more permanent to house the Law.

"You, David, are not the one to build a Temple for me to live in," said God. "That task will fall to one of your sons. I took you from the fields where you were a shepherd, and put you in this palace where you are a king. I have been with you wherever you have gone, I have defeated your enemies for you, and now I will make you one of the most famous leaders the world has known."

And so it was. David proved to be a brave soldier, a fine statesman and a great leader. But, for all his many qualities, he had his weaknesses.

DAVID AND BATHSHEBA

2 Samuel 11:1 – 12:24

The Israelites were fighting the Ammonites, and King David, in constant contact with his commander-in-chief, Joab, was in Jerusalem planning his next move. One evening, from the palace roof, he saw a beautiful woman bathing down below.

"Who is that?" he asked his servants.

"Bathsheba, the wife of Uriah the Hittite," they answered nervously.

"Send her to me," he ordered. Bathsheba was duly brought to the palace where David took her to his bed. In time, she discovered she was pregnant with his child and sent David a message telling him so.

Immediately, David instructed Uriah, one of his best generals, to return home on leave. The next day, however, David was informed that Uriah had spent the night sleeping at the door of the palace.

"Did you not see your wife?" asked David.

"How can I do that, Your Majesty?" he replied. "Joab and our men are camped in the open fields, waiting for the next stage of their attack. The Ark of the Covenant is there too. By all that is holy, I could not go home to eat, drink and sleep with my wife while our people are fighting."

There and then David devised a wicked plan to rid himself of Uriah. The next morning, he sent Uriah back to the battle with a letter for Joab. Little did Uriah know that it contained his death warrant. "Put Uriah in the front line, where the fighting

is heaviest," the letter read. "Then retreat, leave him exposed and let him die."

Joab sent Uriah and his men to spot where the enemy was strongest. The tiny force was no match for the Ammonite troops, who cut them down where they stood.

When Bathsheba heard of her husband's death, she was full of grief. Once her period of mourning was over, David sent for her again and made her his wife. In time, she gave birth to a son. But God was not pleased with what David had done and sent the prophet Nathan to speak to him.

When the two met, Nathan began telling him a story. "There were two men living in the same town," he began. "One was rich and the other was poor. The rich man had many cattle and sheep, while the poor man had only one lamb, which he loved as a daughter. He gave it scraps of his food, played with it, and even let it drink from his cup.

"Then one day, a traveller arrived at the rich man's house. The stranger needed food, but the rich man did not want to kill one of his animals. Instead he took the poor man's lamb, roasted it and fed it to his guest."

"Any man who could do such a cruel

thing should die," said David furiously.

Nathan paused, then said calmly, "But you have done just the same. You are that man."

David went pale as Nathan continued. "Listen! These are the words of God: 'I made you king of Israel and rescued you from Saul. I set you to rule over Israel and Judah and this is how you repay me. Why have you disobeyed my commands? Why did you have Uriah killed? Why did you steal his wife? Terrible punishment awaits you.'"

"I have sinned against the Lord," said David.

"The Lord forgives you," replied Nathan. "You will live, but for your sins, your son will die."

The child of Bathsheba and David became very ill and David begged the Lord to make him better. The king refused to eat anything and every night went to his son's room where

he lay beside his bed. He did not wash, comb his hair or change his clothes. All he could do was to pray that his son would survive. A week later, the boy died.

When he was told the news, David washed, combed his hair and changed his clothes. Then he said his prayers and ate a meal. His servants were puzzled and asked him why he was eating when previously he had been weeping and fasting. "It is true that I fasted while the boy was alive," he replied. "I thought that the Lord would answer my prayers and spare him. But now that the boy is dead, why should I fast any more? I cannot bring him back to life. I will some day go to where he is now, but he will never come back to me."

DAVID AND ABSALOM

2 Samuel 14:25 – 18:33

Of David's sons, Absalom was the most handsome and David loved him dearly. His rash behaviour often upset his father, who always forgave him, nonetheless. But Absalom's ambition to be king himself was to prove his downfall.

Absalom's plan was clever. First he bought a chariot and horses, and assembled an escort of fifty men. Every day, he stood by Jerusalem's city gate, where he established himself as the people's friend, helping them on matters of law and offering his services as a representative of the king.

Then one day, he approached his father and asked to go to Hebron to worship the Lord. "Go in peace," said David. But Absalom had other intentions. He sent messengers to all the tribes of Israel saying, "When you hear the sound of trumpets, shout, 'Absalom has become king in Hebron!'"

The plot against the king quickly gained strength. Even Ahithophel, one of David's principal advisors, joined in the rebellion. At last, with Absalom's army growing in number day by day, David decided to leave Jerusalem with his family and head for the safety of open country. It was now civil war and David was a fugitive once again.

But first he went to pray at the Mount of Olives, saddened that Ahithophel had joined Absalom's army. "Turn his advice against him," he prayed. Then he looked up and saw his trusted friend, Hushai.

In a flash, David realized how he might turn the situation to his advantage. "You will be of no use if you come along with me," he said. "Better for you to go to Absalom and pretend to be on his side. Tell him you will serve him as you served me. Do all you can to counteract Ahithophel's advice."

At first, Absalom was puzzled that Hushai had abandoned David to join him, but he overcame his doubts and invited him to join his team of advisors.

"Let me choose twelve thousand men and set out tonight," said Ahithophel. "We will have the advantage of surprise and we can snatch David while he is exhausted and on the defensive. This way we can target the king and spare everybody else."

"I like the idea," said Absalom. "What do you think, Hushai?"

"I'm not so sure," he replied. "David and his men are fierce fighters and they will put up resistance despite their exhaustion. And, besides, David is experienced enough not to make himself a sitting target by staying with his men. He is probably hiding in a cave somewhere. No, my advice is to wait until we have amassed a much bigger

army. Then we can crush him by sheer force of numbers."

Absalom took Hushai's advice, enabling David, who had been warned of the plan by friends, to escape and consolidate his forces. Before finally going into battle, however, David warned his men to spare Absalom.

The bloodshed was terrible and twenty thousand men lost their lives that day. As the fighting spread out into the woodland, Absalom suddenly found himself cut off from his men. He tried to gallop away, but his long hair became caught in the branches of an overhanging tree and he was left dangling in the air. The soldiers remembered David's orders and spared him, but as soon as Joab heard of Absalom's plight, he rushed to the spot and hurled three spears into his enemy's heart. As Absalom fell to the ground, ten of Joab's men closed in to finish him off.

When the news was broken to David, he was inconsolable. "Oh, my son Absalom," he wailed. "Absalom, Absalom! If only I could have died in your place."

And so it was that a day of victory turned into a day of mourning.

SOLOMON THE WISE

1 Kings 1 – 3

King David was now a very old man, and it was time to find his successor. David insisted that his son Solomon should be king. He was escorted to the Spring of Gihon where Zadok, the priest, anointed him. The trumpets sounded and the people shouted, "Long live King Solomon!"

Shortly before he died, David gave Solomon his last instructions. "Be strong and keep the Lord's commandments," he said. "If you obey God, your reign will be blessed." And so it was. After David's death, Solomon's kingdom prospered.

One of the first things he did was to make an alliance with the Egyptian Pharaoh by marrying his daughter. He brought her to Jerusalem and set to work on the construction of his palace. Most important of all, he drew up plans to build a Temple to the Lord – a Temple where sacrifices could be made and where the Ark of the Covenant could find a permanent home.

One night, the Lord appeared to Solomon in a dream. "What would you like me to give you?" asked God.

"I am young and inexperienced," Solomon replied, "and I have responsibility for many people. So give

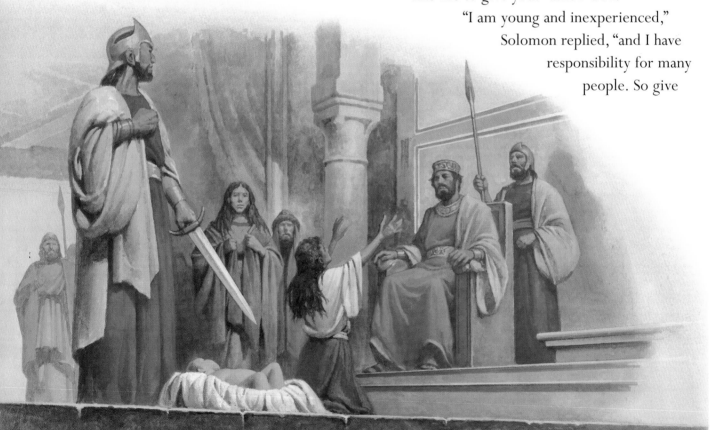

me the wisdom I need to rule with justice, and the ability to tell good from evil."

This pleased the Lord, who said, "I am glad you chose wisdom rather than wealth or long life. For that, your reward will be more wisdom and understanding than anyone has ever had before. And I will also give you what you have not asked for: wealth, fame and a long life – on condition that you obey me!"

At this, Solomon awoke.

One day, Solomon was called on to judge a very difficult case involving two women and a baby.

The first woman said, "Your Majesty, this woman and I share a house and both of us gave birth to baby boys at about the same time. One night, this woman accidentally rolled over in her sleep and smothered her son. Immediately, she got up and switched the two children, so that my baby was sleeping next to her and her dead child was lying beside me. As soon as I woke up, I knew what had happened, but whom could I tell? There was no one else in the house."

"She's lying!" cried the other woman. "The dead baby is hers."

"No, it is not! The living child is mine," said the first woman.

And so the argument went on.

"Bring me a sword," said Solomon gravely. "You both say the living child is yours, so I will cut the baby in two and give you both half."

The first woman almost fainted with shock. "No, Your Majesty," she pleaded, her heart full of love for her child. "Please do not kill the baby. Give it to her."

But the other woman said, "No. Cut it in two and give us half each."

Immediately, Solomon knew who the real mother was and he handed the baby, unharmed, to the first woman. When the people of Israel heard of Solomon's judgment, they were deeply impressed by his wisdom.

As God had promised, the people of Judah and Israel grew in number until there were as many of them as grains of sand on the seashore. Under Solomon they prospered and lived in peace with the neighbouring countries. His kingdom stretched from the River Euphrates in the east to the borders of Egypt in the west. The supplies he needed every day were colossal: thousands and thousands of kilos of flour and grain; dozens and dozens of cattle; hundreds of sheep, deer, gazelles and chickens; plus all the barley and straw needed to feed the animals.

In his lifetime, his people were safe and well fed and each family had its grapevines and fig trees. And all the while, God gave Solomon wisdom and knowledge too great to be measured. He was wiser than the wisest man who had ever lived, and he composed three thousand proverbs and over a thousand songs. He knew everything there was to know about plants and animals – so much so that kings from all over the world sent people to him to learn from his wisdom.

His knowledge was to be of great use to him in his most important project of all – the construction, in the heart of the City of Jerusalem, of a massive Temple to the Lord.

THE TEMPLE

1 Kings 5 – 8

After four years of prosperity and peace in the land, Solomon knew that it was time to build a great temple for the worship of the Lord. The finest cedar and pine wood was rafted down the coast from Lebanon and the work began.

A team of eighty thousand men quarried rock from the mountains, then another seventy thousand men transported it to Jerusalem, where the foundations of the Temple were laid. At the rear of the Temple, a special room was built, a perfect cube covered on all sides with pure gold. This was the inner room, the Holy of Holies, the heart of the Temple. Here the Ark of the Covenant, the sacred vessel containing the laws of God, was to be placed.

In an outer room, lined from floor to ceiling with beautifully carved cedar wood, stood an altar. Beyond this were courtyards with bronze pillars and special bronze tanks resting on stands carved in the shape of bulls.

At the end of seven years, the Temple was complete. Solomon gathered his people together and, after the sacred Ark of the Covenant had been formally installed, he faced them and said, "Praise the Lord of Israel and obey God's commands." Then he prayed, saying, "Lord, look down on your people of Israel and hear us when we call to you for help. And may we be always

faithful to your word."

With that, the Temple was finally dedicated and, after a week-long celebration, the people returned home happy.

THE QUEEN OF SHEBA

1 Kings 9:1-9; 10:1-13

olomon's fame spread far and wide and soon everyone had heard of his great wisdom and knowledge. The Queen of Sheba, intrigued by his reputation, decided to travel to Jerusalem to see whether all she had heard was true.

She brought camels loaded up with spices, gold and precious stones to give to the king. When the two met, she asked him all the questions she could think of, but there was not a single one he could not answer.

She then wandered around his palace. Everything, from the food on his table to the uniforms his servants wore, took her breath away. "Everything I have heard about you is true," she told him. "I would not have believed it unless I had seen it with my own eyes.

"Your people are fortunate to have such a wise ruler. The Lord must be very pleased with you to have made you their king. God's love for Israel is eternal, so you are greatly honoured to be chosen to reign over it, maintaining the Law and ruling with justice."

Just then Solomon recalled a recent dream, and as the queen spoke, he remembered what the Lord had said to him: "If you obey my laws and do as I have commanded, then I will keep the promise I made to your father, and allow his descendants to rule over the land of Israel forever. But if you or your descendants cease to obey me and choose to follow other gods, then I will tear the people from this land and abandon the Temple that has been dedicated to me. The once proud people of Israel will become a laughing stock and this fine Temple will collapse into ruins, so that people will look at it and say, 'What did Israel do to bring this upon itself?' But in their heart of hearts they will know that this was the punishment for straying from the word of the one true God."

At this point King Solomon became aware of the silence that had settled on the room.

"Is anything the matter, Your Majesty?" the queen asked.

"No, nothing," he replied. "Now, before you leave, is there anything else I can do for you?"

"Please accept these gifts," she said. Her servants appeared with gold, spices and precious stones and presented them to Solomon in such quantities as he had never seen before.

"Thank you, Your Majesty," he said, and in return he showered her with presents and gave her everything she desired. Then she and her servants left Jerusalem and returned to the land of Sheba.

The Divided Kingdom

1 Kings 11:26-40; 12 – 13

Solomon had many wives — women from foreign lands who worshipped their own strange gods and persuaded the king to do so too. This angered the Lord, who predicted the destruction of Solomon's kingdom — not in his lifetime, but in his son's.

Solomon had ordered the rebuilding of Jerusalem's eastern wall, and had put a talented young man called Jeroboam in charge of the labourers. One day, a prophet told Jeroboam that because Solomon worshipped foreign idols, the kingdom was to be divided. Jeroboam would have ten tribes and become the king of Israel in the north. Solomon's son, Rehoboam, would have only one tribe and become king of Judah, ruling from Jerusalem in the south.

When Solomon learnt of the prophecy, he tried to kill Jeroboam, but the young man fled to Egypt.

In time, Solomon died. Rehoboam became king, but soon faced a revolt by the people, with only the tribe of Judah pledging him loyalty. The remaining ten tribes of Israel rejected him and moved north into a separate territory.

With Solomon now dead, Jeroboam left Egypt and travelled north, where he was invited to be king of Israel. Just as God had warned, the kingdom was divided into two.

However, Jeroboam feared that his people, who regularly travelled south to the Temple in Jerusalem, would transfer their allegiance to Rehoboam. To prevent this, he constructed two enormous golden bulls and encouraged everyone to worship them.

This angered the Lord, who sent a prophet from Judah to Bethel in Israel, where Jeroboam was offering sacrifices to the golden bull gods. The prophet arrived as these sacrifices were taking place.

Fearlessly he shouted, "Listen! The Lord has told me to tell you this: a child, who will be named Josiah, will be born to the family of David and he will put an end to this pagan worship. Then your priests will be sacrificed on your own altars."

When King Jeroboam heard this, he ordered his men to seize the prophet, but as he stretched out his arm towards him, it became temporarily paralyzed. At that very moment, the altar smashed into a thousand pieces — a clear sign of God's displeasure.

More worrying prophecies followed, one of which struck terror into King Jeroboam.

"I chose you to be king of Israel," said God, "and look how you have repaid me. For your sins I shall punish you and your descendants. Israel will be uprooted from this land and scattered on the wind forever."

ELIJAH AND THE RAVENS

1 Kings 16:29 – 17:24

For forty years after Jeroboam's death, the northern kingdom of Israel was ruled by a series of kings who turned away from the Lord and worshipped other gods. But they were all surpassed in wickedness by King Ahab, who built a temple to Baal, the Canaanite god of fertility.

Ahab and his Canaanite wife Jezebel did more to anger God than any of their predecessors. Jezebel, in particular, was a cold-hearted, cruel woman who ruthlessly exterminated anyone who challenged her husband's authority.

The prophets who dared to do this were brave and devout men. They served God and kept the commandments, often in secret. But the price they paid for questioning the idolatry of Israel was constant persecution.

Queen Jezebel hated these troublesome prophets, and regularly tried to hunt them down, slaughtering them wherever they were found. One man, however, managed to survive these attacks and continued to be a thorn in the side of the wicked king

and queen. He was God's prophet Elijah.

One day, Elijah went to King Ahab to warn him of a terrible drought. This was bad news for the king. It was the last thing he wanted to hear and Elijah was the last person he wanted to see.

"I speak in the name of the one true God," said Elijah fearlessly. "Mark my words. There will be neither rain nor dew in this land for the next few years. Until I say so, not a drop of moisture will touch the earth."

Then God said to Elijah, "Now you must leave. Go east, beyond the River Jordan, to the Brook of Cherith and live there in secret. For now the brook will supply you with all the water you need and I have commanded ravens to bring you food."

So Elijah did as the Lord had commanded

and went to the brook. Every morning and every night, ravens would arrive carrying scraps of bread and meat in their beaks to keep him alive. But in time even the brook dried up because of the lack of rain.

All the time, however, Elijah trusted in the Lord, confident that he would be carefully looked after. And, sure enough, God spoke to him, telling him to go to the town of Zarephath near Sidon, where a widow would feed him.

He set off and, approaching the town gate, saw a woman gathering firewood. He asked her for a drink of water and, as she was going to fetch it, he asked her to bring him some bread too.

"I swear by the Lord Almighty, I have none," she said. "All I have is a cupful of flour and a few drops of olive oil in a stone jar. I came here to find what little wood I could to bake one last meal for my son and me. After that we will starve."

"Don't worry," Elijah said. "Go ahead and prepare your meal, but before you do, bake a small loaf and bring it to me. Then use the rest of the flour and oil to feed you and your son. Trust me. For the Lord, the God of Israel, says, 'The cup will not run out of flour and the jar will not run out of oil until the day on which I, the Lord, send rain from the sky.'"

The widow followed Elijah's instructions and all three of them had enough food for days. Just as the Lord had told Elijah, there was always just enough flour and oil to feed them all.

But one day the widow's son fell seriously ill. His condition got worse and worse until at last he died. The woman was so upset that she turned on Elijah and said bitterly, "Man of God, why did you do this to me? Did you come here to remind me of my sins and so bring about my son's death?"

For once, the prophet was lost for words. The widow stared at him accusingly until finally he said, "Give the boy to me."

Then Elijah took the boy upstairs to the room where he was staying and laid him gently on the bed.

"Oh Lord, my God," Elijah prayed, "why have you done such a terrible thing to this woman? She has been so kind to me and now you have rewarded her by killing her son."

Three times he prayed over the boy saying, "Oh Lord, my God, please bring the boy back to life."

In the stillness that followed, Elijah became aware of a sound in the room. It was the sound of the child breathing. God had answered Elijah's prayer. The boy had been brought back to life.

Gently Elijah took the boy's hand and led him downstairs to his mother, who could hardly believe her eyes.

"Here he is," said Elijah. "Your son is alive again." The boy smiled and ran straight to his mother.

Tears filled the woman's eyes as she held her son in her arms and said to Elijah, "Now I know for sure that you are a man of God and that you speak the truth." And, with that, Elijah said farewell to the two of them. He left the widow's house and set off — though he did not yet know it — towards the biggest challenge of his life.

THE PROPHETS OF BAAL

1 Kings 18:1-46

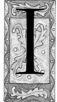 t was the third year of the drought and King Ahab, in desperation, accused Elijah of being the cause of Israel's trouble. "You are the troublemaker," Elijah said. "It is thanks to your idol worship that the Lord is punishing us."

Elijah knew that the only way to settle the matter once and for all was to prove that God was stronger than any foreign idol. He threw down a challenge.

"Meet me on Mount Carmel," he said. "Summon all the people of Israel to be there, along with the four hundred and fifty prophets of Baal."

King Ahab agreed. The scene was set for a spectacular demonstration of God's power.

"Will you worship God or Baal?" Elijah shouted, as the people assembled on the mountain top. "You cannot worship both. Let us see which of the two is truly the everlasting God Almighty."

The people remained silent.

Then Elijah looked at the prophets of Baal and said, "I am the only prophet of the Lord here. One man against hundreds of you!"

Elijah told the people to prepare two bulls for sacrifice. Then he instructed his opponents to build an altar. "Lay your bull on the altar," he said, "but do not light the fire. Let the prophets of Baal pray to their god, then I will pray to the Lord. Whichever answers by sending fire is the one true God."

The prophets of Baal built their altar,

and Elijah said, "You can begin."

"Hear us, Oh Baal!" they shouted, and began to dance around the altar. All morning, they repeated their prayers… but nothing happened.

By noon, Elijah had started to make fun of them. "Pray a bit louder," he laughed. "Perhaps your god's asleep and needs waking."

The prophets were now working themselves up into a great frenzy, but still nothing happened.

Then Elijah said to the people, "Come closer and watch." Now it was Elijah's turn to build an altar. A bull was placed on top and the firewood was drenched with water.

Then Elijah approached the altar and prayed, "Oh Lord, God of Abraham, Isaac and Jacob, prove that you are the God of Israel and that I am your servant."

And with that, the wet firewood exploded into flames, sending sparks high into the air and scorching the earth all around.

When the people saw this, they threw themselves on the ground and cried out, "The Lord is God! The Lord alone is God!"

The prophets of Baal were now very worried and they tried to get away. But

Elijah ordered them to be rounded up and put to death.

Then Elijah went to King Ahab and told him he could hear the sound of a storm approaching. The drought was finally over.

Elijah's servant, who had been scanning the horizon for signs of rain, confirmed it. "I've just seen a cloud no bigger than a man's hand," he said. "It is coming towards us from the sea."

Ahab decided to leave immediately, returning home in his chariot before the rain cut him off. In no time at all dark clouds filled the sky and the torrential downpour began. Elijah was so excited that he wrapped his clothes tightly around himself and, filled with the power of the Lord, sprinted ahead of Ahab's chariot, racing him back to the palace through the pouring rain.

THE WIND AND THE WHISPER

1 Kings 19:1-18

 **T**his had been a triumphant day for Elijah. He had proved himself to be a faithful prophet with an amazing display of God's power. But triumph was soon to turn to disappointment. Bad news awaited him at the palace.

Queen Jezebel had by now learnt of the public humiliation and execution of her personal priests and she was beside herself with fury. She decided to exact her revenge on Elijah, who was now forced to flee for his life.

Exhausted and miserable, he walked for a whole day, further and further into the desert, until he stopped in the shade of a juniper bush. There his strength gave out and he collapsed onto the ground, wishing he would die. "Oh Lord," he prayed, "I am so miserable. I cannot bear this. I am so tired and confused. Take my life away, I beg you."

Then he fell asleep.

After many, many hours, an angel awoke him and, pointing to a loaf of bread and a jar of water, told him to eat. After he had eaten, he immediately fell asleep again. The angel of the Lord watched over him, then awoke him a second time. "Get up and eat," said the angel, "or your journey will be too much for you."

Elijah got up, ate and drank, then walked for forty days and forty nights to Mount Sinai. There, feeling alone and abandoned by everyone, he spent the night in a cave. All this time God was trying to reach him, but Elijah had cut himself off completely.

So the Lord sent a furious wind, which split the rocks and startled Elijah. But the Lord was not in the wind. Then there was a gigantic earthquake, which made the ground tremble beneath Elijah's feet. But the Lord was not in the earthquake. After the earthquake, there was a fire. But the Lord was not in the fire.

And after the fire came a still small voice, like a whisper from the silence. When Elijah heard it, he wrapped his face in his cloak and stood by the cave's entrance.

"Elijah," the voice said, "what are you doing here?"

"Lord God Almighty, I have always served you," he replied. "The people of Israel have broken their covenant with you. They have killed your prophets and I am the only one left."

"Travel to Damascus," said the Lord. "There you will find a man named Elisha, who will follow in your footsteps as my prophet." Elijah obeyed and set off to anoint his successor.

NABOTH'S VINEYARD

1 Kings 21:1-19

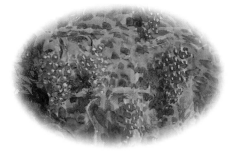

***C**lose by King Ahab's palace in Jezreel was a vineyard owned by a man named Naboth. One day, Ahab approached Naboth and asked him whether he would be willing to sell the vineyard, or accept a better one in exchange.*

Naboth declined the offer, because the vineyard had been in his family for many generations. Ownership of the land was a visible sign of God's blessing. It would be an insult to God to sell it.

Ahab went home depressed and angry. He lay on his bed sulking, and refused to eat. His wife, Jezebel, was worried and asked him what was troubling him.

"It's Naboth," he said. "I offered to buy his vineyard, but he's refusing to sell it to me. It would make a nice vegetable garden for us. And he won't let me have it."

"But you are the king," she replied. "Pull yourself together and I will see to it that you get the vineyard."

She wrote letters to all the officials and noblemen of the city, inviting them to take part in a fake ceremony with Naboth as the guest of honour. "Round up some criminals," went the letter, "and get them to accuse Naboth of blasphemy and treason. Then we can have him executed." She signed the letters in Ahab's name and sealed them with his official royal seal.

Those contacted agreed to the plan. They organized the ceremony and gave Naboth pride of place. As planned, two disreputable scoundrels emerged from the crowd and accused Naboth of speaking against God and the king. Naboth was taken outside the city walls, where he was stoned to death.

As soon as the queen heard of Naboth's killing, she said to Ahab, "Good news. Naboth is dead. Go and claim his vineyard."

But Ahab had only been in the vineyard for a few moments when Elijah appeared and confronted him with his wickedness.

"You have murdered the man," Elijah said, "and now you are taking his property as well? The Lord will bring disaster upon you for this."

God's Curse on Ahab

1 Kings 21:19-29

Standing in the vineyard that had once belonged to Naboth, King Ahab listened in terror to Elijah's words. "This is what God has told me to tell you," Elijah began. "On the very spot where the dogs licked Naboth's blood, they will one day lap up yours."

The king was speechless as Elijah went on. "You have devoted yourself to evil and have done what is wrong in God's eyes. For this, the Lord will curse you and bring disaster on your descendants. You must die — along with every male, young or old, of your line. And as for Jezebel, your wife, she will die in this city and her body will be eaten by the dogs.

"Like your wife, any of your relatives who die will be deprived of burial. Those who die in the city will be eaten by dogs; those who die in the country will be eaten by vultures. And all because you have led Israel into sin."

When Ahab heard the prophet's words, he was appalled. He knew he had done wrong and he was overcome with shame for his terrible actions. But how could he put things right? He tore his clothes and dressed himself in sackcloth. He refused to eat and could not sleep, and a deep depression came over him. His conscience troubled him day and night.

The Lord saw Ahab's sorrow and humility, and spoke again to Elijah. "Have you noticed how Ahab has changed?" God said. "For this change of heart I will spare him. I shall not bring disaster on his family in his own lifetime. Instead, I shall wait until the lifetime of his son. Then my punishment will fall."

ELIJAH AND THE WHIRLWIND

2 Kings 1 – 2

King Ahab died in battle – his blood licked up by dogs, as God had promised – and the Israelites were governed by a new king, Ahaziah. He sent his troops after Elijah, but the prophet was invincible. He commanded a thunderbolt to come down from Heaven and strike them dead.

But Elijah was an old man now and he knew that God was about to take him up into Heaven. He set out on his last journey, accompanied, as always, by Elisha, whom he had anointed as a prophet of God some years earlier.

The two were inseparable, but knowing he was going to die, Elijah asked Elisha to go with him no further. Elisha loved his friend and wanted to stay with him. "I will not leave you," he said, and the two continued on their way to Bethel.

At Bethel, a group of prophets came out to Elisha and said, "Do you know that the Lord is going to take your master today?"

"Yes, I know," Elisha replied, "but do not speak of it." At this, Elijah turned once more to Elisha and said, "You must stay here, while I go alone to Jericho." But again Elisha refused to leave him.

Finally, they arrived at the River Jordan. Elijah took off his cloak, rolled it up and struck the surface of the water with it. Immediately, the water parted and the two prophets crossed the river, walking on dry ground to the other side. When they

had crossed, Elijah turned to his companion and said, "What can I give you before I am taken away?"

"A double portion of your power and spirit," Elisha replied.

"That is a hard thing to grant," said Elijah, "but if you see me when I am taken up to Heaven, you shall have your wish."

Suddenly, as they were walking along and talking together, a chariot of fire appeared in the sky – the fiery chariot of Israel pulled by flaming horses – and it separated the two of them. Elisha watched as Elijah was taken up to Heaven in a mighty whirlwind. As Elijah disappeared, Elisha cried out, "My father, my father!"

Elisha was grief-stricken. Slowly, he picked up the cloak that had fallen from Elijah and walked back to the river's edge. He rolled it up, as Elijah had done, and struck the water. As before, it parted, allowing him to walk across the dry river bed.

A group of prophets from Jericho were watching. "Indeed, Elisha has been given Elijah's power," they said, and bowed down before him.

ELISHA AND THE WOMAN OF SHUNEM

2 Kings 4:8-37

lisha travelled from place to place, teaching and performing miracles in God's name, and soon his reputation as a prophet spread throughout the land. He could be fierce at times, but he was always kind to those in need.

One day, as Elisha was passing through the town of Shunem, he struck up a conversation with a wealthy woman, who invited him for a meal. They became friends and every time Elisha passed through, he stopped by to eat at her house.

"I am sure he is a holy man," the woman said to her husband. "Let's make a small room for him on the roof. We can put a bed in it, and a chair and a lamp, and every time he comes to town, he can stay with us."

When Elisha returned to Shunem, he was delighted by the woman's hospitality. One afternoon, as he was resting in his little room, he told his servant Gehazi to go downstairs and bring the woman to him.

"Ask what I can do for her in return for her kindness," he said.

When Gehazi spoke to her, she answered, "Nothing, sir. I have all I need here in the town."

Gehazi told this to Elisha, but added, "There is one thing. She does not have a son and her husband is an old man."

"Tell her to come here," said Elisha.

The woman stood in the doorway and listened to what Elisha had to say.

"This time next year you will be holding a son in your arms," Elisha said.

"Please, sir, don't make things up like that," she replied. "You are a man of God."

But twelve months later, as the prophet had said, she gave birth to a baby boy.

Years later, tragedy struck. It was harvest time and the child was helping his father in the fields when, all of a sudden, the boy stopped and put his head in his hands. "Father, help me," he cried.

"What's the matter, son?" his father asked.

"My head," he moaned. "It hurts so much."

Immediately his father ordered a servant to carry the boy home to his mother.

All morning, the boy sat on his mother's lap in great pain. His mother put her arms around him, rocking him from side to side to comfort him. But nothing she did could ease the boy's agony and by midday he was dead.

She took his lifeless body upstairs and laid it on Elisha's bed. Then she left the room, closing the door behind her.

Outside, she had her donkey saddled and set off as fast as she could to Mount Carmel, where she knew she would find

Elisha. He saw her in the distance and
sent Gehazi to meet her. When she finally
reached the prophet, she was in such
distress that she threw herself at his feet.

"What is it?" asked Elisha.

"It's my son," she said.

Elisha knew immediately what had
happened. He sent Gehazi on ahead with
his stick. "Don't stop to talk to anyone,"
he ordered. "There's not a moment to lose.
Get back to the boy and hold my stick over
his face until I join you."

"I will stay with you, Elisha," said the
woman.

When they finally reached her house,
Elisha rushed upstairs and saw the boy's
body lying motionless on the bed. Gehazi
was standing there holding the stick.
When Elisha came in, the servant turned

to his master and shook his head.

"Leave us alone for a moment," said
Elisha, and Gehazi left the room.

Closing the door behind him, Elisha
knelt and began to pray to the Lord. Then,
very carefully, he lay down on top of the
boy, putting his mouth against that of the
child. As he did so, he felt warmth
returning to the body. Elisha stood up
and paced around the room. Suddenly, he
heard the boy sneeze. And sneeze again,
and again – seven times in all. Then the
boy opened his eyes.

Elisha called Gehazi and told him to fetch
the boy's mother. When she entered the
room, Elisha said simply, "Here is your son."

The woman immediately fell to her knees
at Elisha's feet. Then she got up, took her
son by the hand, and quietly left the room.

NAAMAN IS CURED

2 Kings 5

Naaman was the commander of the Syrian army. He was highly respected in his country and much valued by the king of Syria, who rewarded him well for all the victories he had won. But he had one problem. He suffered from a terrible skin disease called leprosy, for which there was no cure.

Naaman's wife had a young servant girl, an Israelite who had been captured by the Syrians. One day she said to her mistress, "If only my master would travel to Israel. I know of a man there who could make him better. He is a great prophet and a healer."

Naaman went to the king and told him what the servant girl had said.

"Of course you must go," the king said, assuming that this great prophet must be the king of Israel himself. "Here, take this letter to him. He will know exactly what to do."

Naaman went to the king of Israel and showed him the letter. It read, "This is

Naaman, one of my subjects. I have sent him to you so that you can cure him of his dreadful disease." The king was baffled.

"What on earth does this mean?" he asked. "How can I cure a man of leprosy? Am I God? Does he think I have the power of life and death? The king of Syria is trying to pick a fight with me."

When Elisha heard about this, he said to the king, "Send Naaman to me. I will show him there is a prophet in Israel."

Naaman arrived at Elisha's house, but Elisha did not appear. Instead, he sent a servant to Naaman to tell him to go down to the River Jordan and bathe in it seven times.

But Naaman was outraged. "He could at least have come out in person, prayed to God and touched me," he thought.

In a rage, he turned to leave.

But his servants ran after him and said, "Sir, please do as the prophet says. If he had asked you to do something difficult, you would have done it, wouldn't you? Well, he is only asking you to bathe in the Jordan. That's not such a hardship, is it? Why not do as he says and you will be cured."

So Naaman went down to the Jordan and bathed in it seven times, just as Elisha had said. When he came out, his skin was as smooth and clean as a child's. All the sickness had gone. He took his servants and immediately went back to Elisha.

"Now I know that there is no god but the God of Israel," he said to the prophet. "Please accept a gift from me." And he pointed to the gold and silver and fine clothing he had brought along with him.

"By the living God whom I serve, I cannot accept anything," Elisha replied.

"I understand," said Naaman. "But in Syria, I shall worship only your God."

And he set off for home.

Naaman had only gone a short distance before Elisha's servant Gehazi thought, "My master has let Naaman go without paying a penny. I will go after him and get something."

Immediately, he set off, and before long he had caught up with Naaman's chariot.

Naaman stopped, got down, and asked what the matter was.

"My master sent me to tell you that some of his friends, all prophets like himself, have turned up unexpectedly," Gehazi lied. "Some silver and two sets of clothing would be useful for us."

"Of course," said Naaman. "Take what you like. How much do you want?"

Naaman gave him twice what he had asked for, and sent two of his servants to help Gehazi take all the money and clothing back to Elisha.

"Where have you been?" asked Elisha when the servant returned.

"Nowhere, master," he replied guiltily.

"I don't believe you," said Elisha. "You know it is not right to accept gifts at a time like this."

Gehazi knew only too well.

"Naaman's disease will cling to you and your descendants forever," said Elisha.

And, as the servant left Elisha's presence, he looked at his arm and saw a tiny patch of his skin flaking away.

JEHU AND JOASH

2 Kings 9 – 12; 17:5-23

he northern kingdom of Israel was the scene of many wars and uprisings. Ahab was dead, but his son Joram was just as bad, disobeying God and preferring to worship foreign gods. And Joram's mother, the evil Jezebel, was still alive.

One day, in an effort to put a stop to this wickedness, Elisha summoned one of the younger prophets and told him to go to the town of Ramoth, where he would find an army commander named Jehu. He was to take along a jar of olive oil and anoint Jehu, in God's name, as king of Israel.

The prophet hurried to Ramoth and found Jehu. Then he anointed him, giving him God's instructions. Jehu was to kill the king and to ensure that all of Ahab's family perished, in order to punish Jezebel for murdering God's servants.

Now, it so happened that King Ahaziah of the southern kingdom of Judah was staying with King Joram. Ahaziah was the grandson of Ahab and Jezebel, and he, too, was a wicked man. News came to the two kings that Jehu wanted a meeting, so they climbed into their chariots and drove out to meet him near Naboth's vineyard.

Jehu was waiting there with his troops. "Do you come in peace?" asked Joram.

"How can there be peace," replied Jehu, "when Israel is full of witchcraft and idol-worship – all thanks to your mother, Jezebel?"

"Treachery!" Joram cried. He turned

to run, but it was too late. Jehu drew his bow and fired an arrow with all his strength into the king's back, piercing his heart and killing him immediately.

Ahaziah fled for his life. He drove his chariot off at full speed, but Jehu and his men gave chase and slew him.

Jehu rode to Jezreel, where Jezebel lived. When the queen heard he was coming, she painted her eyes, arranged her hair and waited for him at the window of her palace. As Jehu stormed in below, she called down to him, "Have you come in peace, murderer?"

Jehu did not answer. He looked up at the terrified palace officials standing beside her. "Are you on my side or not?" he shouted to them. "Throw her out of the window!"

And with that, Jezebel was hurled into space, crashing to the ground below and spattering the horses with blood. Jehu had not finished. He raced down the palace steps and jumped into his chariot, then drove it over Jezebel's corpse.

Jehu returned to the palace and sat down to a hearty meal. Then for a moment his conscience disturbed him. "That infernal woman!" he thought. "Even in death she is a thorn in my side." Jehu called to his men. "Go and fetch her body," he said. "Give it a proper burial. After all, she was a king's daughter."

But all they could find was her skull and a few scattered pieces of her body. Just as God had said, Jezebel's body had been eaten by the dogs.

After that, Jehu sought out and killed all the relatives of Ahab, Jezebel and Ahaziah. Their heads were put in baskets and piled up in two heaps by the city gates.

But Jehu had also been chosen by God to rid Israel of its pagan idols, and he reserved his greatest anger for the worshippers of Baal. He called them together for what they thought was going to be a great sacrifice – but it was a trick. They themselves were sacrificed, put to the sword by Jehu's men.

Meanwhile, in the southern kingdom of Judah, news of the massacres had reached King Ahaziah's mother, Athaliah. As soon as she realized her son was dead she gave orders for the rest of the royal family to be killed, so that she herself could be queen.

But one member of the royal household survived. Ahaziah's baby son, Joash, was spirited away to the Temple, where he was kept in hiding for six long years, being cared for by the chief priest.

At last, in the seventh year, the priest summoned an elite squad of soldiers loyal to the family of David. He told them that the young boy was the last of David's line and the rightful successor as king. The following week, on the Sabbath, the soldiers went to the Temple. They formed a circle around Joash with their swords drawn to protect him. Then, to loud cheers from the people, the priest anointed him king. Joash was seven years old.

When Athaliah heard the cheering, she ran to the Temple to see what was happening – only to see Joash standing there before her in the robes of the king.

"Treason! Treason!" she cried, but nobody listened. Instead, soldiers were dispatched to escort her to one of Jerusalem's city gates, where she was killed.

The reign of Joash in Judah lasted forty years, and did much to undo the harm that previous kings had caused. He had been well trained by the chief priest to follow God's ways and keep the commandments and, as he grew up, he did not forget his training.

One of his first tasks was to repair Jerusalem's Temple, which had been greatly neglected for many years. Money was collected to pay for wood and stone, craftsmen were hired to repair the damaged interior, and soon the Temple was returned to the service of God. Joash also reduced the number of pagan temples in the country. After all the wickedness and bloodshed in both kingdoms, the southern kingdom of Judah settled, for a time, into a relative state of peace.

For the northern kingdom of Israel, where wickedness still flourished even after Jehu, there was much worse to come. In the east, the empire of Assyria grew strong, and its invincible armies began to approach Israel's borders. At last, ninety years after Joash's death, Assyria invaded. Israel's cities were destroyed and its people taken into exile. They were never heard of again.

GOD PROTECTS JERUSALEM

2 Kings 18 – 19

After the destruction of Israel, the Assyrians threatened Judah with the same fate. Judah's king was Hezekiah. He was faithful to God and had destroyed pagan temples and shrines. But the Assyrian king, Sennacherib, was closing in fast.

Nothing could stop the invaders. They tore right through Judah until their army surrounded Jerusalem. Then Sennacherib's commander looked up at the city walls.

"Neither Hezekiah nor your God can save you!" he bellowed. "Give up now and you will live. Otherwise, you die."

There was no reply. Inside the walls, however, Hezekiah was worried. He consulted the prophet, Isaiah, who told him to stand firm and trust in the Lord.

At last they sent a message to Sennacherib.

"This is what the Lord says," the message read. "The city laughs at you. You will go back the way you came. For I, the Lord Almighty, will protect Jerusalem."

That night, the angel of the Lord passed over the Assyrian camp, and by morning many thousands of enemy troops lay dead. Sennacherib withdrew and the city was saved.

ISAIAH THE PROPHET

Isaiah

Imagine the Lord seated on a throne, surrounded by winged angels shining brightly! Imagine the angels' voices calling out, praising God so loudly that they make the foundations of the Temple shake and the building fill with smoke! This is what the prophet Isaiah saw and heard.

At first, Isaiah had no desire to be a prophet. "I am a sinful man," he said, as the brightness of the angels overwhelmed him. "I am a sinful man surrounded by a sinful people." But he knew there was no running away from God's call.

Then one of the angels flew down to Isaiah, carrying a burning coal from the sacrificial altar. With it the angel touched Isaiah's lips and said, "Your sins are forgiven."

Then the Lord spoke and said, "Whom shall I send to the people as my messenger?"

"Send me, Oh Lord," said Isaiah. "Here I am! Send me!"

"But no one will listen to you," said God. "Their eyes will be blind and their ears will be deaf. You will be talking for many, many years to people who do not want to listen."

"How long, how long?" asked Isaiah.

"Until every city in the world has been destroyed, until every house on the face of the earth is uninhabited, until the land has been transformed into desert. Until the whole world seems to have been forsaken – except for the small handful of people who truly want to hear."

After that, Isaiah had many visions, visions of what the future could be like if the people followed God, and visions of the catastrophes awaiting them if they turned away from God's laws.

One of the first messages he received was an urgent warning to Israel, whose ungodly behaviour Isaiah blamed for the constant attacks by the Assyrians.

"You sinful nation!" he thundered. "You are doomed. Why do you keep turning your backs on the Lord? Your country has been devastated, your cities have been torched and your land has been overrun by foreign invaders. Remember what happened to the people of Sodom and Gomorrah! That will happen to you too unless you abandon your evil ways.

"But if you decide to obey the Lord, everything can be put right. At the moment your hands are stained red with sin. But they could be washed clean again to become as white as snow. For that to happen, you must see that justice is done. Help the oppressed. Feed the poor."

On another occasion, Isaiah had a vision

of how Jerusalem could be a beacon of hope to the rest of the world.

"Towards the end of human time," God told him, "the hill on which the Temple now stands will be higher than the highest mountain top. All the nations of the world will come to it to learn the ways of the Lord. All my teaching comes from Jerusalem, and all my laws can be heard on Mount Zion.

"In that time I shall sit in judgment over all the nations of the earth. They will beat their swords into ploughshares and their spears into pruning hooks. Never again will they go to war. Descendants of Jacob, let us walk in the light of the Lord!"

On many occasions Isaiah went to the king of Judah to advise him what to do and to warn him of what would happen to the nation if it continued to rebel against God's laws. He warned that, though they might temporarily escape destruction by the Assyrians, they would be taken captive by the Babylonians and spend long years in exile in a foreign land.

Alongside his warnings, however, were promises of hope for the future. He foresaw the time when the Temple would be rebuilt and the Israelites would return to their land.

And he foresaw a time when a great king would be born to save the people. This royal Saviour would usher in a new age of peace and harmony.

"The people who once walked in darkness," he said, "have seen a great light. It has shone on a people who once lived in the shadow of death. Oh Lord, you have given them joy by removing the heavy burdens that they carried. You have set the people free.

"And a child will be born to us all. A son will be given to us! And his name will be Wonderful Counsellor, Mighty God, Everlasting Father, Prince of Peace. He will be King David's successor, ruling with justice until the end of time.

"The spirit of the Lord will fill him with wisdom. He will judge the poor fairly, defend the weak, and punish those who do wrong. In his reign the wolf will live at peace with the lamb, the leopard will lie down with the baby goat, and the calf will eat with the lion cub. And a little child will lead them. Children will be safe to roam and the earth will be full of the knowledge of the Lord."

Isaiah had many hard things to say to the people of Israel, but ultimately he brought them hope. "The spirit of the Lord is with me," he said. "God has anointed me to bring good news to the weak, to heal the broken-hearted, to free the captive and to comfort all those who mourn.

"God has anointed me to comfort those who mourn in Zion. Beauty will replace their reddened eyes, joy will replace their sorrow, and praise will replace their grief. They will be trees of righteousness and glory planted by the Lord.

"And I will take pleasure in the Lord's work. My soul will be joyful and I will be clothed in salvation – like a bride and groom on their wedding day. And just as a garden produces trees and flowers, God will produce goodness and praise among all the nations of the world."

THE STORY OF JONAH

Jonah

One day, God spoke to the prophet Jonah. "Go to the great city of Nineveh," said the Lord, "and tell the people there to change their evil ways." But Jonah did not want to go, and got on a ship sailing in the opposite direction.

Out at sea, a violent storm hit the ship. The crew was terrified and prayed to their gods to save them. Jonah, meanwhile, was asleep in the ship's hold, unaware of the commotion.

The captain rushed below. "Get up!" he shouted. "The ship is in danger. Pray to your God to spare us." The sailors drew lots to find out who was responsible for the storm, and Jonah's name was drawn.

"It is true," Jonah said. "I have brought trouble on us all. You see, I worship Almighty God. This storm has been sent

to punish me for disobeying the Lord's instructions. If you throw me overboard, the storm will stop."

The sailors tried unsuccessfully to row for shore. Reluctantly, they agreed to throw Jonah over the side and the sea grew calm.

Jonah was sure he was going to drown, but, at God's command, a huge fish rose from the sea and swallowed him alive.

For three days Jonah survived in the fish's belly, praying to God. At last, the Lord came to his rescue and commanded the fish

to throw him up onto the beach.

Safe on dry land, Jonah set off for Nineveh, where he announced that, in forty days, the city would be destroyed. For once the people listened. They turned their backs on their evil ways and worshipped God properly. Seeing this, God spared them.

Jonah left the city and sat on the ground not far off. He felt very angry.

"Lord," he said, "I knew this would happen. That's why I tried to run away. I knew you would spare these wicked people even though they deserved to be punished."

As he sat there, God provided Jonah with a leafy plant to shade him from the heat. Jonah liked the plant and his spirits rose.

The next morning, however, the plant had died. Once again, Jonah was angry.

"Lord, why is this happening to me?" he moaned. "Just as I was getting fond of this plant, it dies."

"What right have you to be angry?" said God. "You did not water the plant or help it grow, yet still you feel sorry for it. Should I not feel sorry for the thousands of people in Nineveh?"

JOSIAH THE KING

2 Kings 22 – 23; 25

When King Hezekiah died, Judah reverted to its old, evil ways and the pagan places of worship were restored. The kings and the people worshipped the moon and bowed down to the stars. They began to perform all kinds of witchcraft and magic and even practised human sacrifice.

After about fifty years of this idolatry, the people had forgotten what real worship was. The prophets tried to warn them that, if they continued to disobey God, they would face the same fate as the people of Israel – but this advice was ignored. At last, through the prophets, God said, "I will punish Jerusalem as I punished Israel. I will abandon the people and hand them over to their enemies, who will take them into captivity."

But no one listened.

Then Josiah became king. Like Joash before him, Josiah was only a boy when he came to power, but he was to rule Judah for thirty-one years. In that time, he would reintroduce the true worship of Almighty God. When he was twenty-six, he decided it was time to repair the Temple, so he sent the chief priest, Hilkiah, to organize the workmen.

As Hilkiah was walking around the Temple, he came across some old scrolls that had been discarded and left to gather dust amid all the rubble. Closer inspection, however, revealed that they were no

ordinary scrolls at all. Here was the Book of the Law, copied by scribes generations earlier and containing details of the laws God had handed down to Moses on Mount Sinai after the Israelites had left Egypt. Hilkiah recognized the scrolls instantly, and he handed them to one of Josiah's advisors, who read them aloud to the king.

Josiah tore his clothes in dismay. "The Lord is clearly angry with us," he said, "because we have not done what the Law says. Consult the prophetess Huldah to see what we must do now."

Huldah wrote down what the Lord told her and sent the message back to the king. It read, "I am going to punish Jerusalem and everybody in it. The people have rejected me and offered sacrifices to other gods. I am angry with them. But as for the king himself, he listened to me and obeyed what was written in the scrolls. I have heard his prayer and he will be spared. The punishment will not come upon the city until after his death. I shall allow him to die in peace."

Immediately, King Josiah gathered

together the prophets, the priests and the people, and read out loud to them from the Book of the Law. There and then he renewed the covenant, promising to keep God's laws and commandments with all his heart and soul.

Then Josiah ordered every object, ornament, statue and symbol that had ever been used for the worship of Baal to be removed from the Temple. Everything was piled into carts and taken out of the city to the Kidron Valley. There the objects were heaped up and either burnt or melted down in a huge fire. Any priest who had offered sacrifices to the moon or the stars was removed from office and killed, and any pagan altar was smashed into a thousand pieces. Josiah went throughout the country, destroying places where child sacrifices had taken place, and even pulling bones from the tombs of pagan priests and burning them.

Then, when everything had been purified, Josiah ordered the people to celebrate the Passover in honour of the Lord, their God. There had never been a Passover festival like it in the history of the nation.

But Josiah was not finished yet. In order to enforce the laws written in the book, he removed every medium and fortune-teller from the city. Witches and magicians were driven out, and anybody who had a statue of a pagan god at home had to destroy it. For many years, Josiah served the Lord with all his heart and mind and strength, and there had never been a king like him before.

But God was still angry that Judah had descended into such wickedness in the first place. After Josiah's death that wickedness would be punished. Already, hundreds of miles away to the east, King Nebuchadnezzar of Babylonia had his eyes on Jerusalem as a spider has its eyes on a fly.

JEREMIAH

Jeremiah; 2 Kings 24:1-16

 osiah was still the king of Judah when God called Jeremiah to be a prophet. At first he was reluctant to become one, saying that he was too young and too shy to speak in public. "Do not worry," said God. "I will protect you and tell you exactly what to say."

Jeremiah had a difficult job ahead. He was to serve the Lord under four more kings, often telling them things they did not want to hear. These were dangerous times. The Assyrians from the north were at war with the Babylonians from the east, the Egyptians to the south were being drawn into the fighting and the tiny kingdom of Judah was caught in the middle. Jeremiah constantly reminded the people of Judah that they were not making things any easier for themselves by turning away from God. Destruction would come upon them if they did not change their wicked behaviour.

"You steal, murder and commit adultery," Jeremiah thundered from the steps of the Temple. "You tell lies and worship foreign idols – all the things the Lord hates. Stop this or the city will be destroyed and you will be taken into captivity!"

No one listened.

On many occasions Jeremiah was in great danger. People plotted against him and wanted him dead – simply for telling the truth. Jeremiah himself was often puzzled by this and asked God why wicked men were allowed to prosper when good people were persecuted for speaking out honestly.

The Lord said, "Jeremiah, do not be disheartened, because I have more work for you to do. I have already abandoned Israel. My chosen people turned against me, so I turned against them. I have handed over those I love to their enemies. Tell the people of Judah that the same thing will very soon happen to them."

"But I am so unhappy," said Jeremiah. "I have to argue and quarrel with everyone I meet. They think I'm mad, talking about doom and destruction all the time. They all hate me for it. I wish I had never been born."

But God stood firm and said, "I will rescue you from your enemies. Now go, and do as I have commanded you."

One day, the Lord sent Jeremiah to a potter's house. He watched the man scooping up clay, throwing it onto the wheel and shaping it with his hands into pots and bowls. If the potter made a mistake at any time, he simply stopped the wheel, squashed the half-finished bowl back into a lump and started again, fashioning the shapeless clay into something new.

"That is how I will treat my chosen people," the Lord said to Jeremiah. "They are like clay in my hands. I can build them up, but I can just as easily squash them flat and start again."

Jeremiah continued to tell the people what the Lord had said, but they refused to listen. One day, during the reign of Josiah's son, Jehoiakim, he stormed into one of the Temple courtyards and began to address the people there. When the priests heard him, they immediately had him arrested, beaten and put in chains. But it did not stop Jeremiah from warning them. "The Lord will hand over Judah to the king of Babylonia," he said. "And your fate will be captivity or death."

After this incident Jeremiah was banned from the Temple, so he found it difficult to get across God's message. But some time later, God gave Jeremiah an idea. "I may not be allowed to speak God's message," he thought, "but I can certainly write it down." So he sent for his assistant, Baruch, and dictated to him everything the Lord had

said. Baruch wrote it down on a scroll and took it to the Temple, where he read it aloud to the people.

Temple officials soon heard of this and Baruch was immediately summoned to explain what was going on.

"Read out what it says on the scroll," the officials said.

Baruch did as he was told.

"That's Jeremiah's handiwork," they said. "He dictated it to you, didn't he?"

"Yes, he did," said Baruch.

"Well, you had better give us the scroll," they said. "And if you know what's good for you, lie low for a while. Tell Jeremiah to do the same."

Then they went along to the royal apartments and read out the contents of the scroll to the king. He was so angry with what he was hearing that he snatched the scroll from them and threw it into the fire. It was a useless gesture, because Jeremiah merely dictated another one, this time prophesying that Jehoiakim's rule would shortly be coming to an end.

And so it proved. Very soon the armies of Babylon, under their king, Nebuchadnezzar, were marching on Jerusalem. At this crucial time, Jehoiakim died. Within months, the enemy had captured and plundered the city. They took Jehoiakim's family into captivity, and deported eight thousand skilled and able-bodied men of fighting age to Babylonia. For good measure, they also took gold and other valuables from the Temple. This was the price of Judah's disobedience to God – but worse was to come.

DESTRUCTION AND EXILE

2 Kings 24:17 – 25:26; Jeremiah

The Babylonians gave Judah a new king, Zedekiah, and forced him to swear loyalty to Nebuchadnezzar. But after some years, Zedekiah rebelled and allied himself with Egypt. At this, Nebuchadnezzar set out to teach Judah a final lesson.

At first it seemed that Jerusalem would be safe. Egyptian reinforcements were on their way and the Babylonians decided it would be wiser to retreat. But Jeremiah knew that they would soon be back, and he went to see the king to tell him so.

"I warn you," Jeremiah said, "the city is in great danger because of its disobedience to God. The Egyptian army will soon turn back and Nebuchadnezzar will return in strength. You will not defeat him."

The king ignored him, so Jeremiah

decided that his work in the city was done. He was about to leave, when he was stopped by an officer and accused of desertion. He was arrested, beaten and locked up in a cell.

The situation looked bad for Jeremiah because the officials now wanted him dead. "He's a traitor," they said. "He spends all his time trying to persuade the soldiers to give in to the Babylonians. He's undermining their confidence. Kill him!"

For a while it looked as if they would get their way. The prophet was flung into a deep

— 124 —

well and left without food, slowly sinking up to his knees in the mud at the bottom.

Fortunately for Jeremiah, a friend asked the king to have him lifted to safety before he starved. Indeed, once he was out, the king arranged secret talks with him to try to work out the best course of action.

"Surrender," Jeremiah said. "It is the only way. If you surrender, they will save us. If you don't, the city will burn."

"I shall decide that," Zedekiah replied. "Now, go!"

Some weeks later, news reached the city that the Egyptian forces had turned back. The Babylonians closed in and put the city under siege. For two years, Jerusalem held out, until the people were starving in the streets. Day and night the Babylonians

pounded the walls of the city until, finally, they broke through. Zedekiah fled, but the Babylonians captured him near Jericho.

Zedekiah's sons were put to death before his eyes, then he himself was blinded and taken to Babylon in chains. But Jeremiah was treated mercifully and went to Egypt in exile.

Meanwhile, in Jerusalem, the Temple was looted and set alight. All the gold and silver Solomon had used to build the house of God was removed and piled into carts to be taken off to Babylonia, far away. Houses were burnt and people killed where they stood. Only the poorest were allowed to stay. The rest were taken into captivity, never to see their homeland again. As God had warned, Jerusalem had fallen and the exile in Babylon had begun.

EZEKIEL AND THE VALLEY OF BONES

Ezekiel

Ezekiel lived in exile in Babylon, among the thousands of people taken into captivity when Nebuchadnezzar first took control of Judah. One day, as he was walking by the river, he noticed a storm approaching. Looking up, he saw a vision.

Amid the sheets of lightning, Ezekiel saw four creatures shining like polished bronze in the darkening sky. Each one had four faces and four wings. Above these was a throne of precious jewels, and on it was the outline of a man. Ezekiel flung himself on the ground, knowing that he was in the presence of God.

"Mortal man," said a voice from above. "Be a prophet to my people, the Israelites."

After that, Ezekiel had many visions, often of Judah's disobedient past, but once of what could be its glorious future. He was standing on a hillside looking into a valley full of thousands of skeletons, when God told him to preach to the bones.

"Tell them I will put flesh on those dry bones and breathe life into them," said God.

Then there was a loud rattling noise as all the bones joined together. Flesh covered them and they became living beings again.

"Tell my people that they are like these bones," said God. "They think they are withering in exile without any hope. But if they follow my laws, I will breathe new life into them and lead them back to Israel."

THE FIERY FURNACE

Daniel 1 – 4

Daniel was a young man when Nebuchadnezzar first attacked Jerusalem. Along with other handsome and intelligent young men from the city's richest families, he was taken to Babylonia and given special training to prepare him for service at court.

He and his three friends, named Shadrach, Meshach and Abednego, were all from noble families in Judah. They were treated well, taught the Babylonian language and given good food. But God had told the Israelites that they could eat only certain foods, and Daniel and his friends believed that it was wrong to eat what the Babylonians ate. So they asked their guardian to serve them just vegetables and water.

"But you will all get thin and waste away," he said. "And I will be in trouble."

"Try it for just ten days," said Daniel.

After ten days they were as fit as ever – if not fitter – so the matter was settled. The four friends excelled at their studies and soon became valued advisors at the court.

Some years later, Nebuchadnezzar built a huge golden statue to one of his own gods. It was unveiled in front of all the important people in the land, except for Daniel, who was detained at the palace on business.

As soon as the trumpets sounded, the king ordered everyone to bow down to the statue. Anyone who refused would be thrown into a blazing furnace and burnt to death.

As the fanfare sounded, everyone knelt, except Shadrach, Meshach and Abednego.

"On your knees," shouted the guards.

"No!" they said. "God forbids it."

When the king heard of their disobedience, he was livid. "Very well," he said. "You know what the penalty is."

He ordered the furnace to be heated up until it was seven times hotter than usual and had Shadrach, Meshach and Abednego thrown in. The furnace was so hot that it killed the soldiers who took them there.

After a few minutes, Nebuchadnezzar looked into the fiery furnace and could not believe his eyes.

"How many did we throw in?" he asked.

"Three men, Sire," the guards replied.

"Then who is that with them?"

The guards looked into the furnace and saw a fourth figure beside the men.

"It looks like an angel," said the king. "It is protecting them. Let them out immediately!"

When the three men emerged, they were completely unharmed. Their clothes were not even singed. "Praise be to the God of Shadrach, Meshach and Abednego!" said Nebuchadnezzar and commanded everyone to respect the Lord God Almighty.

BELSHAZZAR'S FEAST

Daniel 5

Nebuchadnezzar died and his son, Belshazzar, became king of Babylonia. One evening, he organized a stupendous banquet for a thousand of his noblemen. It was to be an evening of great festivity, but none of those present could have guessed that it would end in terror and death.

When the guests were seated in the banqueting hall, Belshazzar ordered wine to be served to his guests in gold and silver goblets. But the goblets he used were not his own – his father had plundered them from Jerusalem's Temple, where they had been used for the worship of God. To make matters worse, Belshazzar and his guests used the goblets to drink to their own pagan idols, praising lifeless wooden statues and stone figures.

Suddenly, at the far end of the hall, a human hand appeared from thin air. Immediately, the blood drained from the king's face. Slowly the ghostly hand began to move and, with its finger, wrote on the wall in the full glow of the lamplight. The king watched in horror as the hand wrote four strange words on the plaster of the wall, before finally disappearing as mysteriously as it had come.

By now Belshazzar's face was deathly white. His knees were knocking and he was shaking with fear. With a trembling voice he called out for his wizards and astrologers and asked them to explain the meaning of this terrifying apparition.

"Whoever can make sense of these words," he announced, "will be clothed in the finest robes and given the highest office in my kingdom."

The magicians and astrologers crowded round the words on the wall, but none of them could understand their meaning. This distressed Belshazzar even more, and his face turned paler still.

Just then the old queen, the wife of Nebuchadnezzar, entered the hall, having heard the commotion.

"Do not be alarmed, Your Majesty," she said. "The man you need to solve this riddle is named Daniel. When your father was alive, he used to send for him whenever he had a problem. He made him chief advisor, honouring him for his wisdom and skill in interpreting dreams. Send for him now and he will tell you what these words mean."

When Daniel finally arrived, the king, who had by now calmed down a little, looked at him intently.

"I hear you are the man my father

brought from Judah," he said. "I am told you are wise and skilled at interpreting signs. So, tell me, what do those words on the wall over there mean?"

Daniel walked over to the wall and studied the letters closely.

"If you can solve the riddle," Belshazzar said, "I will make you a very rich man."

"Keep your gifts," replied Daniel. "I want no reward for telling you what this warning means. But first, let me say that at the end of his life, your father, Nebuchadnezzar, believed in Almighty God. Because of that, he was allowed to rule in splendour over his great empire. But you do not believe. Instead, you dishonour the Lord by praising false idols and drinking from the holy cups used in the Temple."

Daniel turned back to the writing on the wall. "As for the words 'MENE MENE TEKEL UPHARSIN' written here,"

he went on, "they mean this:

"'MENE' means 'number'. God has numbered the days your kingdom will last and they are at an end.

"'TEKEL' means 'weight'. You have been weighed in the scales of obedience and found wanting.

"'UPHARSIN' means 'divisions'. Your kingdom will be divided up and given to your enemies, the Medes and Persians."

Despite this terrible omen, Belshazzar kept his promise. Daniel was clothed in purple robes and a gold chain was hung about his neck. Then he was proclaimed the greatest official in the land.

But Daniel's prophecy came true faster than anyone could have guessed. That very night, Belshazzar was killed. Just as Daniel had prophesied, the Medes and Persians invaded Babylonia and put their own leader, Darius, in control.

Daniel in the Lions' Den

Daniel 6:1-26

Darius soon discovered that Daniel was the most able man on his staff, so he decided to make him one of the three most senior administrators in the land. Before long, because Daniel was more gifted than the other two, he was put in overall charge. This made the other administrators jealous.

Every day, they tried to pick holes in Daniel's work. But this was impossible because he was faithful to the king and very efficient at what he did. "It's no use," they said. "We'll never find fault with his work. The only hope we have is to use his religion against him."

It was well known that Daniel served the Lord with all his heart and said his prayers three times a day. So his enemies hatched a plot to bring about his downfall.

They went to King Darius and said, "Your Majesty, we have been discussing this among ourselves for some time and we think you should pass a new law. For a period of thirty days you should make it illegal for anyone to ask for anything from any god or from any man. All requests should be put to you alone. Anyone breaking the law should be thrown to the lions. This will then become the law of the Medes and Persians and no one will be able to change it."

Darius agreed and passed the law.

Daniel heard that the law had been passed, but went into his room as usual to pray. He stood in front of the windows facing Jerusalem and got down on his knees to give thanks to the Lord. But he did not know that his enemies were hiding nearby and were watching him praying to God.

Immediately, they went to the king and reminded him of the law he had just passed. "Majesty," they asked, "did you not sign a decree making it a crime to ask either god or man for anything?"

"I did," he replied. "And I know that according to the law of the Medes and Persians, it cannot be changed."

"Well," they said, "Daniel, one of the exiles from Judah, is breaking your law. He is ignoring you and praying to God — three times a day! The penalty, as Your Majesty knows, must be firmly enforced. He must be thrown to the lions."

The king was very upset at the thought of losing Daniel and he spent all day trying to find a way to save him. But his law could not be changed. At sunset, he reluctantly signed the order for the execution.

"I hope the God you serve will rescue you," Darius said, as Daniel was taken under

guard to the lions' den. Then Daniel was thrown inside, and the entrance was closed with a boulder so that he could not escape.

That night the unhappy king could neither eat nor sleep. As soon as the sun rose, he ran to the lions' den and shouted out anxiously, "Daniel, servant of the living Lord, was your God able to protect you from the lions?"

"Your Majesty, may you live forever," came the reply. "God sent an angel to stop the lions from harming me. God knew I was innocent and that I had done you no wrong."

The king was overjoyed and ordered Daniel to be removed from the lions' den. And when he was brought out, everyone saw that there was not a single scratch on him. But Daniel's accusers were not so lucky. They were thrown into the lions' den themselves and torn limb from limb.

After that Darius passed another law. "By decree of Darius," it read, "the whole kingdom shall respect the God of Daniel. The rule of the living God is unchanging and will last for ever and ever, until the end of time."

ESTHER

Esther

From his palace in Susa, the capital city of Persia, King Xerxes ruled a mighty empire that stretched from India to Ethiopia. In the third year of his reign, he decided to hold a lavish banquet for his court officials to celebrate the wealth and splendour of his kingdom.

The banquet lasted a whole week, and the guests were able to eat and drink as much as they wanted. On the seventh day Xerxes asked his queen, Vashti, to come and join them, in order to display her beauty to the people. But Queen Vashti refused to come. Xerxes was furious.

"How can she insult me like this?" he said to his advisors. "I am being made to look foolish in front of all my guests!"

"More than that, Your Majesty," they replied. "She has not only insulted you, but every man in your empire. Now women everywhere will start disobeying their husbands. Another queen must be found. Vashti must go!"

And so Vashti was deposed, and all the most beautiful young women in the empire were brought to the palace for Xerxes to choose another queen. As soon as the women arrived, they were pampered with scented massages, clothed in the finest dresses and treated to the best food the palace cooks could prepare. Then, one by one, they were taken to see the king.

The most beautiful of them all was a woman named Esther, the cousin of a man named Mordecai. Esther and Mordecai were Jews, the people who had been exiled from Israel and Judah, and who had settled in many parts of the world, including Persia.

When he saw Esther, Xerxes was amazed at her loveliness, and he immediately made her his queen. Mordecai, meanwhile, who had been appointed to an important position in the court, advised his cousin not to tell anyone she was Jewish, in case she was the target of persecution.

There was a lot of scheming in the palace of Susa and, after some months in the king's service, Mordecai uncovered a plot to murder the king. He told Esther of this and she in turn told Xerxes, who thanked her and had the would-be assassins hanged.

Some time later King Xerxes appointed a man named Haman to be his chief minister and ordered everyone to show him respect by bowing to him. But Mordecai refused.

"I am a Jew," he said, "and I bow to no one."

When Haman heard of this, he became very angry and vowed to take his revenge.

He resolved to destroy not only Mordecai, but every Jew in Persia.

Haman cast lots to decide on the day the extermination should take place, then went to the king to explain his plan.

"There are people in your empire," he said, "who are behaving differently from all your other subjects. Their customs are not like ours and they refuse to obey our laws. They are dangerous. You should get rid of them."

"Very well," said the king. "I hereby authorize you to do with them what you think appropriate."

A proclamation was read out in the city. "On the thirteenth day of the twelfth month," it read, "every Jew throughout the Persian Empire is to be put to death."

Mordecai and his friends were horrified, and they appealed to Queen Esther to go to Xerxes to plead for their lives.

Esther devised a plan. A few days later she was summoned by the king and she took the opportunity of inviting him and Haman to a private banquet she was preparing for the following day. Haman was very flattered to be asked and he lost no time in boasting about the invitation to his friends. But as he was happily leaving the palace, he caught sight of Mordecai sitting at the entrance. Immediately his mood darkened and turned to hatred. He decided, there and then, that when he was at the queen's banquet, he would ask the king for permission to hang Mordecai immediately. He ordered a giant gallows to be built so that he would be ready to act without a moment's delay.

But that night King Xerxes could not sleep. He passed the time reading through the court records, where he came upon the full account of the time that Mordecai had saved him from assassination. The king realized he had never honoured Mordecai for this important service.

"I must see to it that he is rewarded," he said to himself. The next day, he summoned Haman and ordered him to give Mordecai special honours. Haman could hardly conceal his rage, but he consoled himself with the thought that he would soon destroy Mordecai's people.

That evening, Esther held her banquet for the king and Haman. Xerxes, entranced by his queen's beauty, told her she could have anything she asked for.

"Then please save the Jewish people!" Esther pleaded. "Save my people – your loyal subjects – who are about to be destroyed!"

"But who would dare do such a thing?" cried Xerxes.

"He is sitting over there," said Esther, and she pointed at Haman, who had gone white with shock.

King Xerxes burst into a terrible rage. He immediately ordered his men to hang Haman from his own gallows. As for Mordecai, he was promoted to become his chief minister. Then Xerxes issued a new edict. The Jews were to be given special honours throughout the Persian Empire. Thanks to Esther, the tables had been turned on the enemies of the Jews, and her people were saved from destruction.

JERUSALEM IS REBUILT

Ezra, Nehemiah, Haggai

Cyrus, the next Persian king, had ruled Babylonia for less than a year when he issued a decree which delighted the Jews. They were free to return to Jerusalem to rebuild God's Temple. Jeremiah's prophecy had at last come true.

Cyrus returned all the gold and silver cups that King Nebuchadnezzar had taken from the Temple and watched as over forty-two thousand people, young and old, prepared to set off. They piled their belongings onto horses and camels, loaded up food and water for the journey and began the long trek home.

When they finally arrived in the ruined city, there was some opposition from the people who were already living there.

"We worship God, too," they said. "Let us help you rebuild the Temple."

"No," the exiles said. "We will rebuild the Temple ourselves, just as Cyrus commanded."

The work halted as Jewish leaders, Persian officials and the residents of Jerusalem exchanged endless letters, attempting to decide who was in the right. The prophet Haggai tried to end the bickering by appealing to the consciences of the people.

"Some of you say it is not the right time to rebuild the house of the Lord," he thundered. "So why have you started work on your own houses? Is it right for you to live in comfort while God's house lies in ruins?"

The matter was eventually settled by Cyrus himself, who personally intervened to authorize the building work to go ahead.

When the Temple was finally complete, a great Passover festival was held, and there was joy in the city as the Israelites returned to the worship of God. True, the Temple was not as splendid as it had been in Solomon's day, but it was a fine building nonetheless.

News reached Babylonia that the Temple had been completed. But one man there, a scholar by the name of Ezra, was worried that, after so long in exile, the people had forgotten many of God's commandments. Since he knew all God's laws, he asked permission to leave Babylonia to teach Jerusalem the proper way to serve the Lord. The king agreed.

Ezra's worries had been well founded. When he arrived in Jerusalem, he saw that many of the men had married women from neighbouring countries and that these women had brought their own foreign gods with them. Instead of remaining apart from other peoples, the Jews were mixing too freely and, as a result, were watering down their religious practices. Ezra had to teach them many things before they were able to serve the Lord in the correct way.

There were other problems too. In practice, the running of Jerusalem was left to Persian officials and local people, but they did not have the same love for the city as the Jews had. Judah no longer had its own king, but it needed someone to take charge if it was to become a great nation once again.

At last, a Jewish governor was appointed. His name was Nehemiah, and he decided to build up the city's defences. Shortly after his arrival in Jerusalem he went on a secret tour of the ruined city walls at night, inspecting the damage and deciding what repair work needed to be done.

Local people were suspicious when he began to organize a Jewish workforce to rebuild the walls. Some even accused him of plotting against the Persian Empire. They mocked the Jews and laughed at their efforts.

"What kind of wall do they think they will build?" sneered one of them. "Even a fox could knock it down."

There were fears that Nehemiah's men would be attacked. So Nehemiah ordered his workers to arm themselves, and with a sword in one hand and a trowel in the other, they rebuilt the city to the glory of the Lord.

Eventually the wall was complete. A solemn ceremony was held, during which the Jews confessed their sins. Ezra read from the Book of the Law and the people of Israel promised faithfully to live forever according to God's commandments.

JOB

Job

A long time ago in the land of Uz, there lived a good and faithful man named Job, who worshipped the Lord with all his heart. One day his life changed dramatically. For reasons he could not explain, terrible things began to happen to him.

Job had seven sons and three daughters and owned vast herds of cattle, making him the richest man in the east. He worked hard and performed all his religious duties faithfully.

God and Satan were watching him.

"Have you noticed my faithful servant, Job?" the Lord asked.

"I have," said Satan.

"He is a good man," the Lord continued.

"Only because he has an easy life," said Satan. "You have given him everything he needs. Why shouldn't he worship you? If you took it all away, then he would curse you."

"Very well," said God. "We shall see. Job is in your power. But do not harm him."

Satan smiled and vanished.

He wasted no time. In a single day he sent robbers to steal Job's herds and kill his servants, he sent lightning to burn Job's sheep, and, worst of all, he killed Job's children.

Job was beside himself with grief. He flung himself onto the ground. "I was born with nothing," he wailed, "and I shall die with nothing. God gives and God takes away. The Lord's name be praised!"

Despite his grief, he did not blame God.

Then Satan made sores break out all over Job's body. They itched and they bled and they stung until Job went mad with pain. He sat by the city's rubbish heap scratching himself and the more he scratched, the more his sores hurt. Even his wife could not believe that he was still faithful to the Lord. "Why don't you just curse God and die?" she said.

Some days later, Job was joined by three friends who wept when they saw him. Job could take his suffering no more. "I wish I had never been born!" he shouted. "Why let me go on living in such misery?"

One of his friends tried to comfort him. "I know this is difficult to hear," he said, "but can you think of a single case where a good man has been punished like this? Think back. Did you do wrong some time in the past? It is no shame to be corrected by God."

"At a time like this," said Job, "I need real friends. I have done nothing wrong! My pain is too much to bear. I am angry and bitter. Why won't God answer my prayers?"

His second friend spoke next. "God never fails to do what is right," he said. "Somebody in your family must have done something wrong to bring this suffering upon you."

"I've heard that argument before," said Job. "But I'm innocent! Don't condemn me, Lord. Just tell me why I suffer like this!"

Then his third friend spoke. "You say you are pure and faithful," he said, "but perhaps God is punishing you less than you deserve. Put yourself right with God."

"My argument is with God, not with you," said Job. "Oh Lord, I know that we live short, troubled lives. But speak to me. Tell me why!"

Without warning, the Lord spoke to Job out of a whirlwind.

"Who dares to challenge my wisdom and power? Where were you when I made the world, Job? Have you ever commanded a day to dawn or the rain to fall? Have you ever walked on the ocean floor or flown among the stars? Who feeds the ravens? Who makes horses strong?"

"Lord, I spoke foolishly," said Job. "I know you are all powerful. There is no more to say."

Then God spoke to Job's friends. "I am angry with you," said the Lord. "Job is right. You presumed to know how I work. Job assumed nothing. He accepts my power. Human reasons are not my reasons. My reasons surpass human understanding."

With that, God cured Job's sickness, gave him back his wealth, blessed him with more children and let him live to a great old age.

FIVE PSALMS

The Book of Psalms is a hymn book and a prayer book reflecting a people's deepest feelings about their lives and about God. Composed over a long period of Israel's history, it includes hymns of praise, prayers for help, pleas for forgiveness and laments for the people of Israel. Some psalms are numbered differently in different Bibles.

PSALM 1

Happiness

Happy are those who reject the
    advice of the wicked,
And who reject the ways of sinners
    and unbelievers.
Happy are those who take pleasure
    in God's Law,
And who study it day and night.
Those people are like trees planted by
    streams;
They are like trees that flower and fruit
    every year.
Their leaves will never wither,
And they will succeed at whatever
    they do.
The wicked are not so fortunate.
They are like straw blown away on
    the wind.
Unbelievers and sinners will be kept apart
    from God's people.
For the Lord guides the righteous,
And the evil perish.

PSALM 22 (23)

Our Shepherd and Provider

The Lord is my shepherd; I shall
    never be in need.
    The Lord lets me rest in
    green fields
And leads me to quiet pools where
    I can drink.
The Lord builds up my strength
And keeps me on the path of goodness.
Even when I walk through the valley of
    the shadow of death
I will not be afraid,
For you are always with me.
Your rod and staff are my protection.
You prepare a banquet for me in full
    view of my enemies;
You anoint my head with oil;
My cup is overflowing.
I know that your goodness and mercy
    will be with me every day of my life.
And the Lord's house will be my
    home forever.

PSALM 60 (61)

For Help or Protection

Hear my cry, Oh Lord,
and listen to my prayer.
When I am far from home
I will call your name.
When I am in despair,
guide me to a safe place.
I will stay in your house forever,
sheltering beneath your wings.
For you, Oh God, have heard
the promises I have made.
And you have given me your blessings.
Preserve the king
and let him live a long life.
He will serve God forever.
Let your mercy and truth protect him.
And I will praise your name forever
As I serve you every day of my life.

PSALM 136 (137)

The Exiles' Lament

By the rivers of Babylon
we sat down and wept
When we remembered Zion.
We hung our harps on the willow trees.
Our captors wanted us to sing to them.
But how can we sing the Lord's song
in a strange land?
If I forget you, Jerusalem,
let my right hand wither.
If I forget you, never let me sing again.
All this, if I do not set Jerusalem above
my highest joy.

PSALM 150

A Psalm of Praise

Praise the Lord!
Praise God in the Temple.
Praise God in the Heavens.
Praise God's strength and greatness.
Praise God with trumpets, zithers
and harps.
Praise God with drums
and dancing,
Praise God with strings
and pipes.
Praise God with
crashing cymbals.
Let everything
that breathes
praise God.
Praise the Lord!

FIFTY PROVERBS

Here are some of the proverbs of Solomon, king of Israel. They will help you to be honest and fair, and, if you follow them, they will help you get the best out of life. First, though, remember that respect for the Lord is the beginning of all knowledge.

1. Listen to what your father and mother tell you. Their teaching is like a fine piece of jewellery. *1:8*

2. When bad people tempt you, resist them. *1:10*

3. Learn from criticism and listen to good advice. *1:23*

4. Wisdom comes from the Lord, who provides help and protection for the righteous. *2:6*

5. Follow the example of good people and lead a righteous life. God will snatch evil people from the earth like plants plucked from the ground. *2:20*

6. Hold on to loyalty and faithfulness. Tie them round your neck and write them on your heart. *3:3*

7. Trust in the Lord with all your heart. *3:5*

8. Never do anything to hurt your neighbour. *3:29*

9. Never say anything that is not true. *4:24*

10. Lazy people can learn a valuable lesson from hard-working ants. *6:6*

11. Laziness will make you poor; hard work will make you rich. *10:4*

12. Sensible people accept good advice. *10.8*

13. Hatred causes trouble; love conquers all. *10:12*

14. Do not be boastful. *11:2*

15. Wealth will not help you at the hour of your death; a good life will. *11:4*

16. Good looks without good judgement are like gold rings in a pig's snout. *11:12*

17. A good person is kind to animals. *12:10*

18. Thoughtless words can wound like swords. Wise words can heal. *12:18*

19. The truth lasts forever. *12:19*

20. Worrying makes you unhappy, but kind words can raise your spirits high. *12:25*

21. Keep away from foolish people. *14:7*

22. Laughter may hide sorrow. *14:13*

23. Peace of mind will make you healthy. Envy will eat away at your bones. *14:30*

24. A mild word quietens anger. *15:1*

25. We make plans; the Lord fulfils them. *16:1*

26. Think before you speak. *16:23*

27. Kind words are as sweet as honey and healthy for the body. *16:24*

28. Gossip destroys friendship. *16:28*

29. It is better to have control over yourself than over whole cities. *16:32*

30. Starting an argument is like the first hole in a dam; stop before it is too late! *17:14*

31. Being cheerful makes you healthy. *17:22*

32. Humility wins respect. *18.12*

33. Your spirit protects your body. If your spirit weakens, your last hope is gone. *18:14*

34. A partner in life is a blessing from God. *18:22*

35. Admire the strength of youth; respect the wisdom of age. *20:29*

36. Sometimes we can learn from painful experiences. *20:30*

37. Give to the poor, for one day you may be in need. *21.13*

38. It is better to be respected than to be rich. *22:1*

39. Lessons learnt in childhood last for ever. *22:6*

40. Do not mix with gluttons or drunkards. *23:20*

41. Be considerate to your parents. *23:22*

42. Do not envy bad people and do not try to make friends with them. *24:1*

43. Wisdom is better than strength. *24:5*

44. Be strong in a crisis. *24:10*

45. Do not gloat over your enemy's misfortune. *24:17*

46. People who do not keep their promises are like clouds that bring no rain. *25:14*

47. Be patient. Persuasion is more effective than force. *25:15*

48. Getting involved in another's argument is like grabbing a fierce dog by the ears. *26:17*

49. Obey the law. *28:4*

50. Admit your faults – and change them. *28:13*

THE

New

TESTAMENT

ELIZABETH AND ZECHARIAH

Luke 1:5-25, 57-80

Around sixty years before the birth of Jesus, the land of Israel, then known as Palestine, became part of the Roman Empire. The Romans appointed King Herod to rule the Jews and it was during his reign that the story of the Messiah began.

At that time, there lived a priest named Zechariah. He and his wife Elizabeth obeyed all God's laws. But they were unable to have children and, because they were very old, they had given up all hope of ever having any.

One day, while Zechariah was carrying out his duties in the Temple, a strange thing happened. An angel of the Lord appeared at the side of the altar and said, "Zechariah, do not be afraid. God has heard your prayer. You and your wife will have a son and you are to call him John.

"From his birth he will be filled with the Holy Spirit and he will grow up to be a great man, preparing the way for God's Kingdom on earth. He will turn the people's disobedience into faithfulness and make them ready to hear the word of the Lord."

"But that is impossible," said Zechariah incredulously. "Elizabeth and I are too old to have children."

"I am Gabriel," the angel answered. "I stand in the presence of God, who sent me to give you this message. But as you do not believe this, you will remain silent – unable to speak – until you see for yourself that God's promise has come true."

By now the people outside the Temple were wondering why Zechariah was taking so long. When he emerged, he could not speak and was forced to gesture with his hands. But from the expression on his face, they knew that he had seen a powerful vision.

In time, as God had promised, Elizabeth had a son. When the time came for naming the baby, everyone expected the boy to be named Zechariah, after his father.

"No," said Elizabeth. "He shall be John."

"But there is nobody named John in the family," her friends said. But Zechariah, still unable to speak, gestured for a slate and some chalk and wrote down four words: 'His name is John'. And as he did so, his voice returned.

Immediately, he praised the Lord, saying, "The God of Israel has come to set the people free. The Lord has sent us a Saviour, a descendant of David, and you, my son, will prepare the way for him."

Their friends were filled with excitement – but also with fear, because, though they knew that John was filled with God's power, they had no idea what he would do. All would be revealed, however, in good time.

MARY AND JOSEPH

Matthew 1:18-24; Luke 1:26-56

In the town of Nazareth, in the northern province of Galilee, lived a young woman named Mary. She was engaged to Joseph, a carpenter and a descendant of King David. One day, the angel Gabriel appeared to her and said, "Mary, you are blessed. You will have a child and his name will be Jesus."

Mary was stunned. "How can that be?" she asked. "I am a virgin."

"The child is the Son of God," Gabriel replied. "You are pregnant by the power of the Holy Spirit. Your son will be great. Like David, he will be a king, but his kingdom will last forever.

"Do not be so surprised," the angel went on. "Remember your cousin Elizabeth. She thought she was too old to have a child, but she will soon give birth. With God, nothing is impossible. You will be touched by the Holy Spirit and God's power will come upon you."

Mary put her trust in God and accepted what the angel was saying to her.

"I will do everything the Lord tells me," she said. Then the angel disappeared.

Joseph was a good man who always wanted to do the right thing. When Mary told him she was expecting a child, he was sad and decided to break off the engagement secretly, so as not to embarrass Mary in public. But then an angel of the Lord appeared to him in a dream.

"Joseph, do not be afraid to take Mary as your wife," the angel said. "It is by the Holy Spirit that she has conceived this child, and he will save the people from their sins. When he is born, you must name him Jesus."

Joseph awoke refreshed. Straight away he went to Mary to tell her he would marry her and that, together, they would take care of the blessed child.

JESUS IS BORN

Luke 2:1-20

Orders came from the Roman emperor Augustus that everyone had to return to their home town to be registered for taxation. For Mary and Joseph this meant a long journey to Bethlehem, where Joseph had been born – a journey all the more difficult because Mary's child was due to be born any day.

When they arrived in Bethlehem, they were exhausted and desperate for somewhere to stay. They went to a nearby inn, but they were told there was no room. At last, by pleading with the innkeeper, Joseph persuaded him to let them stay in the stable.

That night, Mary's baby was born. She wrapped him up snugly in swaddling clothes and laid him in a manger, among the animals, to sleep.

Meanwhile, in the fields just outside the town, shepherds were guarding their flocks. Suddenly, an angel of the Lord appeared to them and they were bathed in the glorious light of God. At first they were very scared, but the angel calmed them. "Do not be afraid," the angel said. "I have been sent with good news that will bring joy to you and all the world. Tonight the Saviour was born, Jesus Christ the Lord. You will find him near here, in King David's town of Bethlehem, lying in a manger."

Then a great choir of angels appeared in the sky singing praises to the Lord. "Glory to God in the highest," they sang. "Peace on earth. Goodwill to all those who believe in him."

The angels disappeared, leaving the shepherds open-mouthed in astonishment. At last, they gathered themselves and said to each other, "Come on! Let's go to Bethlehem and see for ourselves the child that the Lord has told us about."

They hurried down to Bethlehem and soon found Mary and Joseph in the stable, where the baby was lying in a manger. After gazing at the child, the shepherds recounted what the angel had said. Everyone that heard them was amazed at their story, but Mary held their words close to her heart, turning them over in her mind.

At last, the shepherds took their leave, singing praises to the Lord as they made their way back to their flocks. As their voices faded on the night air, stillness returned to the stable. Mary gazed lovingly at the face of her new-born child, marvelling at every detail of this extraordinary night – the night when Jesus Christ, the Saviour, was born.

Jesus at the Temple

Luke 2:21-38

When Mary's child was eight days old, he was circumcised and named Jesus — the name the angel of the Lord had given him. Soon after that, as laid down by Jewish Law, Mary and Joseph took him to the Temple to dedicate him to God.

At the time there was a man named Simeon living in Jerusalem. He was a devout man who had been told by the Holy Spirit that he would live to see the Messiah, the anointed king born to save Israel and the world. Led that day by the Holy Spirit, Simeon made his way to the Temple, where Mary and Joseph had brought the child.

Simeon took the infant Jesus in his arms and knew immediately this was the Saviour. "Lord, let your servant go in peace," he said, "because my eyes have seen the Saviour you promised. He will be like a light guiding the people of Israel and of every nation of the world."

Mary and Joseph listened in wonder to all the things that Simeon said. He blessed them and, turning to Mary, went on, "This child has been chosen by God for the destruction and salvation of many in Israel. Some people will tell lies and say evil things about him and so reveal the evil within themselves. When they do, however, sorrow will pierce your heart like a sharp sword."

A woman named Anna was also present at Jesus' ceremony of dedication. Widowed young and now eighty-four years old, she had spent most of her life in the Temple, praying and worshipping the Lord. As soon as she saw Jesus, she recognized who he was and thanked God. She began to talk about him excitedly to everyone in the Temple.

After the ceremony, Mary and Joseph set off back to Bethlehem, to collect their belongings and return home to Nazareth.

What they did not know was that some strangers were also making their way to Bethlehem at that very moment, having travelled specially from their homeland far away.

THE WISE MEN

Matthew 2

**S**ome time after Jesus' birth, wise men from the east arrived in Jerusalem. "Where is the child born king of the Jews?" they asked. "We have seen his star in the east and followed it. And we have come to worship him."

News of their arrival reached King Herod, who was alarmed. He was the king of the Jews, and it was troubling for him to think he might have a rival in his own land.

He summoned his chief priests to him. "Tell me," he asked, "where will this so-called Messiah be born?"

"In Bethlehem, in Judea," they answered. "It is written that out of Bethlehem shall come a lord who will rule the people of Israel."

Herod summoned the wise men to his palace to find out more. "This star," he said, "tell me about that. When did you see it?"

Thinking that Herod was genuinely interested, they told him when they had seen it and how it had guided them. Herod was interested – but not in the way they thought. Secretly the king was planning a trap.

"Go to Bethlehem," he said. "And when you find the child, report back to me, so that I can go and pay my respects to him."

With that, the wise men set off, keeping their eyes on the bright star in the sky. It seemed to stand still over Bethlehem, indicating where the child was to be found and filling their hearts with gladness.

But this feeling was as nothing compared to the sheer joy they felt when they finally saw the child in Mary's arms. Immediately, they fell to their knees and worshipped him, before giving him presents of gold, frankincense and myrrh.

Soon it was time for them to leave. But an angel warned them in a dream not to return to Herod. Instead of going back to tell him of the child's whereabouts, they returned to their homes by another route.

An angel also appeared to Joseph in a dream, warning him of the danger they faced if they returned to Nazareth. "Herod will be looking for the child," the angel said, "so that he can kill him. Take Jesus and his mother down to Egypt, and stay there until I tell you it is safe to leave."

Meanwhile, when Herod realized that the strangers from the east were not going to return, he was furious. He ordered his men to go to Bethlehem, and there kill every male child aged two and under. The weeping that day was terrible to hear.

Jesus, Mary and Joseph, however, were safe in Egypt, where they stayed until King Herod died. Then, with their enemy dead, they returned home.

JESUS AND THE TEACHERS

Luke 2:41-52

**E**very year, Mary and Joseph travelled from Nazareth to Jerusalem to celebrate the Passover festival. When Jesus was twelve years old and growing into a fine, strong boy, they decided to take him with them.

After carrying out their religious duties at the Temple as usual, Mary and Joseph set off to Nazareth with a large group of family and friends. When evening came, however, they looked for Jesus among the party, and discovered that no one had seen him all day. He had remained behind in Jerusalem.

Mary and Joseph were alarmed and decided to return to Jerusalem immediately. This meant another day-long journey, and a very tense, nervous journey at that, with Mary anxiously hoping that nothing had happened to her son.

When they arrived in the city, it was still thronging with people who had gathered for Passover. Mary and Joseph pushed their way through the crowds to the Temple, where they asked everyone they met if they had seen their son. No one had.

After a long search, they came across a group of Jewish teachers sitting in one of the Temple courtyards. Then they saw that they were gathered round a young boy who was enthusiastically asking them questions. Mary and Joseph looked at each other in amazement, for the boy was none other than Jesus himself. They stopped some

distance away and watched as their son talked to the scholars.

They could barely believe that a boy of twelve could discuss Jewish law with such educated men. Yet there he was, asking questions and listening carefully to the answers, all the time showing that he had a deep understanding of matters that the teachers had spent a lifetime studying.

Mary moved closer and, picking up the courage to interrupt, said, "Son, why have you done this to us? Why didn't you come back with us? We were terribly worried. We have been searching for you."

Jesus said simply, "But, Mother, why did you search for me? Surely you must have known that I would be here, in my Father's house."

Mary and Joseph were puzzled by this reply and did not know what to say. But Jesus willingly left the teachers and came to them. They went back to Nazareth, where life returned to normal. Jesus was a popular boy and an obedient son. He helped Joseph in his carpenter's shop and, day by day, grew up into a wise and much-loved young man.

JOHN THE BAPTIST

Matthew 3:1-12; Mark 1:1-8; Luke 3:1-20; John 1:19-28

echariah's son, John, knew he had been called to do the Lord's work, so when he was old enough, he left his parents' home to prepare. He lived alone in the desert, praying and listening to the word of God — and surviving on locusts and wild honey.

Eventually the time came for him to preach God's message to the people. "Turn away from your sins and be baptized," he said in a commanding voice. "God will forgive you."

In his rough tunic of camel's hair, John cut a strange and dramatic figure. But he had a powerful message that many people in Judea found hard to ignore. Many of them confessed their sins in the open air and were baptized by him in the River Jordan.

John travelled widely, attracting crowds wherever he went, even though sometimes his message made them feel uncomfortable. "You snakes!" he said. "There is no escaping God's punishment. Mend your ways. Turn your backs on sin!

"And do not say you are excused because Abraham was your ancestor. God can make anything into Abraham's children — even this pile of stones! I tell you, the axe is about to fall and the trees will be cut off at their roots. Every tree that does not bear good fruit will be cut down and thrown into the fire."

"But what should we do?" they asked.

"Share what you have with those in need," John replied. "If you have food, share it with someone who has none."

A group of tax collectors came up to him and asked him what they should do. "Be fair in all your dealings," John said. "Do not collect more than the Law says."

Some soldiers asked the same question. "Do not harm anyone," John said. "Do not lie, and be content with your wages."

As the people listened, their hopes rose and many of them wondered whether John himself was the promised Messiah. All this was very unsettling for the Jewish religious authorities, who sent out priests to investigate who exactly John was.

"Are you the Messiah?" they asked him.

"No," said John. "But I am preparing the way for him. Remember the words of the prophet, Isaiah: 'I am the voice of someone crying in the wilderness. Make straight the way of the Lord.'"

"But if you are not the Messiah," they asked, "why are you baptizing people?"

"I am baptizing with water," John replied, "but the man coming after me will baptize with fire, the fire of the Holy Spirit. I am not worthy even to untie his sandals."

And with that the priests left, feeling puzzled and very uneasy.

THE BAPTISM OF JESUS

Matthew 3:13-17; Mark 1:9-11; Luke 3:21-22

esus set out from Galilee one day and made his way to the River Jordan, where John was baptizing people. As soon as John saw Jesus coming towards him he knew exactly who he was.*

John stopped what he was doing and stood motionless in front of the crowd. The crowd too fell silent, wondering what John was going to do next. But it was Jesus who spoke first and what he said took John completely by surprise.

He asked John to baptize him in the river, there and then, in front of all the people. At first John was reluctant. It did not seem right for him to be baptizing the Saviour. Surely, it should be the other way round.

"I should be baptized by you," he said. "How is it that you have come to me?"

"This is how God intends it to be," said Jesus simply. "Do as I say and we will both be doing what God requires of us."

So John agreed and led Jesus into the waters of the Jordan.

As soon as Jesus came up out of the water he saw Heaven opening and the Holy Spirit descending like a dove. As he looked up, he heard a voice from Heaven saying, "This is my beloved Son, in whom I am well pleased."

After his baptism, Jesus took his leave and travelled alone into the desert, where his first trials awaited him.

THE TEMPTATIONS
IN THE DESERT

Matthew 4:1-11; Mark 1:12-13; Luke 4:1-13

nder the guidance of the Holy Spirit, Jesus walked deep into the desert. There he stayed for forty days and forty nights, praying and fasting in preparation for the task ahead. There also, the devil was waiting to lead him into temptation.

After fasting for so long, Jesus was extremely hungry and the devil used that to try to tempt him into disobedience.

"If you are the Son of God," said the devil, "command these stones to turn into bread. I know you are hungry. Think how delicious they would taste."

Although it was very difficult to do so, Jesus resisted. "The scriptures tell us that man cannot live by bread alone," he said. "Only the word of God keeps us alive."

Realizing that Jesus was not going to do as he had suggested, the devil tried again. This time he took Jesus up to the top of the highest mountain for miles around. From there, just for a moment, they had a glimpse of all the kingdoms in the world spread out beneath them. It was a breathtaking sight.

"Look!" said the devil. "All this power and all this wealth have been handed over to me. But I will give it to you. It is yours if you bow down and worship me."

"The scriptures tell us to worship God and God alone," said Jesus. "We must serve only the Lord."

For the third time, the devil tempted Jesus, cleverly quoting the scriptures as Jesus himself had done. Convinced that this tactic would work, the devil took Jesus to Jerusalem and set him down on the highest point of the Temple. From there the people below looked like tiny ants milling around on the ground.

"If you are the Son of God," the devil began, "throw yourself down. You know yourself it says in the scriptures that God will order the angels to catch you as you fall. No harm can come to you. They will take you safely in their hands, and your feet will not even be grazed on the stones below."

But Jesus was ready with a reply.

"It also says in the scriptures that you should not put the Lord your God to the test," he said.

The devil knew he had lost. He had tried to tempt Jesus to disobey the Lord, but had failed utterly. Finally, Jesus turned to him and said, "Go away, Satan! Be gone from me." And all the devil could do was disappear, defeated.

FISHERS OF MEN

Matthew 13:53-58; Mark 6:1-6; Luke 4:14-28; 5:1-11

After his experiences in the desert, Jesus returned to Galilee, strengthened and refreshed. He taught everywhere he could — in the fields, in the market place, in the synagogues — and soon news about him spread throughout the region. His ministry was just beginning and there was much to do.

But in Nazareth, his home town, he had an unwelcome surprise. It happened on the Sabbath when, as usual, he was worshipping at the synagogue. He stood up to read from the scriptures and was handed the scroll containing Isaiah's words. He read out, "'The spirit of the Lord is upon me. I have been chosen to bring good news to the poor, to set the prisoners free, to restore sight to the blind, to free the oppressed and to announce the coming of the Kingdom of God.'"

Jesus' reading of the passage was very powerful and it impressed all those listening. He was saying the words in a way that brought them vividly to life.

After he had read from the scroll he rolled it up, handed it back to the attendant, and sat down with the words, "The passage of scripture you have just heard has come true today — here in this room."

Everybody stared at him. They were very impressed by his wisdom, but could not accept what he had just said. "What can he mean?" they wondered. "He's just a carpenter's son, Mary and Joseph's boy. His brothers and sisters live round here — we

know them all. What on earth is he talking about?"

Jesus knew that they would reject him. "A prophet is never welcome in his own land," he said. This infuriated his audience, and they threw him out of the synagogue and manhandled him out of town.

This did not stop Jesus from preaching wherever he went. "Turn away from your sins," he would say, "because the Kingdom of Heaven is near."

One day, he was preaching on the shore of Lake Galilee when he saw two boats that had been hauled out onto the sand. Some fishermen were sitting beside them, cleaning their nets. Jesus went up to them.

The two men were brothers. Simon Peter owned one boat and Andrew helped him fish for a living. Jesus asked Simon to row him out onto the lake, from where he preached to the crowd that had turned up on the shore to hear him speak. When he had finished addressing the people, Jesus asked Simon to row out further onto the lake.

"Head for the deep water," Jesus told him. "Then cast your nets over the side.

I promise you it will be worth your while."

"But, Master," Simon protested, "we have both been up all night fishing this very stretch of water and we have caught nothing."

"Do as I say," said Jesus. "You will see."

"Very well," answered Simon. "I'll try."

Simon threw his net over the side and was surprised to feel it tug immediately. When they hauled the net back in, they found that it was teeming with fish, the biggest catch they had ever had. It was so full that Simon and Andrew began to fear that the boat would sink. They called over to their friends, James and John, who were fishing nearby, and asked them for help to get the catch aboard. In the end there were enough fish to fill both boats.

Simon and Andrew rowed back to the shore, followed closely by James and John. They pulled their boats up onto the beach and stood still for a moment, looking at each other in amazement.

Simon Peter knew at once that he was in the presence of an extraordinary man. "No, Lord," said Simon, falling on his knees in front of Jesus. "Leave me alone. I am a sinful man."

But Jesus ignored his protests. "Do not be afraid," he said. "Look at all the fish you have caught today. Follow me and I will make you fishers of men."

Now Jesus had four disciples. Soon he would have twelve – twelve men who would leave everything behind to follow him.

WATER INTO WINE

John 2:1-12

The town of Cana in Galilee was in festive mood. A local couple had just married and practically the whole population had turned out for the wedding. There was great excitement in the air as the guests – among them Jesus, his mother and his disciples – gathered to celebrate.

The wedding feast was in full swing when, all of a sudden, the hosts turned to Mary and told her that the wine had run out. This was going to be highly embarrassing for them – and very disappointing for the guests. Mary spoke to Jesus and explained the problem.

"Dear woman, why are you telling me this?" he asked. "My time has not yet come."

Although puzzled by this remark, Mary went to the servants and said, "Do as my son tells you."

At the back of the room were six huge stone jars, all standing empty.

"Fill the jars with water," Jesus said to the servants. "Fill them right up to the brim."

The men did as they were told and waited for further instructions.

"Now draw off some water," said Jesus, "and serve it to the organizer of the feast in one of the goblets."

The servants looked at each other in disbelief, but they did as they were told. Then they realized the truth. Miraculously, the water had turned into wine! When the organizer tasted the wine, a great smile spread over his face. Immediately he called over the bridegroom and congratulated him.

"I have no idea where this came from," he said, "but it is delicious. Most people serve the best wine first and wait until the guests are drunk before serving the ordinary wine. But you have kept the best until last!"

The guests continued to eat, drink and celebrate, unaware of the miracle that Jesus had just performed. But the few people in the room who did know marvelled at Jesus' work. Turning the water into wine, however, was only the first of many miracles Jesus performed, each one persuading the disciples of his power and glory.

HEALING THE SICK

Matthew 8:1-4; 9:1-8; Mark 1:40-45; 2:1-12; Luke 5:12-26

esus' reputation as a miracle worker spread throughout Galilee. Everywhere he went, he attracted crowds of people. Religious leaders had noticed this and were becoming alarmed, fearing that his popularity would undermine their authority.

On one occasion, Jesus was approached by a man with leprosy, a dreadful skin disease that at the time was incurable.

"Master," he said, "if you want to, you can cure me and make me clean again."

Jesus stretched out his hand and said, "I do want to. Be clean. You are cured."

Immediately, the disease disappeared.

"Do not tell anyone about this," Jesus said. "Go to your priest and let him examine you, and when he has certified that you are cured, offer a sacrifice to God."

But the man was so excited that he told everyone what had happened. As a result, Jesus was regularly surrounded by crowds seeking him out. Indeed, on one occasion the crowd was so large that a sick man had to be lowered on a stretcher through the roof!

Four of the sick man's friends, hearing that Jesus was in the area, had brought him to be healed. He was paralyzed, and they carried him on a mat that acted as a make-shift bed. When they arrived at the house where Jesus was preaching, a huge crowd prevented them from getting inside. So they took the outside steps to the top of the house and made a hole in the roof. Then they gently lowered their friend down to the floor where he lay at Jesus' feet.

Jesus looked up and saw four open, honest, trusting faces. Impressed by the men's obvious faith, he said to the paralyzed man, "My son, your sins are forgiven."

Among those watching were some Jewish legal experts. They were offended by Jesus' words. "How dare he blaspheme like this?" they muttered. "Only God can forgive sins."

Jesus heard them and challenged the men. "Let me ask you a question," he began. "Is it easier to say to this paralyzed man, 'Your sins are forgiven,' or to say, 'Get up. Pick up your bed and walk'?"

There was no answer, so Jesus said, "I will prove to you that the Son of Man has the authority to forgive people's sins."

Turning to the paralyzed man, Jesus said, "Arise. Pick up your bed and walk."

And straightaway the man got up, took hold of the mat he had been lying on and rolled it up. Then he walked out the house.

The people were amazed. "We have never seen anything like this," they said, and began to praise the Lord.

THE SERMON ON THE MOUNT

Matthew 5 – 7

One day, Jesus preached to his disciples and a large crowd on one of the hillsides around Lake Galilee. He spoke to them about many things, and after listening to his sermon, people looked at the world in a completely different way.

His teaching about happiness, for example, was utterly new. They thought that being happy meant being rich. Not so, said Jesus.

"Blessed are the poor in spirit," he said, "because the Kingdom of Heaven is theirs."

And he went on, "Blessed are those who mourn; God will comfort them. Blessed are those who are humble; the whole earth will be theirs. Blessed are those who are merciful; God will be merciful to them. Blessed are the pure in heart, for they shall see God. Blessed are the peacemakers, for they will be called the children of God. Blessed are those who are persecuted for doing God's work. Be glad when insults come your way. A reward is waiting for you in Heaven."

Jesus reminded them that they should follow the example of the prophets of old, suffering great hardship for God's sake. He also said that he had not come to do away with the ancient laws of Moses, laws which they, as Jews, still followed.

"I have come to fulfil the Law, not to destroy it," he said. "As long as Heaven and earth endure, not the smallest detail of that Law will be changed."

Jesus taught them about anger and how to control it; he talked about promises and how to keep them; and he talked about revenge and how to avoid it.

"In the old days," he said, "people wanted an eye for an eye and a tooth for a tooth. So if you blinded someone, you would be blinded yourself. But I tell you, if someone slaps your face, turn the other cheek and let him slap that one, too. You have heard it said that you should love your friends and hate your enemies. Well I say, love your enemies and pray for those who persecute you.

"As for wealth, do not store up riches in this life. Fine clothes will be eaten by moths and ornaments will rust away. No, store up your treasures in Heaven, the treasures that come from a pure spirit and a kind heart. These cannot be destroyed or stolen. And remember, no one can serve two masters. Choose to serve God, not money."

He knew that those listening to him were poor, so he offered them comfort and hope.

"Do not worry about the future," he said. "Do not worry about where your food or clothing is going to come from. True life is much more than those things. Look at the birds in the sky. They do not work in the fields gathering up corn to store. God takes care of them, just as God will take care of you.

"As for your clothing, do not get anxious about it. Consider the lilies of the field. They do not spin clothes for themselves, but even King Solomon in all his glory was not dressed as finely as these flowers.

"Do not worry where your next meal is coming from, either. Your Heavenly Father knows all the things you need and he will provide them. Do not think about tomorrow because tomorrow will take care of itself.

"Do not judge. It is easy to criticize other people's faults while forgetting your own."

And he taught them how to pray. "Do not make a great display of your prayers," he said. "Pray quietly in your room and say:

'Our Father in Heaven,
Hallowed be your name.

Your Kingdom come,
Your will be done
On earth as it is in Heaven.
Give us today our daily bread.
Forgive us the wrongs we have done,
As we forgive the wrongs that others
    have done to us.
Do not lead us into temptation,
But deliver us from evil.'"

As he prepared to send the people away, he gave them this advice: "To get to Heaven, you must pass through a very narrow gate, while the gate to hell is wide and easy to get through. But trust God to help you. Because God knows your needs even before you ask."

Finally Jesus said, "Remember: ask, and you will receive. Seek, and you will find. Knock, and the door to everlasting life will be opened to you."

STORM AT SEA

Matthew 8:23-27; Mark 4:35-41; Luke 8:22-25

After a long day preaching, Jesus suggested to his disciples that they take a boat across the lake to get a few hours' peace and quiet away from the crowds. It was a calm evening and the lake was as smooth as a sheet of glass.

Jesus had been talking all day long. He was very tired. He got into the boat first, while the disciples took their leave of the crowd. Then they began to row towards the other side, noticing that Jesus was already asleep.

"Look over there," said one man, pointing towards a thick slab of black cloud low on the horizon. "We ought to get a move on."

The disciples rowed faster. Suddenly, without warning, a gust of wind shattered the calm evening air, transforming the lake's surface into a foam of angry waves.

The storm worsened quickly. The wind stiffened and the waves broke over the bow and spilled into the boat. By now the disciples were seriously worried. They looked towards Jesus who, oblivious to the commotion, was sleeping at the stern of the boat, his head resting peacefully on a pillow.

"We have got to wake him," they said. "We're all going to drown. How can he sleep through this? It's getting worse."

"Just wake him up," shouted one of them, "or we're finished!"

One of the twelve fought his way against the wind and the water to the stern, where he shook Jesus' arm.

"Master, Master!" he shouted urgently. "Wake up! We are all going to die!"

Calmly Jesus got to his feet, then, stretching out his arms, commanded the wind to be still and the waves to subside. Immediately, a great peace settled on the boat – the winds dropped and the waves were calm. For a time, no one said a word – the disciples' ears were still ringing from the storm – then Jesus broke the silence.

"Why are you so frightened?" he asked. "Where is your faith?"

The disciples began to row again. "What kind of man can command the wind and the waves?" they whispered. "Who is he?"

JESUS CASTS OUT DEMONS

Matthew 8:28-34; Mark 5:1-20; Luke 8:26-39

The shock of the stormy crossing was beginning to subside a little as Jesus and the disciples reached the other side of Lake Galilee. But no sooner had they hauled their boat up onto the sand than another extraordinary event took place.

As Jesus got out of the boat, a wild-looking man ran towards him. He was possessed by evil spirits and lived among the dead in the burial caves nearby. Everybody was afraid of him, because he was tremendously strong. People had often tried to chain him up, but he always broke free. Even though they had put heavy iron shackles around his hands and feet, he had managed to pull them loose and run away, his wrists and ankles bleeding from where the iron had scraped his flesh.

He lived in a world of his own, tormented by frightening voices. When the spirits took hold of him, he wandered, screaming, through the cold, dark tombs, cutting at himself with sharp stones. Nobody dared go near him, so he was left alone, tortured by the waking nightmare inside his head.

As Jesus stepped onto the shore, the man approached and threw himself on his knees.

"Evil spirits, leave this man!" said Jesus.

"Jesus, Son of the Most High God!" cried the man. "I beg you, do not torment me!"

"What is your name?" asked Jesus.

The spirits took control of the man's voice. "There are many of us," they said. "Do not send us away. This is our only home."

Then Jesus noticed a large herd of pigs, some two thousand of them, feeding on the hillside above. The spirits had seen them too.

"Send us to the pigs," they screeched. "Let us enter them."

So Jesus allowed the demons to take possession of the pigs. Immediately, the herd began to squeal uncontrollably, racing down the hillside over a steep crag and into the water, where they drowned.

The men looking after the herd were frightened and ran back to the town to tell everyone what had happened. Before long, the local people had arrived on the shore and saw the man sitting quietly, in his right mind once again. Everyone was so terrified by what had happened that they asked Jesus to leave.

As Jesus was getting into the boat, however, the man asked whether he could go with him.

"No," said Jesus. "Go back home to your family and tell them what the Lord has done for you."

The man did as he was instructed and everybody who listened to him marvelled at the story he had to tell.

— 163 —

NICODEMUS

John 3:1-21

icodemus was a Jewish leader and a member of the group of teachers known as Pharisees. Most Pharisees viewed Jesus with great suspicion. Nicodemus, however, was different. He wanted to talk to Jesus, so one night he secretly paid him a visit.

"Rabbi," he said, "we know you are a teacher sent by God. Nobody could perform the miracles you perform unless God were helping him. But…"

"Listen, Nicodemus," said Jesus. "Listen to me. I tell you that people will not see God's Kingdom unless they are born again."

"What do you mean?" Nicodemus asked. "How can an adult be born again? Once you are born, you cannot go back into your mother's womb to do it all over again."

Jesus patiently explained what he meant. "As you can be born physically, so you can be born spiritually. You will not enter the Kingdom of God unless you are baptized by water and born again – this time of God's Holy Spirit. The wind blows where it wishes. You hear its sound, but you do not know where it has come from. That is how it is with everyone born of the Holy Spirit."

"But how?" asked Nicodemus.

"You are a great teacher," Jesus replied, "but you have much to learn. I speak of what I know, but you do not believe. If you do not believe me when I talk of the things in this world, how will you believe me when I talk about the things in Heaven? No one has ever gone up to Heaven except the Son of Man, who came down from Heaven to earth.

"God so loved the world that he gave his only Son, so that everyone who believes will not perish but have eternal life. God did not send his Son into the world to judge it but to save it. Whoever believes in God's Son will not be judged, but whoever does not believe has already been judged.

"The light has come into the world. People prefer darkness because it can hide their evil deeds. But those who do what is good and true come into the light – the light of God."

THE WOMAN AT THE WELL

John 4:1-41

On his way to Galilee, Jesus stopped at a farm in Samaria. There he sat down by a well to rest. In those days there was bad blood between Jews and Samaritans and the Jews of Judea despised their neighbours. Jesus was different.

As he was sitting by the well, a Samaritan woman came along to draw some water. Jesus asked her for a drink. The woman was surprised because no Jew would drink from the same cup as a Samaritan.

"How can you be asking me, of all people?" she said.

"If only you knew who I am," Jesus replied, "and if only you knew what God would give you if you asked me for a drink in return! I would give you life-giving water."

"But, sir," she said, "the well is deep and you have nothing to collect the water. How would you get that life-giving water?"

"The water I am talking about will quench your thirst forever," said Jesus. "It is an inexhaustible spring. Drink and you will never be thirsty again. Drink and you will have everlasting life."

"Sir, give me that water," the woman said, "so that I will not thirst again."

Jesus paused. "Go and fetch your husband," he said.

"I don't have one," she replied.

"I know," said Jesus. "You have been married five times and the man you are living with is not your husband. I am glad you told the truth."

The woman was amazed. This man seemed to know everything about her.

"I can see you are a prophet," she said. "Is it true that we should worship God only in Jerusalem?"

"The time will come when people will worship God everywhere," he replied. "They will worship the Father as he truly is."

"I know the Messiah will come," she said, "and then he will tell us everything."

"I am that man you speak of," Jesus said.

At that point the disciples, who had been buying food for the journey, returned. They were surprised to see Jesus talking to a Samaritan woman, but no one questioned him. They knew that Jesus taught in ways that no one had ever done before.

The woman went back to the town and told everyone what had happened. "This man knew my entire life story," she said. "Come and see him for yourselves."

The Samaritans begged Jesus to stay on at the town, which he did for two more days. At the end of that time, the people there were convinced that he was Christ, the Anointed One, the Saviour of the world.

THE POOL OF BETHESDA

John 5:1-18

he Jewish religious authorities were irritated by reports of the miracles Jesus had performed. His healing ministry was making him very popular and undermining their authority. So, whenever possible, they tried to use the Law to stop him.

One day, Jesus went down to the Pool of Bethesda by the sheep market in Jerusalem. It was famed for its healing powers and attracted streams of people hoping to be cured of disease. Lining the pool were five porches, where the sick would traditionally gather before bathing in the water. It was usually very crowded, with blind, lame and paralyzed people waiting their turn to be submerged in the pool.

When Jesus arrived, one man caught his eye. He had been ill for thirty-eight years, and was extremely frail.

Jesus walked over and spoke to him. "You are waiting to be cured, aren't you?" he said.

"Yes, sir," the man replied. "But I have no one here to help me into the pool. Every time I try to get closer, somebody pushes in front of me and gets there first."

"Get up," said Jesus. "Pick up your mat and walk."

Immediately, the man was well. He picked up the mat he was lying on and walked away.

Now it so happened that the day on which Jesus performed this miracle was the Sabbath, when according to Jewish Law no work could be done. Some religious leaders caught sight of the man carrying his mat, and they reminded him that it was forbidden to carry loads on the Sabbath.

"Yes, but I have been crippled for years," he replied. "An hour ago I couldn't walk. The man who cured me told me to pick up my mat and walk. So I did as he told me, and look – I'm walking!"

"What was the man's name?" they asked.

"I don't know," he replied. "I've never seen him before. He just vanished in the crowd."

A little later, Jesus came across the man in the Temple and said to him, "You are well now. Be glad – but do not sin any more."

The man quickly left and told the Jewish authorities Jesus' name. As soon as they had this proof, they tracked him down and accused him of healing on the Sabbath.

But Jesus had an answer for them. "My Father is always working," he said, "so I must work too."

This angered the priests even more; not only because he had broken the Law, but because he had said God was his father. That could mean only one thing – that he considered himself equal to God. For this, they thought, Jesus deserved to die.

HEALING ON THE SABBATH

Matthew 12:1-14; Mark 2:23-28; 3:1-6; Luke 6:1-11

Two groups, the Sadducees and the Pharisees, often challenged Jesus as he went about his work. One Saturday, Jesus and his disciples happened to be walking through a cornfield when the disciples picked some of the stalks, rubbed them in their hands to get at the grain, and started to eat.

Some Pharisees had been observing this, as usual taking every opportunity of collecting evidence against them.

"That's harvesting!" they said. "You know that's not allowed on the Sabbath. You are breaking the Law."

But Jesus, who had studied the scriptures since he was a boy, came back at them with a story. "Surely you remember what David and his men did when they were hungry. David went into the Temple and ate the bread that was supposed to be offered to God. Now, everybody knew that was against the Law. But God did not punish David for it."

The Pharisees were lost for words. Jesus was quoting scripture, using it against them!

"And have you not read in the Law of Moses," Jesus went on, "that every Sabbath the priests of the Temple themselves break the Sabbath law? They are working on the day of rest – but they are not punished!

"I tell you that you are standing in the presence of someone greater than the Temple," said Jesus. "The scriptures say, 'It is kindness I want, not animal sacrifices.' If you really understood the Law, then you

would not condemn innocent people. The Son of Man is the Lord of the Sabbath."

The Pharisees could not believe their ears. Yet what could they do? Jesus knew the Law as well as they did. What he had said about the Temple priests was right. They went back into the city, furious that this troublemaker was challenging their authority.

Jesus' next stop was the synagogue where he met a man with a paralyzed hand. Again the Pharisees were lying in wait, watching what he would do.

Looking for an excuse to accuse him, they went straight up to him and asked, "Is it lawful to heal on the Sabbath?"

"What if one of you had a sheep that fell down a deep hole on the Sabbath?" Jesus asked them. "Wouldn't you rescue it? Well, isn't a man worth helping as much as a sheep? Does the Law allow us to do good on the Sabbath, or harm? To save life or destroy it?"

Then Jesus turned to the sick man and said, "Stretch out your arm." He did so and it was as healthy as the other one.

The Pharisees said nothing to this, but secretly they began to plan how to kill Jesus.

Jairus' Daughter

Matthew 9:18-31; Mark 5:21-42; Luke 8:40-56

As Jesus continued his ministry, people throughout Galilee heard about the miracles he performed. More and more people came to him asking for his help. Jairus, an official at a local synagogue, was one of them. His daughter was desperately ill and only Jesus could cure her.

Jairus threw himself down at Jesus' feet. "Please come to my house," he said, "and place your hands on my daughter. If you do, I know that she will recover."

Jesus agreed and asked Jairus to lead the way. By now, the crowd was huge and it was very difficult for Jesus and the disciples to move forward, as they were constantly jostled on every side.

Hidden among the crowd was a woman who had suffered an illness which made her bleed for twelve years. The doctors had prescribed endless, expensive cures which had had no effect whatsoever. She had travelled a long way to be there that day, convinced that, if she could only touch Jesus' clothes, she would be cured.

Jesus was just ahead of her, surrounded by a crush of bodies, each one asking for his help. The woman stretched out her hand and just managed to touch the hem of Jesus' cloak. Instantly, her bleeding stopped. Jesus felt some of his power leaving him. He stopped walking.

"Who touched me?" asked Jesus.

The disciple nearest him, Peter, was puzzled and thought he had misheard his master.

"Someone touched me," Jesus said again. "Who was it?"

"But Master, there are so many people touching you," said Peter. "Just look at the crowd. It could have been anyone."

But Jesus knew differently. He looked around at the crowd. The woman could feel

Jesus' eyes upon her, so she came forward and knelt down in front of him trembling. In front of everyone she told him the whole story.

"I knew that if I could just get near enough to touch you, I would be cured," she said.

"My daughter," said Jesus, looking down at her. "Your faith has made you well. Go in peace."

Jairus, meanwhile, was looking anxiously at Jesus. His daughter was gravely ill and there was no time to lose. But at that very moment, a man pushed his way through the crowd.

"I am sorry to have to tell you, Jairus," he said, "but I have just come from your house. Your daughter is dead."

Jesus heard this and said to Jairus, "Do not be afraid. Only believe, and your daughter will be well."

They hurried on to Jairus' house, still pursued by the crowd. When they arrived, they were faced with a distressing scene. The girl's family were beside themselves with grief. Friends and neighbours had gathered outside the house and the air was filled with the sound of their crying.

Jesus broke away from the crowd and instructed the disciples Peter, John and James to come with him into the house. Apart from them and the girl's parents, everyone else was told to stay outside.

The six of them went into the girl's room. When the mother saw the little body lying on the bed, she let out a terrible cry and fell to the ground.

"Do not weep," said Jesus calmly. "The child is not dead. She is only sleeping."

The mother and father looked at Jesus in some confusion. The child was obviously dead. Her lifeless body was lying in front of their eyes. What could he mean?

But Jesus walked over to the bed and took hold of the girl's hand. With her hand in his he said softly, "Wake up, my child."

Immediately the girl's eyes opened and the life returned to her. She blinked, then looked around the room, wondering why her mother and father and four strangers were looking down at her.

The girl's parents were overcome by joy and astonishment. They could not find words to thank Jesus.

"Do not tell anybody about this," he said to them, and then, turning to the girl, added, "She is hungry. Go and fetch her something to eat."

And with that, Jesus and the three disciples left the house.

But Jesus' work was not over for that day. No sooner had he gone outside than two blind men called out to him. "Have mercy on us, David's son!" they cried.

Jesus waited until he had taken shelter in one of his disciples' houses. Then the blind men came to him.

"Do you truly believe that I am able to heal you?" he asked them.

"Yes, Lord," the men said.

"Then because of your faith, it will be done," Jesus said, and laying his fingers on their eyes, he restored their sight.

Despite Jesus' wish that these miracles should remain secret, the news soon spread and his reputation grew still further.

THE PARABLES

Jesus often told stories to get his message across to ordinary people. Featuring imaginary characters and situations from everyday life, these stories, called parables, seemed straightforward. But they often contained complex hidden meanings that Jesus had to explain.

THE LOST SON

Luke 15:11-32

There was once a man who had two sons. The younger of the two asked him for some money – the money that he would eventually inherit when his father died. His father agreed, but not long after that the son left home suddenly and settled in a far off country, where he wasted all his money on reckless living.

When he had spent everything, a great famine struck and, with no money to his name, he was forced to take the worst jobs simply to survive. From being very rich and wanting for nothing, he was reduced to looking after pigs on another man's farm. At last, when he could bear it no longer, he came to his senses and thought, "Here am I starving, when even my father's servants have more food than they need. I'll go back and apologize to my father for the wrong I've done to God and to him."

And with that, he set off back to his father's house. But while he was still a long way off, his father saw him coming and took pity. He ran towards his son and kissed him. "Father, I'm so sorry," he said, "I'm not fit to be called your son."

But his father told his servants to dress his son in the finest clothes and to put a ring on his finger and shoes on his feet. "Let us celebrate!" he said. "My son has come home. It is as if he has died and come back to life."

Meanwhile his elder son, who had been working in the fields, could hear the celebrations and asked a servant what they were for. His father came out to meet him, but the son exploded into anger and said, "For years, I have served you and done exactly as you've said, but you've never done this for me. Why are you doing it for that son of yours who went off and wasted all your money?"

"My son," said the father, "you are always here with me and everything I have is yours. But it is right to celebrate your brother's return because he was dead and now he is alive. He was lost and now he is found."

THE THREE SERVANTS

Matthew 25:14-30

A rich man was preparing to go on a long journey. He called his three most trusted servants and gave each a sum of money according to his skills. So, the first servant was given five thousand gold coins, the second received two thousand and the third, one thousand.

While their master was away, the first servant invested his five thousand coins and earned another five thousand. The second servant did the same and earned another two thousand. But the third servant was afraid of losing the money and buried it.

"Well done," said the man to the first servant when he returned. "I shall put you in charge of more of my property."

Then he turned to the second servant and said the same. But to the third servant he said, "You lazy, wicked good-for-nothing! At least you could have put the money where it would have earned interest. Give your coins to the first servant. For those who have will be given more. And those who have practically nothing will find that the little they do have will be taken away from them. Now get out of my sight!"

THE PARABLE OF THE SOWER

Matthew 13:3-23; Mark 4:1-20; Luke 8:1-15

Jesus was in Galilee preaching to a large crowd by the lakeside one day when he told this parable.

"There was once a farmer," he began, "who went into his field to sow seed. Some of the seeds ended up on the path running alongside the field and were eaten by the birds. Some fell on stony soil, which prevented the seeds from taking root properly. As a result, they sprouted, but soon shrivelled up when their roots found no moisture. Some of the seeds landed among the thorn bushes, where the young shoots were eventually choked to death.

But some fell on fertile soil and produced a record harvest."

Jesus paused for a moment to let the story sink in. As he did, the disciples asked him why he used parables so often in his teaching.

"The reason I use them," said Jesus, "is that people look but do not see. They listen but they do not hear. To understand these parables, they must open up their eyes and ears. You are fortunate. You have been given an understanding of the Kingdom of Heaven. They have not. So they need to be told in a challenging way."

Then Jesus began to explain the meaning of the parable he had just told them.

"Think of yourselves as different kinds of soil," he said. "If you hear God's message and do not follow it, then you are like the soil on the path. The devil will come and snatch the message of God away – just as the birds came and carried all the seeds away before they could grow.

"If you are like the soil on stony ground, you will follow the message at first, but give up when times are hard. Stony ground will let the seed sprout in the beginning, but it will not let it take root properly and eventually it will wither. If you are like the soil among the thorn bushes, you will be distracted from the message of God by money or possessions. And just as the seed was choked by the thorns, so the message of God will be suffocated by your everyday worries.

"If you are like fertile soil, the message of God will grow strong and healthy just as the seeds in good soil grows into a flourishing plant. And you will be blessed with a record harvest."

THE LOST SHEEP

Luke 15:1-7

One day Jesus was preaching to a crowd that included a number of tax collectors and other people despised by the Jewish authorities. The Pharisees were disgusted by this and said, "Look at this man welcoming sinners and outcasts. He even eats with them."

Jesus turned to the Pharisees and said, "Imagine one of you has a hundred sheep and one of them goes missing. What does he do? Does he not leave the ninety-nine in the field and go looking for the one missing sheep? When he finds it, he is so pleased that he puts it on his shoulder and carries it home. Then he tells all his friends about it.

"Well, in the same way, there will be more joy in Heaven over one sinner who repents than over ninety-nine good people who do not need to repent."

THE GOOD SAMARITAN

Luke 10:25-37

One day, a lawyer stood up in front of Jesus and asked him a question to try to catch him out.

"What do I have to do to get to Heaven?" he asked.

"What does the Law say?" asked Jesus in return.

"That I should love God with all my heart and with all my soul and with all my mind and with all my strength. And that I should love my neighbour as myself," he said.

"Correct," said Jesus.

But the lawyer did not stop there. "But who exactly is my neighbour?" he asked.

So Jesus told him this story.

"A man was travelling from Jerusalem to Jericho one day when he was attacked by thieves who robbed him, beat him and left him for dead. A priest came by, saw the man, but walked past on the other side of the road. Another man came along – also from the Temple – and did the same; he just looked at the traveller and walked on by.

"But then a Samaritan came along..."

At this point the lawyer's face dropped. The Samaritans after all were not popular and the Jews treated them with suspicion. Jesus went on.

"A Samaritan came along and took pity on the traveller. He cleaned and bandaged his wounds, put him on his own donkey and took him to an inn where he had him well looked after.

"When he left the next day, he gave some money to the innkeeper and told him to take care of the traveller. 'If it costs you any more than this,' he said, 'I shall pay you back when I return.'"

Then Jesus asked the lawyer, "Which of those three men was a good neighbour to the injured traveller?"

"The one who was kind to him," he replied, unable even to say the word Samaritan.

"Go, then," said Jesus, "and do the same."

THE FRIEND AT MIDNIGHT

Luke 11:5-10

Jesus was teaching his disciples how to pray when he told them this story.

"Let us imagine you had a good friend whom you had not seen for a long time. Imagine that he stopped by unexpectedly and you had no bread in the house to feed him."

The disciples listened, wondering what Jesus would say next.

"Now imagine you went to another friend's house at midnight and asked to borrow three loaves. What would you do if he shouted back at you, 'Do not bother me. It is late, my door is locked and all my family are in bed'?"

The disciples looked at each other in silence.

Jesus continued, "He might be tired and not feel like getting out of bed so late at night to do you a favour. But if you are his friend, you will not be embarrassed to ask him for the bread a second time. Eventually, he will get up and lend you the loaves because you are not ashamed to keep on asking.

"Prayer is like that. Ask and you will receive, seek and you will find, knock and the door will be opened to you."

THE RICH FOOL

Luke 12:13-21

A man asked Jesus to solve a family dispute. "Teacher," he said, "tell my brother to give me my fair share of the property our father has left us as our inheritance."

"What right have I to divide the property between you?" Jesus asked him. Then he went on, "Guard against every kind of greed, because your true life has nothing to do with what you own, no matter how rich you are."

Then Jesus told this story.

"There was once a rich man who owned fields that produced a good crop. He had so much grain he had nowhere left to store it. So he decided he would tear down the barns he had and build bigger ones. 'Then I can sit back and take life easy,' he thought to himself. 'I can eat, drink and be merry. What a lucky man I will be. I will have everything I could possibly need.'

"But God said to him, 'You fool! Tonight you will die and what good will your wealth do you then?'"

Jesus paused and said, "This is what it is like for people who hoard riches for themselves, but who are not rich in God's eyes."

THE GREAT FEAST

Luke 14:15-24

One day, while dining at the house of a rich man, Jesus told this parable.

"There was once a man who decided to give a great feast for his son's neighbours. When the food was prepared, he sent out his servants to fetch the invited guests but, one by one, they turned him down.

"'I've just bought a plot of land and I need to inspect it,' said one.

"'I've just bought a team of oxen,' said another. 'I need to put them to work.'

"And a third could not attend because he had just got married.

"The man was furious. He told his servant. 'Go out into the street and invite anyone you can find. Fetch me the poor, the blind and the lame. They can eat with me instead.'

"The servant did as he was told. He scoured the streets, then returned to his master and said, 'There is room for more.'

"'Then go and get me more people,' his master said, 'so that my house can be filled. But not one of those men I invite will get a taste of my dinner.'"

THE TENANTS IN THE VINEYARD

Luke 20:9-15

One day Jesus told this story:

"There was once a man who planted a vineyard and put it in the care of tenants. He told them to look after it while he was away and added that he would be gone for a long time.

"When harvest time came he sent a servant to collect a portion of the grapes from the tenants. But the men beat the servant and sent him back empty-handed. So the man sent another servant – and the same thing happened again. He was beaten and sent back without a thing. When the same thing happened a third time, the owner of the vineyard was at a loss. 'What shall I do?' he wondered. 'I know, I will send my own dear son. Surely they will show him some respect.'

"But when the tenants saw him they said, 'Look, it's the owner's son. Let's kill him and the vineyard will be ours.'

"As soon as the owner's son came up to them, they set on him, threw him out of the vineyard and beat him to death."

At this point Jesus stopped, turned to the people, and asked, "And what do you think the owner of the vineyard will do to the tenants?"

NEWS OF JOHN

Matthew 11:1-19; Mark 6:17-20; Luke 7:18-35

he Romans, who controlled Palestine, appointed kings to rule on their behalf and gave them power and status in exchange for their obedience. When Herod the Great died, the kingdom was divided amongst his sons.

One of these was Herod Antipas, who ruled over Galilee. One day, word came to him of John the Baptist's preaching. What he learnt did not please him. "The man is clearly a troublemaker," Herod thought, "preaching about the coming of the Messiah and stirring up the people with false expectations."

He also realized that if John acquired a large following – and there was evidence of this – he could be a threat to public order. The Romans would see this as a rebellion and might intervene to crush it themselves, removing Herod from power at the same time. He was determined not to let this happen and vowed to keep a close eye on John.

At the same time, Herod's eye was attracted elsewhere. He was becoming increasingly fond of his brother Philip's wife, Herodias. In fact he was so attracted to her that he divorced his own wife to have her. Such behaviour was clearly against the Law of God, and when the news got out, John the Baptist was the first to say so publicly. For this he was arrested and thrown into jail.

Locked in his prison cell, John began to lose his confidence and he started to wonder whether Jesus really was the Messiah whose coming he had been chosen to announce. So he arranged for a few of his followers to go to Jesus and ask him some of the questions that were on his mind.

"Are you the one we are waiting for?" they asked Jesus. "Or should we expect someone else?"

Jesus reassured them. "Go back and tell John what you have seen and heard," he said. "Tell him how the blind can see, how the lame can walk, how the dead are brought back to life and how the good news is being preached to the poor."

Then Jesus turned to the crowd and spoke to them about John.

"What did you expect to see when you went to him in the desert?" he asked them. "Did you expect to see a man in fine clothing? Of course not. You went to see a prophet. And what a great prophet John is! He is greater than any man who ever lived. But I tell you this. Once you have entered the Kingdom of Heaven, the least of you will be greater than him."

JESUS SENDS OUT HIS DISCIPLES

Matthew 10; Mark 3:13-19; Luke 9:1-9

Jesus' twelve disciples were Simon Peter and his brother Andrew, James and his brother John, Philip and Bartholomew, Thomas and Matthew, James and Thaddeus, Simon and Judas Iscariot. One day, Jesus called them all together and gave them important instructions.

"Do not go into a non-Jewish country," he said to them, "and avoid the towns of Samaria. Instead, visit the lost sheep of the people of Israel and tell them that the Kingdom of Heaven is near.

"Heal the sick, cure disease, bring the dead back to life and cast out demons. And, since you have been given these powers free of charge, do not accept any payment. Do not carry any money with you – whether gold, silver or brass – do not even carry a bag for your journey, nor a spare coat, sandals or a stick. Like workers arriving for a job, you will be given everything you need.

"When you come to a town or a village, look for a good family to stay with until you leave. Look for people who will welcome you into their home. When you go inside a house, say to the family, 'Peace be with you.' If they welcome you, then let the peace you bring remain with them. If they turn you away, then they turn away your greeting of peace as well.

"If a family or even an entire city turns you away and refuses to listen to you, do not worry. Simply leave the house or city behind, shake the dust from your feet and move on to where you are welcome. That will be a warning to them. I can tell you that, on Judgement Day, God will show more mercy to the sinners of Sodom and Gomorrah than to those people who turn their backs on you."

So the disciples went out to the towns and villages all around, healing, casting out demons and telling the people to turn away from sin. Jesus had told them they would have to suffer many hardships for spreading his message. "I am sending you out like sheep to a pack of wolves," he said. "So be careful. Be as cunning as snakes, but also as gentle as doves. For my sake you will be arrested, beaten and put on trial. But do not worry about what you should say. When the time comes, the right words will come to you – not your words, but those of God.

"Those who love their fathers or mothers more than me are not fit to be my disciples. Nor are those who refuse to take up their cross and follow me. If you try to save your life, you will lose it; but if you lose your life for my sake, you will save it."

THE DEATH OF JOHN

Matthew 14:1-12; Mark 6:14-29

Herod's new wife, Herodias, hated John the Baptist for his public disapproval of her marriage. She wanted him executed, but Herod, who feared and respected the prophet's holiness, refused. Before long, however, Herodias got her way.

It was the king's birthday. Herod had invited all his military commanders and the leading figures of Galilee to a huge feast. There were mountains of food and endless supplies of wine. Then came the high point of the afternoon's entertainment.

A beautiful young woman appeared from behind the court musicians and the whole hall fell silent. It was Herodias' daughter who was about to perform a dance for all the guests. As the music played, the girl moved across the floor in a way that held her audience spellbound. As if hypnotized by her exquisite beauty and her flawless dancing, the guests watched open-mouthed.

When the dance was over, the delighted king made a promise he would later regret.

"Your dance was splendid," he said as the applause died down. "Have anything your heart desires. Take half my kingdom if you wish!" The young woman did not know what to say, so she left the banqueting hall to speak to her mother, Herodias.

"What should I ask for?" she said.

"Ask for John the Baptist's head!" came Herodias' cruel reply.

The young woman hurried back to Herod, who said, "Have you decided? What will you have?"

"I want the head of John the Baptist – served on a platter," she said.

Silence fell. The shocked guests looked at each other in disbelief, knowing that the king could not go back on his promise.

With great sadness, Herod called for a guard. He gave him instructions and sent him off to John's cell. A little later, the guard returned, carrying a plate with John's head on it. In full view of the guests, many of whom turned away in disgust, he presented Herodias' daughter with her reward. She in turn carried it to her waiting mother. Herodias had got her revenge.

When John's followers heard about this, they came to the prison, collected John's body and buried it. Then they went to tell Jesus.

FEEDING THE FIVE THOUSAND

Matthew 14:13-21; Mark 6:30-44; Luke 9:10-17; John 6:1-15

Jesus was very upset when he learnt of John's death, so he and his disciples went off in a boat to spend some time alone. It was not long, however, before the people found out where Jesus was and gathered to meet him. Jesus took one look at this large crowd and was filled with compassion.

"They are like sheep without a shepherd," he thought. So he set about teaching them and healing those who were sick. The day wore on. There was much for Jesus to do. In fact, everyone was so busy concentrating on Jesus' message that it was early evening before the disciples realized that nobody had eaten all day. People were beginning to feel very hungry.

"Perhaps we should send them back to the village," they said. "They can buy some food there."

"There is no need for them to leave," said Jesus. "Feed them with what you have."

"But, Master," they said, "the only one with any food is this young lad. And all he has is five loaves and two fish. It is not enough to feed so many and we do not

have enough money to buy food for the whole crowd. There must be over five thousand people here."

Jesus was not at all concerned. He instructed the disciples to divide the crowd into groups of fifty and to seat them on the grass. The disciples did as they were told, unsure what Jesus had in mind.

When the people were seated in their groups, Jesus took the bread, looked up to Heaven and gave thanks to God. Then he broke the bread and told the disciples to distribute it among the hungry crowd. While they were doing this Jesus prayed over the fish. The disciples passed the food round, and to their amazement the people had more than enough to eat.

But Jesus was not finished yet. "We must not waste anything," he said. "Gather up what is left."

The disciples collected what was left and, to their surprise, discovered that they had filled twelve baskets with the remains. All this from just five loaves and two fish!

Jesus could see that the crowd was very excited by this miracle and he could hear the people murmuring among themselves. "Surely this is the prophet who is come into the world!" they said, and began to crowd in on Jesus and the disciples.

Jesus was afraid that they would seize him to make him their king. So he withdrew, to the hills, where he could be alone.

JESUS WALKS ON WATER

Matthew 14:22-33; Mark 6:45-52; John 6:15-21

After feeding the five thousand, Jesus needed time to be alone. He sent the disciples on ahead, telling them to sail to the other side of the Lake of Galilee. As night fell, Jesus prayed on the hillside overlooking the lake.

It was after three o'clock in the morning when his prayers were at an end. Jesus looked out over the water and saw the disciples still rowing their little fishing boat towards the distant shore. He could see that the wind was against them and that large waves were slapping against the bow.

Inside the boat, the disciples strained at the oars, trying to steer against the wind. Then one man glanced to the side.

"Look!" he cried.

All the disciples turned to see a figure walking towards them on the water. As the mysterious person drew nearer, they were convinced it was a ghost and each man cried out in fear.

By now the figure was close enough for them to recognize the unmistakable face of Jesus, but still they were afraid.

"Be brave," he said. "It is me. Do not fear."

Peter was the first to speak.

"Lord, if it really is you," he said, "order me to walk towards you on the water."

"Come," said Jesus, holding out his hand.

Peter climbed out of the boat and started to walk towards Jesus. But as soon as he felt the strong wind against his face and the cool water beneath his feet, he started to panic. Sinking down into the waves, he shouted, "Help me, Lord! Please save me!"

At once, Jesus reached out and grabbed hold of him. "Peter," he said, "how little faith you have! Why did you doubt me?"

Peter climbed back into the boat, calmly followed by Jesus. The wind died down and the disciples looked at each other in wonder. Then they worshipped Jesus, saying, "Truly, you are the Son of God!"

SIMON THE PHARISEE

Luke 7:36-50

One day, Jesus went to the home of a Pharisee named Simon, who had invited him to share a meal. Jesus took his place at dinner, reclining in the Roman fashion, his legs stretched out behind him. Then, without saying a word, a woman entered the room and stood by his feet.

No one said anything, but everyone knew who she was. She was well known in the town as a woman who had lived a sinful life. She began to cry, and as her tears splashed down onto Jesus' feet, she bent down to dry them with her hair. Then, pouring sweet-smelling oil from her alabaster jar, she gently massaged Jesus' feet.

The guests looked elsewhere, pretending not to notice. Simon, the Pharisee, shifted nervously from one elbow to the other.

"If this man Jesus were a real prophet," he thought to himself, "he would know exactly who this woman is and think twice before allowing her to touch him."

Jesus knew what he was thinking.

"Simon," he said, "let me tell you a story."

"I am listening, Master," Simon replied.

"There were two men who owed money to a money-lender," Jesus began. "One of them owed five hundred pieces of silver and the other owed fifty. Neither of them could afford to pay back the money, so the money-lender decided to cancel both their debts. Now, Simon, which of the two men do you think was more grateful?"

"I suppose the one who had the bigger debt forgiven," said Simon.

"Correct," said Jesus. "I came into your home and you gave me no water for my feet. But this woman has washed my feet with her tears and dried them with her hair. You did not welcome me with an embrace, but she has not stopped kissing my feet since she arrived. You did not anoint my head, but she has bathed my feet in scented oil.

"I tell you, Simon, everyone needs forgiveness. This woman knows that only too well – she has many sins that need to be forgiven. But they are forgiven – the great love she has shown to me today proves that. For whoever has been forgiven little, loves only a little. But those who have been forgiven much, like this woman here, love much."

Then Jesus looked into the woman's eyes and said, "Your sins are forgiven."

The other Pharisees looked at each other. "Who is this man who says he can forgive sins?" they wondered. But Jesus held the woman's gaze as she prepared to leave. "Your faith has saved you," he said. "Go in peace."

JESUS PREDICTS HIS DEATH

Matthew 16:13-28; Mark 8:27 – 9:1; Luke 9:18-27

The disciples loved Jesus, but sometimes they found the things he had to say to them very disturbing. For example, one day, after Jesus had been praying alone, he asked his disciples a question that took them by surprise.

"Who do the people say I am?" he asked.

"Some say you are John the Baptist," they replied. "Others say you are Elijah. And some say you are one of the other prophets of old, miraculously brought to life."

"What about you?" Jesus asked. "Who do you say I am?"

Peter answered. "You are God's Messiah," he said.

Jesus looked at the disciples and told them not to repeat Peter's answer to anyone.

It seemed to the disciples that Jesus was in a strange mood, and what he went on to say disturbed and upset them very much.

"The Son of Man must suffer many things," he said. "He will be rejected by the chief priests, elders and the teachers of the Law."

"What do you mean, Master?" they asked.

"I must suffer much," Jesus continued. "I must go to Jerusalem, where I shall be put to death."

The disciples looked at each other in horror.

"But three days later I shall rise from the dead," said Jesus.

"No, Master, no!" gasped Peter. "This must not happen!"

Immediately, Jesus turned to Peter and said sharply, "Get behind me, Satan. You are in my way. You are like an obstacle standing in my path. What you are saying is not inspired by God, but by human beings."

By now the disciples were becoming alarmed. But Jesus went on.

"If anybody wants to come with me, they must forget themselves, pick up their cross and follow me completely. They must leave everything and everybody behind. Whoever clings to the old life will lose it, but whoever loses their life for my sake will save it. And what good will it do people to win the whole world and lose their soul?"

The disciples knew that Jesus' message was always challenging, and they began to accept the hard things he was saying.

"These are sinful and wicked times," said Jesus finally. "If anyone is ashamed of me or my teaching, then I will be ashamed of him when I come in glory. And I am telling you this – when the Son of Man does come, he will bring people their just reward. There are some here today who will not die before they have seen the power and the glory of the Kingdom of God."

THE TRANSFIGURATION

Matthew 17:1-13; Mark 9:2-13; Luke 9:28-36

About a week after Jesus had spoken of his death, he took Peter, James and John up a high mountain to pray. The three disciples were tired and soon fell asleep. Then, as Jesus prayed alone, a strange and wonderful transformation came over him.

His face shone like the sun and his clothes radiated a dazzling whiteness that was brighter than any light the world had ever seen. The three disciples awoke with a start and, at first, were terrified by what they saw. As they looked on, however, their fear faded and they caught sight of two other figures – the great prophets Moses and Elijah – talking to their master.

Peter was the first to find his voice. "Lord, it is good that we are here," he stammered. "If you wish, we will make three sacred tents – one for you, one for Moses and one for Elijah."

But just then a bright cloud appeared and covered them all. From the depth of the cloud a booming voice rang out. "This is my own dear Son, in whom I am well pleased," it said. "Listen to him."

When the disciples heard the voice, they were filled with fear. Hurling themselves to the ground, they hid their faces. At last, Jesus came to them and touched them to reassure them that all was well.

"Get up," he said. "Do not be afraid."

Slowly the disciples looked up and saw that the figures of Moses and Elijah had vanished, leaving only Jesus standing alone before them.

As they set off down the mountain again, Jesus instructed them to say nothing about the vision they had witnessed.

"Do not tell anyone of what you saw," he said, "until the Son of Man has been raised from the dead."

This reminded the disciples of what Jesus had said a week earlier, when he had spoken of coming back to life three days after his death. They puzzled over it for a while, but at last put such strange ideas from their minds and did as they were told, keeping the secret of Jesus' transfiguration to themselves.

But they had one more question to ask. "The teachers of the Law say Elijah must return before the Messiah comes," they said. "What does that mean?"

"Elijah has already come," Jesus replied. "But the people did not recognize him. They ignored him and treated him very badly."

Then the disciples knew he was speaking of John the Baptist.

"And I tell you this," Jesus went on. "The people will treat me, the Son of Man, very badly also."

JESUS AND THE CHILDREN

Matthew 19:13-30; Mark 10:13-31; Luke 18:15-29

Wherever Jesus went, he attracted crowds of people. Some asked him questions, some wanted to be healed and some just wanted to be near him. But of all the people who came to see him, he was most fond of children.

One day, while he was teaching in the open air as usual, the disciples noticed that he was attracting a very large crowd. On occasions like this they did their best to shield Jesus from too many requests. Today, however, they noticed that people were bringing their children to him, asking Jesus to bless them.

"This is getting out of hand," said one of the twelve. "Look, he is surrounded by children. He will never get away from them."

So the disiples tried to send the boys and girls away, telling their parents to get them out from under their master's feet.

But when Jesus noticed this, he grew angry with his disciples and spoke to them sharply. "Let the little children come to me," he said, placing his hands gently on the shoulders of a boy and a girl standing next to him. "Do not stop them from approaching me. The Kingdom of God belongs to people like these. I can tell you that unless you become like a trusting little child, you will not enter the Kingdom of Heaven."

Jesus mixed freely with the huge crowd of children, putting his hands on each of their heads and blessing them.

As Jesus was preparing to leave, a man came up to him and asked him what he had to do to receive eternal life.

"You know what the commandments are," Jesus said. "Do not murder, do not commit adultery, do not steal, do not lie, respect your parents and love your neighbour as yourself."

"I have followed the commandments," the man replied. "But what else must I do?"

Jesus looked at the young man in a way that made him very uneasy and said, "Go home, sell everything you own and give the money to the poor. You will have riches in Heaven. Then come and follow me."

When the man heard this, he went away feeling sad – because he was wealthy and could not bear to part with his possessions.

Jesus then turned to his disciples and said, "It will be very hard for rich people to enter Heaven. I tell you, it will be easier for a camel to pass through the eye of a needle than it will be for a rich man to enter the the Kingdom of God. Remember too that many who are first now will later be last. And the last shall be first."

Martha, Mary and Lazarus

John 11:1-44

On his travels through Judea, Jesus often stayed in the village of Bethany at the home of Martha, Mary and their brother Lazarus. One day, Jesus received a message from Martha and Mary telling him that Lazarus was dangerously ill.

Instead of setting off immediately to Bethany, Jesus stayed where he was for two days, because he knew that Lazarus had already died.

When Jesus finally arrived, Lazarus had already been buried. His two sisters were very upset, and only Martha came out to meet Jesus. "If only you had been here," she said, "my brother would not have died."

"He will live again," replied Jesus.

"Yes, Lord, I know," she said. "He will rise again on the last day."

"I am the resurrection and the life," said Jesus. "Whoever believes in me will live, even if he dies."

Jesus then asked to see Mary, and when he saw her coming, with her face wet with tears, he was so moved that he too began to weep.

At last, he made his way to Lazarus' tomb, a cave with a stone sealing the entrance, and ordered some men to take the stone away.

"But Master," said Martha, "he has been dead for four days now. The smell will be terrible."

"Only believe and you will see God's power," said Jesus. Then he called in a loud voice, "Lazarus! Come out!"

And the dead man appeared, still wrapped in his burial clothes. To everyone's surprise and joy, he was alive again and well.

Then Jesus turned to the two women and said, "Take off his burial clothes and let him go."

JESUS ENTERS JERUSALEM

Matthew 21:1-11; Mark 11:1-11; Luke 19:1-9, 28 — 40; John 12:12-19

Many people now believed Jesus was the promised Messiah, and word spread that he intended to visit Jerusalem. This worried the disciples. They knew Jesus had powerful enemies in the city, who would try to stop him preaching and healing. At best, they would put him in jail. At worst, he could be put to death.

But Jesus was determined to go. Only in Jerusalem, he said, could his authority as the true teacher of God's word be proved.

On his way, he passed through Jericho, where more crowds gathered. Among the people jostling to see him was the chief tax collector, Zacchaeus. Being a short man, he could not see over others' shoulders, so he ran ahead and climbed a tree to get a better view. Jesus stopped by the tree and saw the tiny figure perched there.

"Come down, Zacchaeus," said Jesus. "Hurry up! I am on my way to your house, where I want to stay for a while."

Immediately, the crowd began to grumble. Jesus should not be visiting such a sinful man as that tax collector! But from that moment on, Zacchaeus was different. "If I have cheated anyone," he said, "I will give back all I have taken, and from now on, I shall give half of what I have to the poor."

Jesus smiled. "Salvation has come to his house today," he said.

Not long afterwards, Jesus made his final journey to Jerusalem. It was Passover and the city was very crowded. As Jesus and his disciples came to the Mount of Olives, Jesus instructed two of them to go ahead to the next village, where they would find a donkey tethered in a field.

"Untie it," said Jesus, "and bring it here. If anybody asks you what you are doing, say, 'The Master needs it, and it will shortly be returned.'"

All this was in accordance with the teaching of the prophet Zechariah, who had told the people of Jerusalem that their king would enter the city, riding on a donkey.

The disciples brought the donkey to Jesus. They threw their cloaks over its back as a make-shift saddle and helped Jesus onto it.

The large crowd that had been waiting for him began to get very excited as he approached. Some spread their cloaks in the road, while others cut palm leaves and threw them in his path. "Praise God!" they shouted. "God bless the one who comes in the name of the Lord!"

It was an extraordinary welcome. People on all sides were shouting and cheering, waving their arms and jumping up and down for a better view. And Jesus was at the centre of it all, riding a donkey into the city. All Jerusalem was in uproar.

Only the watching Pharisees remained unmoved. To them, this man was a threat. Somehow he had to be stopped.

CLEANSING THE TEMPLE

Matthew 21:12-17; Mark 11:15-19; Luke 19:45-48; John 2:13-22

**he Temple in Jerusalem was supposed to be the centre of the nation's religious life. It was a holy place where great respect was to be shown to the Lord. But, when Jesus visited it, he was horrified by what he saw.**

Trestle tables lined the courtyard, with traders selling everything from trinkets to sacrificial animals. Everywhere Jesus looked, he could see money changing hands.

Filled with rage, he charged at the money-changers' tables and began to overturn them. He kicked over stools and knocked down stalls, sending pigeons' cages crashing to the ground, and sheep and cattle running for their lives. Then he grabbed some pieces of rope and, winding them into a whip, drove the animals out of the Temple.

"Get them out of here!" he shouted. "This is my Father's house, not a market-place!"

Some looked at him open-mouthed, furious that this man should dare to cause such uproar. Jesus glared back at them and shouted, "It is written in the scriptures that God's house is a house of prayer. You have turned it into a den of thieves!"

Not everyone was outraged by his actions. Blind and crippled people who had heard the commotion immediately came up to Jesus to be healed. But the chief priests and teachers of the Law were watching, and were not at all pleased by what they saw.

For the moment there was very little they could do. If they arrested Jesus now, they would have a full-scale riot on their hands. But they could not allow this incident to pass unchallenged.

After a time, the priests shouldered their way through the crowd, went up to Jesus, and challenged him with the full force of the Law.

"What miracle can you perform to show us that you are who you claim to be?" they asked.

"I challenge you to tear down this Temple," replied Jesus, striking his chest, "and I will rebuild it in three days."

"You will build it in three days?" they sneered. "It is forty-six years since Herod started rebuilding the Temple – and it is still not finished!"

But Jesus was not referring to the bricks, mortar and stone of the Temple of Herod. What he meant was the temple of his body, which would be restored to life three days after his death. At the time the disciples also misunderstood him. They only understood the significance of his words much later, after the greatest miracle of all.

Questions and Answers

Matthew 21:23-27; 22:15-22; Mark 12:28-34

The Pharisees were determined to trap Jesus and regularly debated with him, hoping he would say something that they could use to have him arrested. But no matter how clever their questioning, Jesus was more than a match for them!

"What right do you have to preach the word of God as you do?" the priests asked Jesus.

"Answer me this and I will tell you," said Jesus. "Where did John's right to baptize people come from?"

The priests were thrown into confusion because they could see that it was a trick question. If they said, 'From God', Jesus would ask why, in that case, they had not believed John's message. But if they said 'From man', the crowd would be furious because they believed John was a prophet.

"We do not know," they said, judging this to be the safest answer.

"In that case," said Jesus, "I will not tell you what right I have to preach."

On another occasion the Pharisees went to Jesus with some of King Herod's officials.

"Teacher," they said smoothly, "we know you speak the truth about God's plan for us. So tell us this. Is it wrong to pay taxes to the Roman emperor? Is it against our Law?"

Jesus instantly saw through their plan. If he said 'Yes, it is wrong', then the Romans could accuse him of rebellion. If he said 'No, it is right', Herod's men could accuse him of disloyalty.

"You hypocrites," he said. "I can see what you are trying to do. Very well, here is your answer. Give me a coin."

The Pharisees did as they were told.

"Whose face is on it?" Jesus asked.

"The emperor's," they replied.

"Give the emperor what belongs to the emperor," Jesus said, "and give to God what belongs to God."

Not all Pharisees were so treacherous. One asked Jesus this question: "What is the greatest of the commandments?"

"Love the Lord your God with all your heart, with all your soul and with all your mind," Jesus replied. "That is the greatest commandment. And the second most important commandment is very like it – love your neighbour as you love yourself. The whole of the Law of Moses and the entire teachings of the prophets rest on these two commandments."

The Pharisee nodded.

"Teacher, you have answered well," he replied. "These commandments are far more important than offering sacrifices to God."

Jesus smiled at him. "You are not far from the Kingdom of God," he said.

JESUS BETRAYED

Matthew 23:37 — 24:14; 26:1-2, 14-16

Although many people heard Jesus' message during his time in Jerusalem, he knew that few truly believed. One day, looking around at the city in great sadness, he said, *"Jerusalem, oh Jerusalem! Prophets and messengers of God have come to warn you, but you have killed them all!*

"How many times have I wanted to put my arms around all your people, like a hen gathering her chicks under her wing! And you would not let me. For refusing to hear the word of God, your Temple will be destroyed and left abandoned and in ruins."

Jesus and his disciples went to the Mount of Olives, where the disciples began to ask Jesus questions about some of the things he had been saying.

"Master, you have spoken about the destruction of the Temple," they said. "But when will it happen? You have spoken about the end of the world, too. How will we recognize the end times?"

"Just be on your guard," he told them. "Do not be deceived by people claiming to be the Messiah. You will hear of wars and rumours of wars, there will be earthquakes and famines too. But do not be afraid. Such things will have to happen, but they do not signal the end of the world.

"The time will come when you will be arrested and punished for my sake. All humankind will hate you because of me. Many people will give up their faith when that moment comes. They will betray each other and hate each other. False prophets will appear and deceive many. And in the face of such evil many people's love will grow cold. But whoever holds out to the end will be saved. This is the good news about the Kingdom of God, and it will be preached throughout all the world. And only after that will the world end."

Meanwhile, the religious leaders of Jerusalem had finally decided to rid themselves of Jesus and were making plans to execute him. Jesus knew this and said to his disciples, "In two days' time, the Son of Man will be betrayed and handed over to be crucified."

The betrayer was none other than one of the twelve disciples, Judas Iscariot. That very day he went secretly to the chief priests to bargain with them.

"What will you give me if I betray Jesus to you?" he asked.

Without replying, they counted out thirty pieces of silver and handed them to him. From then on, Judas looked out for an opportunity to hand Jesus over to his enemies.

THE LAST SUPPER

Matthew 26:17-30; Mark 14:12-26; Luke 22:7-23; John 13:1-35

Two days after Judas' meeting with the priests, the Passover festival began. That evening, Jesus and his disciples met for the Passover meal. Before they ate, Jesus took a towel, filled a bowl with water and began to wash the disciples' feet.

The disciples were shocked. This was a servant's job, not their master's.

"Surely you are not going to wash my feet," said Peter.

"You do not understand now what I am doing," Jesus replied. "But later you will."

But Peter became agitated. "Lord, you shall not wash my feet," he said.

"If I do not do so," Jesus said, "you cannot be called my disciple or be part of me."

"In that case," Peter said, "wash my hands and head as well."

But Jesus said to him, "You are pure and clean already. Only your feet need to be washed. Everyone here is clean – except for one man."

Then Jesus turned to all the disciples and said, "Serve one another as I am serving you." Then he washed the disciples' feet and took his place at the table.

As they were eating, Jesus said, "One of you sitting around this table tonight will betray me."

The disciples were shocked by this. "Will it be me?" they asked, one after the other.

"I will dip some bread into the sauce," Jesus replied, "and the one I give it to will be the traitor. And I tell you it would be better for that man if he had never been born."

Jesus dipped the bread in the sauce and handed it to Judas Iscariot. "Be quick about it," said Jesus, but the other disciples did not understand. Judas immediately got up and left the room, stepping out into the darkness of the night.

The meal continued in silence until Jesus spoke up. "I have wanted so much to have this last supper with you before I die," he said. Then he took some bread and thanked God. He broke the bread and passed it to his disciples, saying, "Take it and eat. This is my body."

Next he poured wine into a cup, thanked God, and handed it to them with the words, "This is my blood, which is shed for you for the forgiveness of sins. It is the sign of the new covenant. I tell you I will never again drink this wine – not until the day I drink it with you in the Kingdom of Heaven.

"My children, I shall not be with you for much longer. You cannot go where I am going. So now let me give you a new commandment – love one another as I have loved you. If you show by your example that you love one another, then you will show the world that you are truly my disciples."

When the supper was over, they sang a hymn and went up to the Mount of Olives.

THE GARDEN OF GETHSEMANE

Matthew 26:31-56; Mark 14:27-52; Luke 22:31-34, 39-53; John 18:1-11

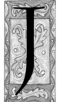

Jesus made his way through the night towards the Mount of Olives. All but one of his disciples went with him. On the way, Jesus suddenly turned to them and said, "Very soon, all of you will run away and desert me."

Before they had a chance to respond, Jesus continued. "The scriptures say that God will kill the shepherd and the sheep will be scattered," he said. "But when I am raised again from the dead, I shall go on ahead of you to Galilee."

The disciples protested loudly at Jesus' words. "I will never leave you," cried Peter, "even if all the rest do!"

Jesus looked at him with pity and said, "I tell you, Peter, that this very night you will pretend you have never known me. Before the cock crows tomorrow, you will have denied me three times."

"No, Master," said Peter. "Never. I shall die with you if need be."

Jesus said nothing.

Eventually they came to the Garden of Gethsemane, which lay on the Mount of Olives. Here Jesus took Peter, James and John with him while he prayed. The others he told to wait nearby. Turning to the three, he suddenly felt a great weight of sadness upon his shoulders. "The sorrow in my heart is like the anguish of death," he said. "Stay here a while, pray and keep watch."

Then Jesus walked a few steps away from them and threw himself down on the ground, praying that, if possible, he might be spared the suffering that was in store for him.

"Father," he prayed, "with you all

things are possible. Take away this bitter cup." He paused a moment. "But in the end, let your will be done, not mine."

In great agony of spirit, Jesus continued to pray, alone in the dark garden, his sweat falling to the ground like drops of blood.

Three times during his prayers he returned to the disciples, each time finding them fast asleep. Tired out by grief, they had not been able to keep their eyes open. "Why could you not stay awake and pray for just one hour?" Jesus asked them. "The spirit is willing, but the flesh is weak."

When he came back the third time, he woke them and said, "Enough! The hour has come. Now is the time for the Son of Man to be handed over to the power of sinful men. Look! Here comes the one who will betray me."

The disciples looked up and, even as Jesus was speaking, saw Judas coming towards them. He was not alone. With him was a large group of Roman soldiers and Temple guards who had been sent by the chief priests. The silence of the garden was shattered, the darkness lit up by bright lanterns and flares.

In the harsh light, the terrified disciples saw that the men were armed with swords and clubs.

Judas stepped forward from the crowd and walked towards his master. What the disciples did not know was that Judas had arranged a special signal to tell the soldiers whom they were to arrest.

"The man I kiss," he had told them, "is the man you want. Seize him."

Now Judas stood in front of Jesus. He paused for a moment, before opening up his arms and kissing him.

"Greetings, Master," he said.

"Is this how the Son of Man will be betrayed?" Jesus said. "With a kiss? Friend, do what you came for."

As soon as the soldiers saw the signal they moved into arrest Jesus. In a second, they had him surrounded.

The disciples had been taken off guard, but Peter quickly drew his sword. He lunged at the High Priest's slave Malchus, and cut off his ear. He would have done worse if Jesus had not spoken out to stop him.

"Put your weapon away," he said. "All who take up the sword, will die by the sword." Then he reached out his hand and healed the slave's wound.

Jesus faced his captors. "Let me tell you that I could call on my Father to save me," he said. "He would send down armies of angels to chase you away. But I will not do that. Instead, what is written in the scriptures will come true."

Then he stared at the soldiers searchingly and said, "Why did you have to come after me with swords and clubs, hunting me down like a criminal? Day after day I have been going to the Temple to preach. You could have arrested me there at any time, in full view of everyone. But you chose not to. Instead you have waited for the darkness to make your move."

The soldiers said nothing. They grabbed Jesus by the arms and marched him back to the city. As for the disciples – they all ran away, just as Jesus had said they would.

Jesus Before the Council

Matthew 26:57-68; Mark 14:53-65; Luke 22:66-71; John 18:13-14, 19-24

 eized under cover of darkness, Jesus was taken to be interrogated by his enemies — the Jewish authorities. If they found him guilty, he would be sent to the Roman governor, Pontius Pilate, who alone had the power to put him to death.

Jesus was taken to the house of the High Priest, Caiaphas, where the elders and the teachers of the Law had gathered. Peter, who had initially fled when the soldiers had snatched Jesus, followed at a distance, blending in with the crowd of guards in the courtyard. He took a seat by the fire and waited to see how events would unfold.

If Jesus was to be executed, the chief priests first had to find evidence against him. But they could find none. A few so-called 'witnesses' came forward to testify, but it was clear their stories did not agree.

Eventually two men came forward and said, "We were in the city one day when we heard the accused speaking to a crowd, telling them that he would destroy God's Temple and rebuild it in three days."

The High Priest looked at Jesus.

"Well," he said, "what do you say to that?"

Jesus said nothing.

"This is a serious charge against you," Caiaphas continued. "How do you answer?"

Again Jesus said nothing.

"Very well," said Caiaphas, "answer me this. And remember you are under oath. Are you the Messiah, the Son of God?"

"I am," Jesus replied. "And you will see the Son of Man appearing in the clouds of Heaven, seated in power by the side of God."

At this the High Priest tore his cloak in shock. "Blasphemy!" he cried. "We need no further witnesses. Did you hear that?"

The other priests nodded grimly.

"Tell me this, though," the High Priest said. "What is it exactly that you say to the people when you preach to them?"

"I have never made any secret of my preaching," Jesus replied. "I have preached openly in public, at synagogues and at the Temple. Ask the people who listened to me. They know what I said."

"This is an insult," the priests said. "He's not taking this Council seriously. It's a disgrace. He refuses to accept our authority."

"Enough!" said Caiaphas. "We must decide. What is your verdict?"

"Guilty!" they shouted. Then they began to spit on Jesus. One priest blindfolded him, and others jeered and beat him.

"If you are the Christ," they taunted, "tell us who hit you!"

"Take him to Pilate," said Caiaphas above the laughter, and Jesus was bundled away.

PETER'S DENIAL

Matthew 26:69-27:10; Mark 14:66-72; Luke 22:56-62; John 18:15-18, 25-27

As Peter was waiting in the darkness, one of Caiaphas' servant girls crossed the courtyard. In the light of the fire she caught sight of Peter's frightened face. "You were with Jesus of Nazareth," she said. "You're one of his followers."

"No, I'm not," Peter said, standing up and moving away. "I don't know what you're talking about."

As he walked towards the courtyard exit, another girl recognized him and said, "He was with Jesus of Nazareth!"

A small crowd formed, with all eyes on Peter, who was becoming very nervous.

"I'm not," he said. "I swear to you. I have never met the man."

Suddenly there was a commotion in the yard. It was the guards, coming out with Jesus. By now it was beginning to get light and they were taking their prisoner to Pilate. They were shouting and pushing Jesus in front of them. A voice called out, "You are his disciple! You are from Galilee too."

Peter looked away from Jesus.

"No, I'm not," he said. "I told you. I have never seen this man before."

Just then a cock crowed loudly. The Lord turned round and looked Peter straight in the face. Peter could feel his eyes filling with tears as he remembered what Jesus had said: 'Before the cock crows tomorrow, you will have denied me three times'.

Then Peter broke down and ran away, crying bitterly.

Across town, Judas had learnt of his master's fate. He knew that Jesus would probably be put to death. He began to regret what he had done and went back to the chief priests to return the thirty pieces of silver.

"I have sinned," he said. "I have betrayed an innocent man. And now he will die."

"That is not our business," they said. "We do not want your blood money. It is unclean."

Judas threw down the coins and ran from the Temple. Beside himself with shame and grief, he went into a field and hanged himself from the nearest tree.

JESUS BEFORE PILATE

Matthew 27:11-26; Mark 15:1-15; Luke 23:1-5, 13-25; John 18:28 — 19:16

Jesus was led in chains to the governor's palace, where Pontius Pilate met him. But the chief priests had a problem. They knew that Pilate would not sentence a man for blasphemy, since he was unwilling to get involved in their religious matters. Instead, they hoped to have Jesus convicted of treason.

"What do you accuse this man of?" Pilate asked.

"We would not have brought him to you if he had not committed a crime," they said.

"If he has committed a crime against your Law," said Pilate, "deal with him yourselves. Why bring him to me?"

"Because we are not allowed to put him to death," they replied. "And because he claims to be king. Surely Rome would object to that."

Pilate had Jesus brought before him.

"Are you the King of the Jews?" he asked.

"Who told you that?" Jesus replied. "My kingdom is not of this world. If it were, my disciples would fight to prevent me from being handed over to the Jewish authorities. No, my kingdom lies elsewhere."

"I will ask you once again," Pilate said. "Are you a king?"

"I came into this world for one purpose," said Jesus, "to speak the truth. Those who love the truth will listen to me."

"What is truth?" said Pilate, exasperated that his questions were getting him nowhere. Then, turning to the Jewish leaders, Pilate said, "I have examined this man here, in your presence, and I can find no reason to convict him. Have him flogged."

The Jews protested. "But he has been misleading the people," they shouted. "His teaching has been causing chaos in Judea. He started in Galilee and now he has come here to stir things up."

At every Passover festival it was usual for the Roman governor to set a prisoner free. Pilate decided he would appeal to the crowd and ask the people directly whom they would like released.

In prison at that time was a convicted murderer named Barabbas. When the people had assembled in front of his palace, Pilate asked them which of the two men, Jesus or Barabbas, he should free.

The chief priests had already stirred up the crowd against Jesus. "Barabbas!" the crowd roared. "Free Barabbas!"

"Then what shall I do with the so-called King of the Jews?" Pilate asked.

"Crucify him!" they shouted.

"But what crime has he committed?" asked Pilate.

"Crucify him!" came the reply.

Pilate was a worried man. His wife had earlier warned him to have nothing to do with Jesus who was, she said, completely innocent. She had had a bad dream about him, making her feel very uncomfortable. With this fresh in his mind, Pilate went back inside the palace and spoke to Jesus.

"Tell me who you are," he said.

But Jesus said nothing.

"Speak to me," Pilate went on. "Do you not realize that I have the power of life and death over you? I am trying to help you."

"You have authority over me only because God has given it to you."

By now the crowd outside was getting unruly and Pilate had to act. He knew that he could not risk disappointing them. Judging by their mood, he could have a full-scale riot on his hands, which would displease the emperor in Rome. Reluctantly, he decided to give in to the baying crowd.

He went out and appealed to them one last time. "I find no fault in him," he said.

They were unmoved. "Crucify him!" they shouted.

So, standing before them, Pilate washed his hands, saying, "I am not responsible for the death of this man. This is your doing."

With that, Pilate set Barabbas free and, after ordering Jesus to be flogged, handed him over to be crucified.

THE CRUCIFIXION

Matthew 27:27-55; Mark 15:16-41; Luke 23:26-49; John 19:16-30

With the death sentence passed, Pilate's soldiers took Jesus into the governor's palace, stripped him and dressed him in a scarlet robe. Then they placed a crown of thorns on his head, put a reed in his hand and mocked him with the words, "We salute you, King of the Jews."

When they had finished taunting him, they led him out to his death. They led Jesus to a place called Golgotha, which means 'The Place of the Skull,' and tried to make him drink wine mixed with myrrh to deaden his pain. But he refused.

There, at nine o'clock in the morning, they crucified him. Roman soldiers divided up his clothing and drew lots to see who would get what. Others nailed a notice above his head. On it was written the accusation brought against him: 'This is Jesus, the King of the Jews.'

People hurled insults as they passed. "If you are God's Son," they shouted, "save yourself and come down from the cross."

Even the chief priests joined in. "He says he has saved others," they jeered, "but he cannot save himself. We will believe he is the Messiah if he comes down from the cross now."

Jesus said, "Father, forgive them. They do not know what they are doing."

Two criminals were also crucified on that day, one on Jesus' right and the other on his left. One of them began to mock Jesus too, but the other silenced him.

"We deserved our punishment," he said. "This man did not deserve his. Remember me, Jesus, when you enter your kingdom."

Jesus said, "I promise you that today you will sit beside me in Paradise."

At noon, the whole country was covered in darkness that lasted for three hours. At three o'clock Jesus cried out, "My God, my

God, why have you forsaken me?"

One man soaked a sponge in vinegar and raised it on a stick for Jesus to drink.

"It is finished," said Jesus.

At that moment, the curtain in the Temple of Jerusalem was torn in two. The earth shook and rocks split apart, as Jesus gave out one last great cry, "Father, into your hands I entrust my spirit."

And then he died.

A Roman soldier heard his shout and felt the earth shake. "Truly this man was the Son of God," he said.

Another soldier plunged a spear into Jesus' side to ensure that he was really dead. Then those who had come to see the spectacle set off home, leaving Jesus' friends from Galilee to watch as his lifeless body was brought down from the cross.

THE EMPTY TOMB

Matthew 27:57 — 28:10; Mark 15:42 — 16:8; Luke 23:50 — 24:12; John 19:38 — 20:18

esus was dead. Those closest to him were paralyzed with grief and could do nothing. However, towards evening on the day of his death, a rich man named Joseph of Arimathea went to see Pilate. He asked for Jesus' body so that it could be buried.

Joseph was a follower of Jesus, but followed him in secret, fearful of what the Jewish Council would do if it ever found out. He himself was a member of the Council, so he was in a difficult and dangerous position. Nevertheless, he went to Pilate and asked for the body.

Pilate agreed to release the corpse and Joseph duly collected it. He wrapped it in a new linen sheet and placed it in his own family tomb, a cave which had been recently dug out of solid rock. Then he rolled a large stone across the entrance to the tomb and went away.

Two friends of Jesus, Mary Magdalene and Mary, the mother of the disciples, James and Joseph, had gone with Joseph of Arimathea to the tomb. Long after he had gone, they sat there in tearful silence. They had hoped to anoint the body with perfumes and spices, as was the custom, but the Sabbath had begun and such work would now have to wait until it was over.

Meanwhile, the Jewish leaders suspected that the disciples of Jesus had an elaborate plan in mind. They thought that they might return to the tomb to steal the body. That way, they could make it look as if Jesus' prophecy had come true and that he really had risen from the dead three days after he had been crucified. The Council decided to take no chances. They persuaded Pilate to send guards to seal the tomb and to keep watch by the entrance.

Early on Sunday morning, the two women went back to the tomb with their friends, carrying the oils and spices they needed to bury Jesus properly. When they arrived, they were dumbfounded. The stone had been rolled away. The Lord had done this, causing the guards to run away in terror. But, for now, the women had no idea that this was what had happened. They looked at each other in surprise.

Nervously they went inside the cave, but found no trace of Jesus' body. Just then two angels appeared beside them and the two women bowed down in fear.

"Why are you looking among the dead for someone who is alive?" the angels asked. "He is not here – he has been raised from the dead, as he said he would be."

Immediately the women ran back to the disciples to tell them what had happened.

At first the disciples refused to believe their story. What the women were saying sounded like nonsense. But Peter and John hurried to the tomb to see for themselves. John was faster than Peter and reached the tomb first. He saw the linen wrappings inside the cave and paused. Peter arrived shortly after and, like John, saw the burial clothes, but no sign of Jesus' body. Although they could not understand, Peter and John knew at once that something miraculous had happened and they ran off to tell their friends.

Mary Magdalene, who had followed the two disciples, remained by the tomb, gently weeping. Turning round, she saw someone approaching and assumed at first that it was the gardener. "Why are you crying, woman?" the stranger asked.

"Sir, they have taken away my Lord," she replied. "If you have taken

him, tell me where he is so that I can go to him."

"Mary," the stranger said simply – and she realized at once that it was no stranger at all. It was Jesus – alive!

She was so overcome with joy that she stepped forward to embrace him, but Jesus drew back. "Do not touch me," he said softly, "because I have not yet gone back to my Father in Heaven. Tell my friends you have seen me. Tell them I will shortly return to my Father who is their Father, to my God who is their God."

Full of happiness, she went back to the disciples and told them she had seen the risen Lord.

THE ROAD TO EMMAUS

Luke 24:13-35

esus had been crucified and, just as he had foretold, had risen from the dead. Some of his friends had seen him, some had not and news of his resurrection was only just beginning to circulate. There was uncertainty in the air.

Later that Sunday, two of Jesus' followers were heading for the village of Emmaus, a short distance from Jerusalem. As they walked along the country road, they talked about what had happened over the past few days. Just then a stranger approached. It was Jesus, but they did not recognize him.

As they walked on, Jesus asked them what news they had. The two stopped dead in their tracks. One of them, Cleopas, said, "You must be the only person in Jerusalem who hasn't heard!"

"What?" asked the stranger.

"Have you not heard of Jesus of Nazareth? You must have. He was a prophet, a man with God-given powers to heal and teach. We all hoped he would set Israel free, and we loved to hear him talk. Everybody did. Except the chief priests, that is, who handed him over to the Romans to be crucified.

"Some of the women from our group told us that his tomb was empty. They went there this morning and said that his body was gone. There was talk of angels and things I do not really understand. Then some others went to the tomb and found it exactly as the women had described it. But no sign of Jesus. We do not know what to think now."

The stranger said, "How much will it take for you to believe? Have you forgotten that this is just what the prophets said would happen? The Messiah had to suffer all those things before he returned to his Father."

Then Jesus explained everything the scriptures had said about him, beginning with Moses and the writings of the prophets.

The two listened with great interest and, when they arrived at the village, did not want the stranger to leave.

"Stay with us," they said. "It is getting late." So Jesus sat down to eat supper with them.

He took the bread and said the blessing; then he broke it and handed it to them. In that instant their eyes opened and they recognized Jesus. But when they looked again, he was gone.

They gazed at each other with joy and amazement. "It was like a fire burning inside when he spoke about the scriptures," they said. "We must tell everyone!" Hurrying back to Jerusalem, they found the eleven disciples and told them the amazing news. Everyone hugged each other, saying, "The Lord is risen! The Lord is risen indeed!"

Jesus and Thomas

Matthew 28:16-20; Luke 24:36-49; John 20:19-29

It was late on Sunday evening. The disciples had gathered together in a room and locked the door, afraid that the Jewish authorities might be searching for them. Suddenly Jesus appeared in the room. They thought they were seeing a ghost!

Jesus immediately reassured them. "Peace be with you," he said, showing them the wounds in his hands, feet and side.

"Look," he said. "Don't be alarmed. How can a ghost be made of flesh and bones?"

But the disciples still could not believe what they were seeing.

"Is there anything to eat?" Jesus asked.

They gave him a piece of cooked fish and watched as he ate it in front of them. They needed no more convincing. There was now no doubt in the disciples' minds that this was their Lord, and they were overjoyed.

"Peace be with you," said Jesus a second time. "Just as my Father sent me to do his work, so I am sending you to do mine. I want you to go out and preach the message of repentance and forgiveness of sins. Take this message to every nation on earth. Tell them that whoever believes and is baptized will be saved. And tell them that believers will be able to do miracles in my name."

"But where will we get the power to do all this from?" they asked.

"Never fear," Jesus replied. "Go to the city and wait until that power comes."

One of the disciples, Thomas, was not at this meeting, and when he was told about it, he was sceptical. "Unless I can see the wounds the nails made in his hands," he said, "and unless I can put my hand in the wound in his side, I will not believe."

A week later the disciples again assembled in a locked room. Again Jesus appeared.

"Peace be with you all," he said and made straight for Thomas.

"Put your finger here," he said. "Look at the wounds on my hands. Now stretch out your hand and touch the wound in my side. Stop doubting and believe," Jesus said.

Thomas looked at Jesus and said, "My Lord and my God."

"Thomas," Jesus replied, "you believe because you have seen me with your own eyes. Blessed are those who have not seen me, but who still believe."

Some time later, Jesus spoke to the disciples and told them once again what they should do. "Go to all peoples everywhere and make them my disciples," he said. "Baptize them in the name of the Father, the Son and the Holy Spirit and teach them to obey me. And I will be with you always, until the end of time."

JESUS AT THE LAKE

John 21:1-19

After his encounter with Thomas, Jesus appeared to the disciples again, on the shore of the Lake of Galilee. As usual they did not recognize him at first and, as usual, he had a surprise for them.

Peter had decided to go fishing. Some others said they would go too. So they all got into the boat, sailed out into the middle of the lake and fished throughout the night. They did not catch a thing.

As the sun was coming up, a man appeared at the water's edge. The disciples saw him, but did not give him a second thought. The boat approached the shoreline and the stranger called out to them.

"Have you caught anything?" he shouted.

"Not a single fish," they replied.

"Then throw your nets out to the right," he said. "You'll soon have a catch."

They did as they were told and caught so many fish that it was a struggle to heave them aboard. They were amazed and looked at the stranger on the shore more closely.

"It's the Lord!" John said to Peter in a sudden flash of recognition. "It's Jesus!"

Jesus had already lit a fire on the shore and had brought along some bread. "Come and eat," he said. "Bring some of your fish and we will have breakfast together."

After they had eaten, Jesus turned to Peter and asked him a question.

"Do you love me?" he asked.

"Lord, you know that I do," Peter replied.

Three times Jesus asked the same question. Three times he received the same reply.

"In that case," said Jesus finally, "take good care of my followers."

THE ASCENSION

Luke 24:50-53; Acts 1:1-11

By now, Jesus had appeared to the disciples a number of times and none of them was left in any doubt that their master had truly risen from the dead. For the moment, he was with them on earth. But the final farewell was not far off.

It was now forty days since the resurrection, and in that time Jesus had often spoken about the kingdom of Heaven. He gathered the disciples together for one last time and gave them their instructions.

"Go back to Jerusalem," he said, "and stay there. The gift my Father promised you and the gift I have often talked about will soon be yours. You will recognize it when it comes. The prophet John baptized with water, but you will be baptized with the Holy Spirit. Stay in the city and wait."

They had many questions for Jesus and knew that they did not have much time left to put them all to him.

"Will you restore the kingdom of Israel to its former glory?" they asked.

"That will be decided by my Father in his own good time," Jesus replied. "It is not for you to know when. But when the Holy Spirit comes upon you, you will be filled with power, and you will take my message to the people of Jerusalem, Judea and beyond. Travel to the ends of the earth to tell people everywhere what I have done."

Those were Jesus' last words on earth. At that moment he was taken up into Heaven.

The disciples watched as a cloud enfolded him and hid him from their sight. They were still looking into the sky when two figures dressed in white appeared by their side.

"Men of Galilee," the strangers said, "why are you standing here gazing at the sky? Jesus has gone back to Heaven to be with God. But he will return."

The disciples made their way back to the city, filled with great joy. They worshipped Jesus and spent all their time in the Temple, praising God and giving thanks.

Before they could begin the task Jesus had set them, the disciples had to find a replacement for Judas Iscariot, who had killed himself after betraying Jesus.

The new disciple had to be someone who had accompanied Jesus right from the beginning. At this time, his followers numbered a hundred and twenty, including Jesus' mother Mary and many other women. There were two main candidates to choose between, named Joseph and Matthias.

"Lord," the disciples prayed, "show us which of these two you have chosen to serve you as an apostle." Then they cast their lots and Matthias became the twelfth apostle.

TONGUES OF FLAME

Acts 2:1-42

On the day of Pentecost, all Jesus' friends were gathered together in a house in Jerusalem. Suddenly there was an incredible sound, like a strong wind blowing, which filled the whole room. Then tongues of flame came down and touched everyone.

An incredible sensation came over all those present. The fire flickered and danced, but did not burn them. Instead, it filled them with a strange power – the power of the Holy Spirit – and they began to speak in other languages. There was so much commotion that a large crowd assembled to see what was going on.

It so happened that staying in Jerusalem were Jews from as far afield as Egypt and Persia, Rome and Arabia, Mesopotamia and Crete. They were astonished to hear Jesus' followers speaking their own languages.

"These men and women are from Galilee!" they exclaimed. "How is it that they are speaking in languages that we can understand?"

Some onlookers made fun of them.

"They're drunk," they said. "That's all it is."

But Peter stood up and said, "We are not drunk. It is too early in the morning to start drinking! We are just fulfilling the words of the prophet Joel. Remember what he said God would do in the last days: 'I will pour out my Spirit on everyone. Your sons and your daughters will prophesy, your young men will see visions, and your old men will dream dreams. I will show you signs and wonders in the sky and on the earth. And whoever calls out to the Lord will be saved.'

"Listen, fellow Israelites!" Peter went on. "Jesus of Nazareth was a man sent by God to do miracles. You know that. You yourselves saw what he did. God's plan was to send him down among us and have him handed over to you to be crucified by wicked men.

"God raised him from the dead. Death could not hold him!"

The people listened in silence, feeling a mounting sense of dread and guilt. Deeply troubled, they asked Peter what they could do. Peter looked at them and said, "Each of you must turn away from your sins and be baptized in the name of Jesus Christ. That way, your sins will be forgiven."

Many people heard Peter's message and believed it, so that in a single day the number of Jesus' followers grew by over three thousand. A new community of believers was born – men and women who studied, ate and prayed together, united by a shared love of Jesus Christ, the Saviour.

THE STONING OF STEPHEN

Acts 2:42-47; 3 — 5:12-42; 6:8-15; 7

 **D**ay by day, the Christian community grew. Believers met regularly in each other's homes and shared all they had. They sold their belongings and used the money to support one another, all of them receiving exactly what they needed to live.

One day, Peter and John went to the Temple to pray. A beggar there, who had been lame all his life, asked them for money. Peter looked him straight in the eye and said, "I have no money to give you, but I will give you what I have. In the name of Jesus of Nazareth, get up and walk!"

He took the man's hand and helped him stand. To the crowd's amazement, his legs were strong again and he could walk.

"Why are you so surprised?" Peter asked the crowd. "The God of Abraham, Isaac and Jacob has passed on divine glory to his son, Jesus. It was the power of his name that healed this man. His faith in Jesus made him well."

Just then some Sadducees arrived, angry that Peter and John were preaching in Jesus' name. The disciples were promptly arrested and thrown into jail. The next day they were brought in front of the Jewish Council.

"Where did you get the power to heal the lame man?" the Jewish leaders asked.

"From Jesus Christ," Peter answered.

"Do not mention that name ever again," they said, sending Peter and John away.

Back at home, the disciples prayed for courage. Day after day, they returned to the Temple, defying the authorities, working miracles and teaching about Jesus. Before long, they were brought back to the Council.

"We warned you not to teach in the name of that man," the priests shouted, unable even to mention Jesus by name. "And that is exactly what you are doing! This time you will be severely punished."

Many members of the Council wanted to have them executed on the spot, but a Pharisee named Gamaliel, a highly respected teacher of the Law, intervened.

"We must be very careful," he said. "Remember all the other so-called prophets who have claimed great things for themselves. They have all come to nothing.

"My advice is to take no action against these two. If what they are doing is inspired by men, it will soon pass away and we will hear no more of them. But if their power comes from God, then there is nothing we can do to stop them."

The Council followed Gamaliel's advice and the apostles were whipped, not killed.

The number of believers was growing all the time and the apostles did all they could

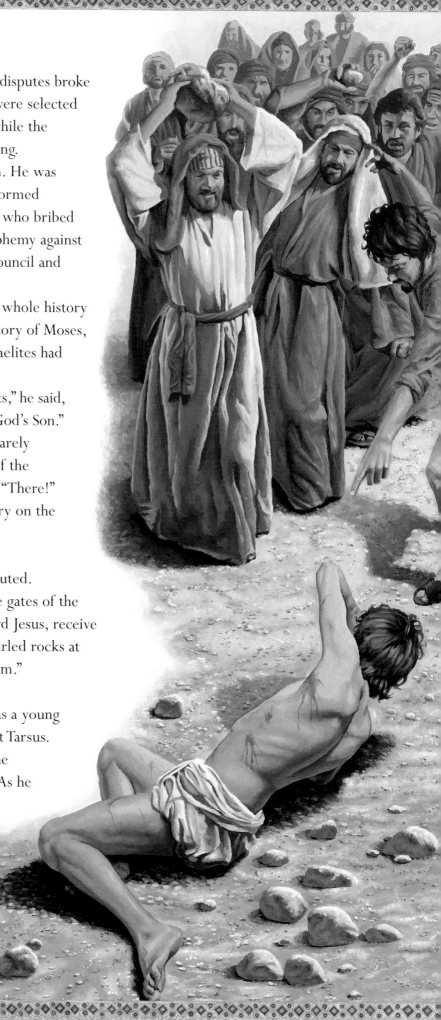

to keep them in order. But occasionally disputes broke out that needed solving. So seven men were selected to deal with these practical problems, while the others gave all their attention to preaching.

One of the seven was named Stephen. He was a devoted follower of the Lord and performed many miracles. This made him enemies, who bribed dishonest men to bring a charge of blasphemy against him. Stephen was brought before the Council and forced to defend himself.

In his speech, Stephen recounted the whole history of the Israelites. When he came to the story of Moses, he reminded the Council of how the Israelites had often turned their backs on God.

"Our ancestors ignored God's prophets," he said, "and you have done it too by crucifying God's Son."

The members of the Council could barely contain their anger. Then Stephen, full of the Holy Spirit, looked up towards Heaven. "There!" he cried. "I can see Jesus standing in glory on the right hand side of God!"

At this, the priests' anger exploded.

"Take him out and kill him!" they shouted.

Stephen was seized and led out to the gates of the city, where he was stoned to death. "Lord Jesus, receive my spirit," he cried out, as the crowd hurled rocks at him. "Do not hold this crime against them."

And with that, he died.

Watching from a discreet distance was a young man named Saul, a Pharisee from distant Tarsus. Although he did not throw any stones, he wholeheartedly approved of the killing. As he stood there among the murderous crowd, no one, least of all Saul himself, could possibly have guessed what God had in store for him.

THE CONVERSION OF SAUL

Acts 8:1-3, 9:1-31; 22:6-16; 26:12-18

On the day that Stephen was killed, a campaign of persecution began against the church in Jerusalem. House-to-house searches were made as believers were hunted down, dragged out of their homes and thrown in jail. The man behind all this was the young Pharisee, Saul.

For some time, Saul had suspected that a group of believers was meeting in Syria. So he set off one day for the capital city of Damascus, hoping to root them out and bring them back to Jerusalem in chains. As he was approaching the city, a bolt of light shone out of the sky and flashed all around him. He fell to the ground blinded, and heard a voice saying, "Saul, Saul, why are you persecuting me?"

"Who are you, Lord?" he asked.

"I am Jesus, the one you are persecuting," the voice replied. "Get up and go into the

city, where you will be told what to do."

Saul got to his feet and opened his eyes. He could not see a thing, so the men who were travelling with him took him by the hand and led him into the city. For three days he was unable to see, and in that time he neither ate nor drank.

In Damascus there lived a believer named Ananias, who had a vision in which the Lord appeared to him.

"Go to a house on Straight Street," God said. "There you will find a man from Tarsus by the name of Saul. He will be praying. I have told him that you will place your hands on him and make him see again."

"But Lord," said Ananias, "I have heard terrible things about this man. He has harmed many of us in Jerusalem and he has come here to do the same. The chief priests have given him the authority to arrest any one of us."

"Go," said the Lord. "I have chosen him as my servant. He is to take my message to Gentiles, kings and Israelites alike. I will show him what he must suffer for my sake."

So Ananias went to where Saul was and placed his hands on him. "Brother Saul," he said, "Jesus, our Lord, has sent me so that you might see again and be filled with the Holy Spirit."

Immediately, scales fell from Saul's eyes and he could see again. He stood up and was baptized.

In that instant his life was turned around. From being an enemy of the teachings of Jesus, he became a true believer. Once his strength had returned, he wasted no time in going to the synagogues to preach that Jesus was the Son of God.

Those who heard him were amazed. After all, here was a man who had come to Damascus to arrest Christ's followers, and yet now he was siding with them and spreading Jesus' teachings. Saul had a thorough understanding of Jewish Scripture and this helped him to preach even more powerfully. His argument that Jesus was the Messiah was extremely convincing and the Jews in the synagogues found it hard to answer him back.

But all this went down very badly with the Jewish authorities, who had learnt of Saul's change of heart. This was nothing less than a betrayal by one of their own people. It could not be tolerated. At the earliest opportunity they made a plan to have him killed.

Guards lay in wait at all the gates of the city. Saul would not be allowed to leave Damascus alive. But word of the plan had reached Saul and his friends, and he was lowered down over the city walls in a basket. Straightaway, he set off for Jerusalem as fast as he could.

The disciples were at first reluctant to welcome him. They were afraid that he had not changed. But when they were told about how boldly Saul had preached in the name of Jesus, they were finally convinced.

Under the guidance of Saul and the apostles, the new church began to thrive. Over the next few years, it spread throughout Judea, Galilee and Samaria, and, blessed by the Holy Spirit, increased in numbers and strength day by day.

PAUL'S FIRST MISSION

Acts 13 – 14

The early followers of Christ were mainly Jewish – like Jesus himself – and, at first, they argued that things should stay that way. But eventually it was agreed that God's message of salvation through Christ should be preached all over the world, to Jews and non-Jews alike.

Saul and the apostle Barnabas were teaching in the city of Antioch in Syria. Then the Holy Spirit spoke to them, summoning them to spread the message of Jesus far and wide. So, after praying and fasting, they departed on a great missionary journey.

Their first stop was the island of Cyprus, where they preached in the synagogues. At the town of Paphos, they met a magician named Bar-Jesus, a false prophet with a strong influence over the island's governor.

The governor, Sergius Paulus, was an honest man who tried to follow the word of God. He sent for Barnabas and Saul (who by this time was known as Paul) and asked them to preach – much to the annoyance of Bar-Jesus, who did his utmost to turn Sergius Paulus against them.

Paul was more than a match for Bar-Jesus. Filled with the Holy Spirit, he glared at him and said, "You child of the devil! You are the enemy of goodness. The Lord will punish you for trying to tempt people away from the truth with your evil tricks. As a result of your wickedness you will go blind!"

Instantly a dark mist came over the magician's eyes and he could not see. Sergius Paulus was so impressed by God's power that he became a follower of Jesus there and then.

Eventually, Paul and Barnabus left Cyprus to set sail for the mainland. At the city of Antioch in Pisidia, they preached to both Jews and Gentiles. Some Jews turned their backs on their message, however, and threw Paul and Barnabas out of town. The two were not dismayed, because they knew that many Gentiles had accepted the message of Christ. So they shook the dust off their feet and went on their way.

In the town of Lystra they healed a man who had been crippled since birth. This so amazed the crowds that Paul and Barnabas were treated like Roman gods.

"We are men just like you!" they said. "We are preaching the word of the one true God."

It was then that Paul had a narrow escape. Some Jews from Antioch turned the crowd against him and he was stoned and left for dead. But his friends carried him away and healed him, and before long he and Barnabas were travelling home to Syria, preaching just as powerfully as ever.

Paul's Second Mission

Acts 16 — 18

aul soon set out on a new missionary journey, this time with a companion named Silas. Together they travelled overland to Troas, then sailed across to Philippi in Macedonia, bringing news of Christ to the continent of Europe for the first time.

Their first convert there was a woman named Lydia, a businesswoman who worked in Philippi as a dealer in textiles. Together with her entire family, she was baptized by Paul and Silas and became a good friend of theirs, inviting them to stay at her house.

But if they made friends along the way, they also made enemies. At Philippi they met a slave-girl who was possessed by evil spirits, which enabled her to read fortunes and see the future. She followed the pair around for days, until Paul, upset at her cries and taunts, commanded the spirits to leave her. Instantly she was cured.

But when the spirits left her, so too did her ability to predict the future. Her owners were furious, because people had paid a lot of money for her predictions, and now this income would dry up. So they dragged Paul and Silas to the town square and paraded them up before the Roman authorities.

"These men are troublemakers," they shouted. "They are Jews spreading dangerous ideas, contrary to Roman law."

The officials agreed and had the two men publicly flogged. After their beating they were thrown into jail.

At about midnight, Paul and Silas were praying when an earthquake struck the prison, causing all the doors to burst open. The jailer thought that the prisoners had escaped, and was about to kill himself in shame when Paul called out from the cell.

"Do not harm yourself," he cried. "We are all here. Nobody has tried to escape."

The jailer was so relieved that he became a believer on the spot. Soon after, Paul and Silas were freed.

In Athens, Paul noticed many statues to foreign gods. This upset him greatly and he told the people so, debating in public with many of the thinkers there. The Greeks were skilled debaters who listened to Paul with interest, but in the end only a few were convinced of the truth of Jesus' message.

At Corinth, Paul stayed with a Jew named Aquila and his wife, Priscilla, earning his keep by helping them make and repair tents.

One day, he had a vision. The Lord told him to persevere with his work in the city. He stayed on for a year and a half, watching the small Christian community he had founded grow steadily in strength day by day.

PAUL'S FINAL JOURNEYS

Acts 19 — 28

Aquila, Priscilla and Paul left Corinth and set sail together for the city of Ephesus. Paul then left to report back to the Christian communities in Jerusalem and Antioch, but soon returned to his friends. They stayed in Ephesus for two years.

During this time, God performed wonderful miracles through Paul. Any handkerchief, apron or towel that Paul had touched was able to cure the sick and drive away evil spirits. This did not pass unnoticed by some of the false healers, who tried to use the name of Jesus for their own ends.

On one occasion seven brothers, sons of a Jewish high priest, approached a man possessed by demons and said, "In the name of Jesus, we command you to leave!"

But the evil spirits spoke back. "We know Jesus and we know Paul," they hissed, "but who are you? You have no power over us."

And immediately the spirits gave the man superhuman strength. He attacked all seven brothers and chased them away.

All the Jews and Gentiles who heard about this were terrified and they treated the name of Jesus more respectfully from that day on. Many sorcerers confessed their sins, bringing books of magic to be burnt on a big bonfire in the town square. The message of Jesus was spreading day by day.

But Paul and his followers had many enemies. A silversmith named Demetrius had long held a grudge against Paul and accused him of ruining his trade. Like the other silversmiths in Ephesus, he earnt his living selling silver statues of the goddess Diana. All this talk about Jesus was bad for business and sales were going down!

Demetrius called a meeting of his fellow silversmiths and whipped up the crowd into such a frenzy that the city soon had a riot on its hands. Two of Paul's friends were dragged to the open-air theatre by a mob baying for their blood. It was several hours before officials managed to calm the crowd down.

After this incident, Paul decided it was time for him to move on. He travelled to Jerusalem, but no sooner had he got there than he was caught up in another riot!

He had gone to the Temple to preach the message of Jesus and some Jews visiting from Asia were angry at seeing him back. Violence was threatened, but Roman soldiers arrived just in time and arrested Paul for his own safety. But even in custody he was not safe. The Romans got wind of a plan to kill him, so they took him off to the city of Caesarea.

Here, Paul spent two years in jail while waiting for his case to be heard. Eventually,

— 218 —

he was told that, as a Roman citizen, he had the right to appeal to the emperor in person. This meant he would have to be taken by prison ship to Rome.

At sea the weather was bad, and by the time they neared the island of Crete, it had got much worse. For days and nights on end the crew could not see the sun or the stars and had no way of knowing where they were. Strong winds and driving rain buffeted the ship, threatening to break it up at any moment.

Paul reassured the crew and passengers. "Take heart," he shouted above the din of the storm. "God has told me that we shall all be safe. Only the boat will be destroyed. But for now we must all eat to get our strength up for the trials ahead."

Paul blessed the food and they ate. After that, they threw all the cargo overboard in order to lighten the boat and make it less likely to run aground on the nearby sandbanks. But the ship was already doomed.

As it began to break into pieces, the order was given to abandon ship. Soldiers, prisoners and crew all jumped into the sea, then swam or clung to wooden planks until they made it to the shore. Just as Paul had said, everyone survived. They had been shipwrecked on the island of Malta, where they stayed until it was safe to return Rome.

Paul was given a hero's welcome by the Christian community there. For the next two years, under house arrest while waiting trial, he continued to preach zealously about the Saviour, Jesus Christ.

PAUL'S LETTERS

*Paul was one of the greatest Christian leaders of all time.
His letters, a mixture of religious teaching and practical advice,
were written to individuals and groups, as a way of keeping in
touch with Christian communities all over the Mediterranean
and the Middle East.*

TO THE ROMANS

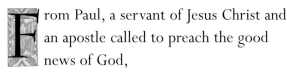

Romans

From Paul, a servant of Jesus Christ and an apostle called to preach the good news of God,

I write to all of you in Rome. May the grace and peace of God our Father and the Lord Jesus Christ be upon you. I pray that I might soon be able to visit you, preaching the good news. I have complete confidence in the gospel of Christ, which has the power to save Jews and Gentiles from sinful ways.

When we were baptized, we died with Jesus Christ and were buried with him. And, just as he was raised, so we were born again to a new life. What we are suffering at this present time is nothing compared to the glory that will be revealed to us. Up until now the whole of creation has been groaning in agony. We have been groaning, too, waiting for God to set us free. But if God is for us, who can be against us?

I am convinced that nothing, neither death nor life, neither angels nor rulers, neither the present nor the future, neither height nor depth, nor anything in creation, will be able to separate us from the love of God, which is ours through Christ.

Moses wrote that whoever obeys the commandments and the Law will live. But the scriptures now say that if you confess that Jesus is Lord and believe that God raised him from the dead, you will be saved.

So I appeal to you to offer yourselves as a living sacrifice to God. Do not behave as the world expects. Let God transform you completely. Share what you have generously with others, work hard, be cheerful and show kindness to others.

Do everything to live in peace with your neighbour. Do not take revenge – that is for God alone. If your enemies are hungry, feed them. Do not let evil defeat you; instead conquer it with good. We whose faith is strong should help the weak carry their burdens.

I send my warmest greetings to you all and urge you to stay true to the teachings of God through Jesus Christ. Amen.

TO THE CORINTHIANS

1 Corinthians

From Paul who was called by God to be an apostle of Jesus Christ,

I have heard that you have been quarrelling among yourselves. I appeal to you not to let divisions tear you apart.

Do not be proud, do not despise anyone. Do not boast about your talents. They are not yours to boast of – they are gifts given to you by God. I am writing this not to make you feel ashamed, but to instruct you, as if you were my own dear children.

Remember that Christ's church is like a single body made up of many parts. Each part of a body, great or small, needs the other parts to function. Together we, as Christians, make up one body and we need each other. Are we all prophets? Can we all teach? Can we all perform miracles? No. So why should we be envious of those who can and dismissive of those who cannot? I will tell you a better way to live our lives together.

Without love we are nothing.

Love is patient and kind. It is not jealous or conceited, it is not loud or selfish. Love is pure and takes pleasure in the truth, not in evil. Love bears all things, believes all things, hopes all things, endures all things.

Knowledge is not everything. Love is. We look at the world now as if through darkened glass; soon we will see it as it is. All things will pass away, but faith, hope and love will survive. And the greatest of these is love.

The grace of our Lord Jesus Christ be with you. Amen.

TO THE GALATIANS

Galatians

From Paul, an apostle called by God, I am surprised at you! In no time at all you have deserted the gospel of Christ and have gone back to your old ways.

Let me remind you, brothers and sisters, that I was brought up to follow the Jewish religion – I was devoted to it. But the way I follow now is different. Why? Let me ask you a question. Do you receive God's Spirit by doing what the Law requires, or by hearing the gospel and believing it? Before Christ came, the Law kept us prisoners. Now the Law no longer rules us.

Christ has set us free. Do not become slaves again. The whole Law is now summed up in one commandment: 'Love your neighbour as you love yourself.'

The grace of Christ be with you. Amen.

REVELATION

Revelation 1:9-20; 20:1-10; 21-22

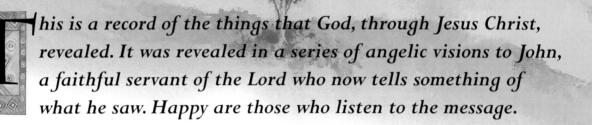

This is a record of the things that God, through Jesus Christ, revealed. It was revealed in a series of angelic visions to John, a faithful servant of the Lord who now tells something of what he saw. Happy are those who listen to the message.

On the Lord's day, on the island of Patmos, the Spirit took control of me, and I heard a loud voice that sounded like a trumpet.

"Write down what you can see," it said. "Send it on a scroll to the churches in these seven cities – Ephesus, Smyrna, Pergamum, Thyatira, Sardis, Philadelphia and Laodicea."

When I looked around, I saw seven golden lampstands and, among them, a figure wearing a long robe and a gold sash around his chest. His hair was as white as snow and his eyes blazed like fire, his feet gleamed like brass and his voice sounded like a rushing waterfall. His face shone like the sun.

When I saw him, I collapsed like a dead man. But he placed his right hand on me and said, "Do not be afraid. I am the first and the last. I was dead, but now I am alive and I shall live forever. I have broken the power of death and hell and I have authority over them."

In another vision, I saw an angel coming down from Heaven, holding a key and a chain. The devil was blocking his path. Quickly, the angel seized him and put him in chains, using the key to lock him away in a dark dungeon, where he stayed for a thousand years. At the end of that time, the devil was let loose from his prison and gathered his forces for one final battle against God. But the devil's army was destroyed and he was

thrown into a lake of fire and sulphur where he was punished for ever and ever.

Then I saw a new Heaven and a new earth. And I saw a new Jerusalem coming down from Heaven, like a bride dressed for her husband on their wedding day. I heard a voice speaking from a throne, saying, "God has now come to live among men and women. God will wipe away all tears and there will be no more crying. There will be no more pain and no more death. All the old things have passed away."

And the figure seated on the throne said, "Now I will make all things new. To anyone who is thirsty, I will freely give the water of everlasting life."

Then an angel took me up to the top of a high mountain and showed me Jerusalem, the Holy City. It shone like a precious jewel, and the river of the water of life ran through it, flowing down from the throne of God. On either side of the river stood the tree of life, yielding its fruit for all. The city had no need of sun or moon because it was lit by the glory of God and of Jesus Christ, the Lamb of God. And people from every nation walked in its light.

This is the record of what I, John, have seen. May the grace of our Lord Jesus be with you all. Amen.

THE *Reference* SECTION

IN THE BEGINNING

INTRODUCTION

The Bible is a detailed account of the changing relationship between God and humanity, stretching from the earliest recorded history up to events that happened two thousand years ago. All the events in the Bible are set in the Fertile Crescent, an area stretching from Egypt up along the Mediterranean Coast to the Euphrates and Tigris Rivers. Some of the world's first civilizations sprang up in the rich farmland of this region, and great empires fought constantly to control it.

    The Old Testament (or Hebrew Bible) is a record by the Israelite people of their journey to the Promised Land of Canaan and, once there, of their struggles to keep it. They must continually fight human enemies and wrestle with their own tendency to disobey the Laws of God. After the first few chapters of Genesis, which describe the creation of the world and the first people, this epic account begins with the story of Abraham, the father of Israel.

THE BIBLE LANDS

The harsh conditions of the Sinai Desert, where the Israelites spent forty years, helped prepare them for a life of obedience to God. Mt Sinai is seen here in the background.

THE EXODUS

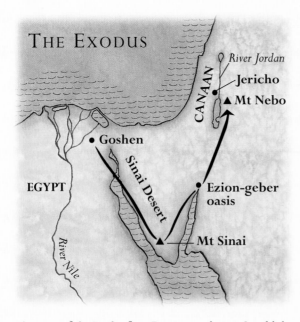

The route of the Exodus from Egypt is not known. It is likely that the Israelites crossed the northern tip of the Red Sea, perhaps in a marshy area. Moses renewed God's covenant on Mt Sinai. He died at Mt Nebo before reaching Canaan.

The Promised Land of Canaan was situated between the great empires of Egypt, Assyria and Babylonia, in the middle of the Fertile Crescent. Abraham was originally a native of Ur, in Babylonia. He had resettled in Haran, where he eventually received God's call.

Mt Ararat (left), in modern-day Turkey, is the site where, according to tradition, Noah's ark came to rest after the great flood.

▲ Mt Ararat

• Nineveh

ASSYRIA

River Euphrates

River Tigris

PERSIA

• Babylon

BABYLONIA

• Susa

• Ur

Persepolis •

Possible route of Abraham

CAPTIVITY AND FREEDOM

Abraham, Isaac and Jacob, known as the Patriarchs or founding fathers of Israel, lived nomadic lives in Canaan, perhaps around 1900–1750BCE. This ended in Joseph's time, when his people fled to Egypt to escape a terrible famine. Many generations later, according to tradition, the Israelite numbers had grown so great that the Egyptians made them their slaves. Under Moses, the Israelites escaped from Egypt. The Bible tells us that Moses then received God's laws on Mount Sinai, and renewed the covenant with God.

Ziggurats, or stepped pyramids (left) were temples built in great cities such as Babylon, Ur and Nineveh. They were the most distinctive buildings of the time, and the Babylonian ziggurat may have been the model for the Tower of Babel.

A CHOSEN PEOPLE

Israel's story begins with God's call to Abraham to leave his homeland and set out on a journey of faith, which, many generations later, would lead to the Promised Land of Canaan. In return for his obedience to the one true God and his rejection of other gods, he was told he would be the father of a great nation. That nation would prosper if it served God faithfully, but it would be judged and punished if it did not.

Abraham accepted the offer. In so doing, he committed his descendants to a binding agreement, or covenant, with God.

Although the Israelites were at first made welcome in Egypt, they were eventually enslaved. Many Egyptian wall-paintings (above) show slaves at work. Here they are depicted working on building projects. Egyptian records do not mention the Exodus. No one knows for certain which pharaoh opposed Moses, although Rameses II (1279–1212BCE) and Thutmose III (1479–1425BCE) have been suggested.

FROM TRIBE TO NATION

THE PROMISED LAND

After the death of Moses, leadership of the Israelites passed to Joshua, a brilliant military commander. According to the Bible, Joshusa crossed the River Jordan, destroyed Jericho, and went on to capture large areas of Canaan.

Military success was seen as a direct result of the people's faithfulness to God. The settlement of Canaan was the fulfilment of God's first promise to Abraham.

The land was distributed among the twelve tribes of Israel (the descendants of the twelve sons of Jacob). But they were surrounded by many hostile tribes, which presented a constant threat to their survival.

THE LAND OF CANAAN

• Hebron:	Settlements
Simeon:	Israelite tribes
Edomites:	Other peoples

The land of Canaan (left) is centred on the lush valley of the River Jordan, which winds south from the mountains of Lebanon, through Lake Galilee, into the Dead Sea. Joshua's crossing of the Jordan marked the symbolic beginning of the Israelite settlement of Canaan.

OLD TESTAMENT TIMELINE

Most dates from the biblical period are approximate. At times the Bible itself uses conflicting dating systems and an exact chronology of events described is almost impossible to construct. Early events, such as the lives of the Patriarchs and the Exodus, are particularly uncertain, but independent historical records confirm the dates of some major events, such as the falls of Israel and Judah.

This map (above) shows the distribution of the Israelites and their neighbours, many of whom, the Bible says, are distantly related to the Israelites themselves. Although Joshua conquered a large area, many regions remained disputed, with different peoples living close together.

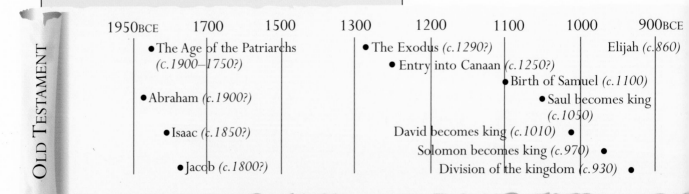

OLD TESTAMENT

1950BCE	1700	1500	1300	1200	1100	1000	900BCE

• The Age of the Patriarchs (c.1900–1750?)

• Abraham (c.1900?)

• Isaac (c.1850?)

• Jacob (c.1800?)

• The Exodus (c.1290?)

• Entry into Canaan (c.1250?)

• Birth of Samuel (c.1100)

• Saul becomes king (c.1050)

David becomes king (c.1010) •

Solomon becomes king (c.970) •

Division of the kingdom (c.930) •

Elijah (c.860)

THE PHILISTINES

The Philistine people, who had migrated from Crete to settle on the southern coast of Canaan, were a constant military threat to the Israelites. At different times they captured the Ark of the Covenant and killed Saul, Israel's first king. Saul's successor, David, defeated the Philistines, swinging the balance of power decisively in favour of the Israelites. This Egyptian relief shows a group of Philistine soldiers wearing plumed helmets.

STRANGE GODS

Canaanite tribes worshipped a wide variety of gods associated with things such as the weather and fertility. The Israelites brought with them monotheism – the worship of one God. Their religious pracitices were totally different from those of the neighbouring tribes.

Early Israelite society was thus threatened in two ways: by direct military attacks, and by the creeping influence of foreign religions, which undermined their worship of the one true God. The Israelites' strength as a nation depended on united obedience to God. If that was tainted by idol worship, as the second commandment warned, they would become divided, and their military fortunes would decline.

This bronze figurine (left) *may show Baal, the Canaanite fertility god. Worship of such gods was strongly condemned by the prophets of Israel. In a dramatic confrontation between Elijah and the followers of Baal, the Canaanite god is proved to be powerless in the face of God's might.*

THE JUDGES

As the Israelite tribes settled in Canaan, local leaders known as judges emerged. These were dynamic figures who had won the respect of their people and who could interpret the Law, settle disputes and take charge of local government.

Some, such as Deborah, were chosen for their wisdom; some, such as Samson, for their physical strength – but all were considered to have special gifts that God could use to build up a great nation. In time, however, with threats on every side, the people longed for a king, a central figure of authority to whom all the twelve tribes could swear allegiance.

800BCE	700	600	500	400	300	200	100BCE

● Isaiah *(c.750)*

● Jerusalem's Temple rebuilt *(c.536–516)*

● Conquest of Israel by Assyria *(722)*

Romans conquer Palestine *(63)* ●

● Judah becomes vassal of Babylonians *(c.601)*

● Jerusalem first surrenders to Babylonians *(c.598/7)*

● Judah and Jerusalem fall to Babylonians. Exile begins *(587/6)*

● Israelites return to Judah *(c.537–445)*

THE KINGDOM'S RISE AND FALL

THE AGE OF KINGS

Around 1050BCE, the Israelites sought security against their enemies by uniting under the first king, Saul. He built up their armies and achieved many successes before his death at the hands of the Philistines.

The next king, David, strengthened the monarchy and transformed Israel's twelve tribes into a unified nation, centred on his new capital, Jerusalem. By bringing the Ark of the Covenant to the city, he made it both the religious and political heart of his kingdom. His son Solomon, who constructed the Temple to house the Ark, presided over a secure age of great prosperity.

Jerusalem (above) was a small fortified hilltop before King David captured it from the Jebusite tribe and established his capital there. It became the religious centre of Israelite life.

Solomon's kingdom was divided into Israel, under King Jeroboam, and Judah, under King Rehoboam. After the fall of Israel in 722BCE, Judah survived alone for another 135 years.

Phoenicia

Syria

Samaria

Israel

Jerusalem

Philistia

Judah

Moab

ISRAEL AND JUDAH

This stone relief (right) shows Assyrian warriors piling up the heads of their defeated enemies. With their reputation for ruthless cruelty, the Assyrians struck fear into the hearts of other peoples. After defeating Israel, the Assyrians deported much of the population, to prevent them from rebelling.

THE DIVIDED KINGDOM

By the end of Solomon's reign, the ten northern tribes had become unhappy with rule by Jerusalem. As a result, in 930BCE the kingdom was divided into two: the northern kingdom of Israel and the southern kingdom of Judah.

After one hundred years, the two small kingdoms became caught in the power struggles of the great Egyptian and Assyrian empires. Prophets like Elijah saw the growing threat of invasion as a punishment for the Israelites' worship of foreign gods. At last, in 722BCE, Israel was invaded and destroyed by the Assyrians.

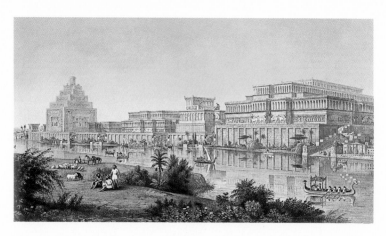

A reconstruction of the palace of King Sennacherib in the Assyrian capital, Nineveh. Assyria was the most powerful empire in the ancient world until it was defeated by the Babylonian king Nebuchadnezzar II in 605BCE.

EXILE AND RETURN

After the fall of Israel, the southern kingdom of Judah survived for many years, although the threat of invasion always remained. Many of its kings worshipped foreign gods, and prophets such as Jeremiah predicted that this disobedience would bring ruin.

In 586BCE, Judah was conquered by the armies of the Babylonian king, Nebuchadnezzar II. Solomon's Temple was destroyed and many people were deported and taken into exile.

For nearly fifty years, the Judeans lived far away from their homeland under Babylonian rule. During this time, they never forgot their faith in the one God, nor their home in Jerusalem. Finally, when Babylon was itself conquered by the Persians, the exiles were allowed to return. Their first task was to rebuild the Temple, which became the focus for the new nation. Although Judah was rarely independent in the centuries that followed, the Jewish faith, centred on Jerusalem, flourished and developed.

The Persian king, Cyrus the Great (559–29BCE), who conquered Babylon in 539BCE, allowed all the people held captive in the city to return to their homes. On this clay cylinder are written details of Cyrus' decree that allowed these exiles, including the Jews, to leave.

THE PROPHETS

Throughout Israel's history, prophets had an important role to play in communicating God's word to the people. They were wise individuals – usually men – to whom God spoke. The Bible tells us that some were able to work miracles.

The prophets all insisted that God should be at the centre of everything and warned that disobedience to God's laws would bring about disaster, both for individuals and for the country.

The first, and perhaps greatest, prophet was Moses, who was able to talk with God face to face. Later prophets were often obscure figures attached to local shrines, where they gave out advice on spiritual matters. Others were famous for their wisdom and became advisers to leaders and kings on political matters.

As the times became more unstable, the role of prophets became more important – and dangerous – since they often had to speak out against the wickedness of kings. Men such as Elijah warned that Israel would fall if the people ceased to follow God's word, while Jeremiah and Isaiah foretold the Babylonian exile.

But even in the worst times, the prophets still repeated God's message of hope. During the exile in Babylon, Ezekiel looked to the time when the Temple in Jerusalem would be restored.

THE TIME OF JESUS

ROMAN OCCUPATION

About sixty years before the birth of Jesus, the area where the Jews lived – now named Palestine – became part of the Roman Empire. It was ruled by Roman governors alongside Jewish kings appointed by Rome.

All Jews resented this occupation. Some – the Zealots – plotted armed rebellion and were crushed by the Roman army. But most accepted Roman rule and tried to make the best of it.

Jewish groups such as the Sadducees co-operated with the Romans in exchange for the freedom to run their own affairs. They feared that any disruption might cause the Romans to withdraw that freedom. In Jesus, the Sadducees saw just such a disruptive influence.

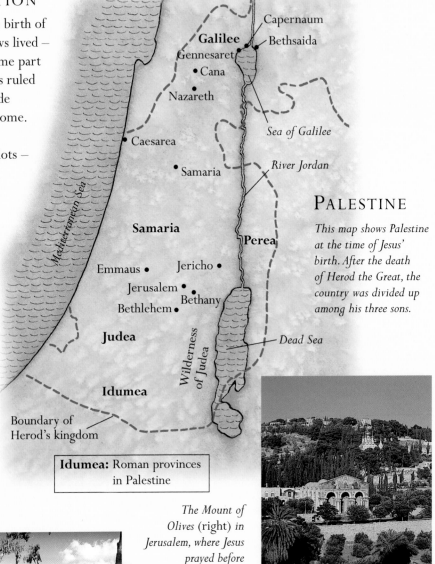

Mediterranean Sea

Capernaum
Galilee · Bethsaida
Gennesaret
· Cana
· Nazareth

Caesarea

Sea of Galilee

· Samaria

River Jordan

Samaria

Perea

Emmaus · Jericho ·
Jerusalem · ·
Bethlehem · Bethany

Wilderness of Judea

Dead Sea

Judea

Idumea

Boundary of
Herod's kingdom

Idumea: Roman provinces
in Palestine

PALESTINE

This map shows Palestine at the time of Jesus' birth. After the death of Herod the Great, the country was divided up among his three sons.

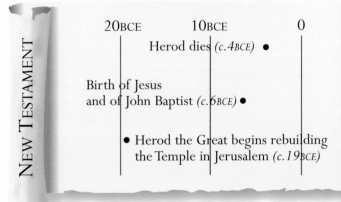

The Mount of Olives (right) in Jerusalem, where Jesus prayed before his arrest.

Jesus did most of his preaching and teaching in Galilee, in the north of Palestine. It was near the shores of the Sea of Galilee (above) that he chose the first disciples, gave the Sermon on the Mount, and fed the five thousand.

NEW TESTAMENT

20BCE	10BCE	0
	Herod dies *(c.4BCE)* ●	
Birth of Jesus and of John Baptist *(c.6BCE)* ●		
	● Herod the Great begins rebuilding the Temple in Jerusalem *(c.19BCE)*	

Bethlehem (above) *a hilltop village, was Jesus' birthplace. It was the site of David's birth, and it had long been prophesied that a Saviour King would be born here again.*

THE LIFE OF JESUS

Jesus was born in Bethlehem in Judea and grew up in Galilee. Little is known about his early life and it is only at the age of about thirty, when his public ministry began, that a picture of him emerges.

He was a healer and a gifted teacher with a thorough knowledge of Jewish Law. He appealed to ordinary people and conveyed his message in ways they could easily understand. His natural authority won many devoted followers, drawn from the outcasts of society.

But his claim to be the Son of God upset the religious leaders of the day, who considered him to be a blasphemer and a troublemaker. It was only a matter of time before they acted to silence him.

RELIGIOUS TENSIONS

There were two main Jewish groups in Jesus' time: the Sadducees, who were in charge of the Temple and who interpreted the Torah (the first five books of the Hebrew Bible) literally; and the Pharisees, who tried to make the Torah more relevant to people's lives.

All Jews, however, believed in the idea of the 'Messiah', the one 'anointed' to be king or high priest, who would deliver the Jewish people into freedom. The claims that Jesus was the 'Christ' ('anointed one' in Greek), caused both excitement and outrage.

The 'Garden Tomb' in Jerusalem (above) *gives an idea of the kind of tomb in which Jesus would have been placed after the crucifixion.*

NEW TESTAMENT TIMELINE

None of the key events in the New Testament can be dated with complete certainty. Although our system of dating stems from Year O, when Jesus was supposed to have been born, it has long been thought that he was born a few years earlier, about 6BCE. By 70CE Christianity was beginning to spread throughout the Mediterranean world.

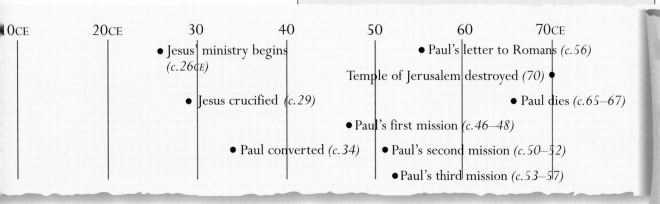

0CE	20CE	30	40	50	60	70CE

- Jesus' ministry begins (c.26CE)
- Jesus crucified (c.29)
- Paul converted (c.34)
- Paul's first mission (c.46–48)
- Paul's second mission (c.50–52)
- Paul's third mission (c.53–57)
- Paul's letter to Romans (c.56)
- Temple of Jerusalem destroyed (70)
- Paul dies (c.65–67)

PAUL AND THE EARLY CHURCH

THE FIRST CHRISTIANS

It may seem strange today, but the early Christians were Jews. Jesus was a Jew, and his disciples would have been steeped in Jewish customs and religious practices. After Jesus' crucifixion, his followers formed a small, close-knit group that prayed and worshipped in Jerusalem.

The Bible tells us that the character of the group changed forever on the day of Pentecost. The disciples were visited by the Holy Spirit, who gave them powers to speak foreign languages and to heal the sick in Jesus' name. This was the first vital step in the transformation of a small Jewish sect into a worldwide missionary movement.

The Lion's Gate (left) in Jerusalem is said to be the site where Stephen, the first Christian martyr, was stoned to death. Paul, then known as Saul, was in the crowd. Although he did not take part in the murder, he approved of it.

The Christian community in Corinth (above) fell into immoral ways and was criticized by Paul. His letters would have been written on papyrus, like this ancient example (right).

THE APOSTLE PAUL

A key figure in the spread of Christianity was Paul, a Jew born in Tarsus in what is now south-eastern Turkey. Saul (his name at birth) hated the early Christians and persecuted them, until one day, on the road to Damascus, he had a vision of Christ as Lord. After this conversion, he devoted his life to spreading the word of Jesus.

Paul believed passionately that Christianity should not be for the Jews alone, but that non-Jews, or Gentiles, should also hear the message. To this end, he travelled tirelessly throughout the Roman Empire.

ROME AND CHRISTIANITY

The Romans treated their emperor like a god and expected people to worship him. But Christians refused to do this and were persecuted for their disobedience. Many, like Paul, were executed for their faith, and others died painful deaths in amphitheatres such as Rome's Colosseum (*right*). Christians would meet in each other's houses to pray and eat, thereby attracting less attention and controversy from the authorities.

PAUL'S JOURNEYS

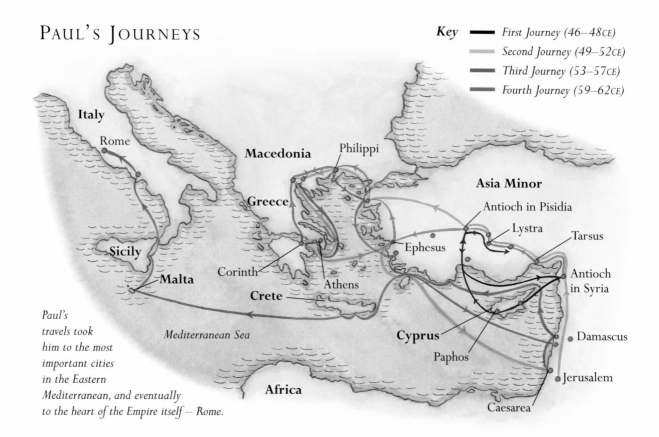

Key
— First Journey (46–48 CE)
— Second Journey (49–52 CE)
— Third Journey (53–57 CE)
— Fourth Journey (59–62 CE)

Paul's travels took him to the most important cities in the Eastern Mediterranean, and eventually to the heart of the Empire itself – Rome.

In a period of just over fifteen years, Paul made a series of journeys around the Mediterranean, helping to establish local Christian communities. He would often visit these in person, giving them guidance and encouragement, but also criticizing them if they did not live up to the Christian ideal. He also kept in touch with each community through letters, which would be read out in public and which, rather like a sermon today, would explain important aspects of the Christian life.

TRIALS OF THE NEW FAITH

Spreading the gospel of Christ brought great danger for Paul and other early missionaries. Many people viewed the new faith with deep suspicion. Paul often spread his message to Jews at local synagogues, and this made him unpopular with Jewish religious leaders. Several times he was arrested and put in jail.

In a letter to the church in Corinth, Greece, Paul described the hardships he had experienced. He had been whipped, stoned and shipwrecked; he had faced danger from floods, robbers and wild animals; and he had often been hungry and exhausted.

According to tradition, Paul was eventually executed in Rome, around 65 CE. But his example continued to inspire the ever-growing numbers of Christians across the Empire.

Despite occasional persecution by the Roman authorities, Christian churches sprang up in cities throughout the Empire. In 312 CE, the Emperor Constantine was himself converted, and Christianity became the Empire's official religion. This sixth century CE Roman mosaic (above) depicts the miracle of the loaves and fishes.

THE HOLY BOOK

ONE BIBLE?

Christians and Jews order the books of the Bible differently, but have one section in common (known to Jews as the Hebrew Bible and to Christians as the Old Testament). Christians add to this the New Testament – an account of the work of Jesus and his followers.

Jews divide the Bible into three sections: the Torah (the first five books which are the basis of Jewish religion, Law and teaching), the Prophets (major and minor), and the Writings (including the histories, the Psalms and the Wisdom Literature). The Christian Old Testament has four sections: the Pentateuch (another name for the first five books), the Histories, the Wisdom Literature and the Prophets.

Two thousand years old, the Dead Sea Scrolls are the oldest existing Bible texts.

THE DEUTERO-CANONICALS

Over the years, each tradition has agreed on the list of books acknowledged to be the revealed word of God. This list is called the canon. However, there are a number of later additions to the canon, which are still judged by some to qualify for inclusion in the sacred literature. These are known as 'deutero-canonical' ('deutero' means 'secondary'), and they are included in the Roman Catholic canon. Jews and other Christians do not include them in their canons.

This fourth-century CE manuscript (left) is the oldest surviving Christian Bible. It was discovered in 1844 at St Catherine's Monastery (above) on Mount Sinai.

The rolled scrolls of the Torah (right) are treated with reverence when they are taken out for Jewish worship.

THE OLD TESTAMENT

PENTATEUCH
GENESIS · EXODUS · LEVITICUS · NUMBERS · DEUTERONOMY

HISTORICAL BOOKS
JOSHUA · JUDGES · RUTH · 1 SAMUEL · 2 SAMUEL · 1 KINGS · 2 KINGS · 1 CHRONICLES · 2 CHRONICLES · EZRA · NEHEMIAH · ESTHER

WISDOM LITERATURE
JOB · PSALMS · PROVERBS · ECCLESIASTES · SONGS OF SONGS

PROPHETS
ISAIAH · JEREMIAH · LAMENTATIONS · EZEKIEL · DANIEL · HOSEA · JOEL · AMOS · OBADIAH · JONAH · MICAH · NAHUM · HABAKKUK · ZEPHANIAH · HAGGAI · ZECHARIAH · MALACHI

THE BOOKS OF THE BIBLE

The Old Testament

The Pentateuch

The first five books, known collectively as the Pentateuch, form the basis of Jewish Law and religious instruction, or Torah.

GENESIS

'Genesis' means 'beginning'. The first book of the Bible contains an account of God's creation of the universe and the early history of the Israelites, including Abraham, Isaac and Jacob (the Patriarchs) and Joseph and his brothers.

EXODUS

This book describes the oppression of the Israelites by the Egyptians and the Exodus from Egypt under the leadership of Moses. It contains the renewal of the covenant on Mount Sinai and the handing over of the ten commandments.

LEVITICUS

The third book of the Bible lists the rules that the Israelites had to follow, if they wished to be a holy people living in obedience to God. Among its rules are procedures for sacrifice and details of what foods can and cannot be eaten (the so-called 'kosher' dietary laws). But the most important rule in the book is 'Love your neighbour as yourself' (Leviticus 19:18), which is later quoted by Jesus (Mark 12:28-34).

NUMBERS

The fourth book of the Bible begins with the first census of the people of Israel. It also describes their construction of the tabernacle, the tent which housed the Ark of the Covenant, and their long, tense journey across the desert towards the Promised Land.

DEUTERONOMY

The fifth book of the Bible continues the description of the Israelites' desert journey and includes Moses' many speeches, which urge faithfulness to God's covenant. It ends with the death of Moses.

The Historical Books

These books contain accounts of the history of the Israelites, from the invasion of Canaan to the return from exile in Babylon.

JOSHUA

This book describes the conquest of Canaan by the Israelites under Joshua, and the division of the Promised Land among the twelve tribes of Israel.

JUDGES

An account of the Israelites' relationships with neighbouring tribes, especially the enemy Philistines, over a period of about three hundred years. It stresses the importance of obedience to God as the key factor in the nation's survival, and ends with a period of anarchy that prompts Israel to seek a king.

RUTH

A short story about the Moabite woman Ruth and her Israelite mother-in-law Naomi, illustrating the eternal values of kindness and social responsibility.

1 AND 2 SAMUEL

These two books give accounts of the prophet Samuel and the first two kings of Israel, Saul and David. God's plan is shown working through the kings, although if they sin, they too are punished.

1 AND 2 KINGS

This history covers four hundred years, beginning with King Solomon and his construction of the Temple in Jerusalem. It follows the fortunes of the divided kingdom, and the tense relationship between God's prophets and the nation's rulers.

DEUTERO-CANONICAL BOOKS

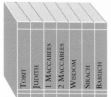

TOBIT · JUDITH · 1 MACCABEES · 2 MACCABEES · WISDOM · SIRACH · BARUCH

THE NEW TESTAMENT

MATTHEW · MARK · LUKE · JOHN

ACTS

ROMANS · 1 CORINTHIANS · 2 CORINTHIANS · GALATIANS · EPHESIANS · PHILIPPIANS · COLOSSIANS · 1 THESSALONIANS · 2 THESSALONIANS · 1 TIMOTHY · 2 TIMOTHY · TITUS · PHILEMON · HEBREWS · JAMES · 1 PETER · 2 PETER · 1 JOHN · 2 JOHN · 3 JOHN · JUDE · REVELATION

GOSPELS   ACTS

EPISTLES

1 AND 2 CHRONICLES

These books restate themes and histories described elsewhere in the Hebrew Bible, beginning with Adam and ending with the return from the Babylonian exile.

EZRA

An account of the Jews' return from exile and the rebuilding of the Temple. It describes the need for personal and collective repentance if disaster is to be avoided in future.

NEHEMIAH

An account of the rebuilding of Jerusalem's city walls. It stresses how holiness can be attained through obedience to God's laws.

ESTHER

A dramatic story of a Jewish woman in exile who is made queen of Persia and who saves her people from destruction.

Wisdom Literature

These books contain both practical advice about the best ways to live, and speculation about the meanings of eternal human concerns, such as love, death and suffering.

JOB

A reflection on the nature of suffering and God's justice.

PSALMS

A series of sacred songs or poems expressing the hopes, fears, prayers and celebrations of the Israelites. Some are designed for public use, while others are deeply personal. They cover the widest range of human emotions.

PROVERBS

A collection of wise sayings.

ECCLESIASTES

A reflection on the purpose and value of life and on the importance of belief in God to give life meaning.

THE SONG OF SONGS

An extended love poem celebrating love between a man and a woman, and God's love for Israel and for the world.

The Prophets

The prophetic books were written during the period from 750 to 350BCE. They include the major prophets, Isaiah, Jeremiah and Ezekiel, and many minor prophets.

ISAIAH

The prophet calls to the kings and the people to be faithful to God. He also looks beyond the sadness of the exile to a period of hope and salvation.

JEREMIAH

A collection of the prophet's sayings and sermons calling on the people of Judah to repent. He warns that lack of trust in God will result in punishment, not only for individuals but for the kingdom as a whole.

LAMENTATIONS

A collection of poems expressing sadness at the destruction of Jerusalem and the misery that comes from being rejected by God.

EZEKIEL

Written at the time of the exile, the book stresses the consequences of sin in personal and national life. In a series of dramatic visions, however, the prophet looks to a glorious future when Jerusalem and the Temple are restored.

DANIEL

A series of exciting stories about life at the Babylonian court. The stories stress the importance of maintaining faith in times of persecution. It also contains a series of visions which predict the downfall of four powerful earthly kingdoms, and the eventual triumph of the kingdom of God.

An Assyrian relief (left) *showing Jews taken into captivity. The Bible tells us that the ordeals of the Israelites are a direct result of disobedience and unfaithfulness. God will bless the Israelites and make the nation prosper only if they uphold the covenant. When they sin, they are punished by death and exile.*

HOSEA

A personal account of the prophet's marriage as a symbol of God's relationship with Israel. Hosea's wife, Gomer, was unfaithful to him and caused him great anguish. His pain mirrors God's pain at being rejected by Israel.

JOEL

The book was written at a time when drought, locusts and enemy attack all afflicted the land of Judah. The prophet declares that only after repentance will the Lord intervene to save the people.

AMOS

A plea for justice and fairness in society. The prophet criticizes unfair treatment of the poor and argues that fairness for all is part of God's divine plan.

OBADIAH

The shortest book in the Hebrew Bible and a reflection on God's promise to deliver the people of Israel from their enemies.

JONAH

The vivid story of Jonah, the reluctant prophet, who eventually preaches to the people of Nineveh. The book shows that God's love is not only for the Israelites, but for all humanity.

MICAH

A plea for justice and a warning against disobedience.

NAHUM

The prophet condemns the cruelty of Assyria, but says that even such powerful empires will eventually fall. God, however, will exist for all time and will reward the faithful.

HABAKKUK

A book in which the prophet asks questions of God and is reassured that the people will always be cared for if they remain faithful.

The Wisdom Literature of the Hebrew Bible takes elements of everyday life, such as work (left), play, love and family, and weaves them into a profound meditation on the purpose of existence and the nature of God's creation.

ZEPHANIAH

A condemnation of the sinful behaviour and idolatry of the people of Judah and a call to repentance.

HAGGAI

An encouragement to the people of Jerusalem to rebuild the Temple, which is still in ruins years after the return from exile.

ZECHARIAH

Instructions to the people of Jerusalem to build up a holy community once again.

MALACHI

A call to repentance after the Israelites have returned from exile and resumed their sinful ways.

Deutero-canonical Books

These are a series of biblical books that do not form a universally accepted part of either the Hebrew Bible or the New Testament. They are thought to have been written some time between the third century BCE and the second century CE. These books are also sometimes known as the Apocrypha, from the Greek word meaning 'hidden away'.

TOBIT

This book describes a godly man, who is blinded and longs to die. In a far-off country lives Sarah whose seven husbands have died. Tobit's son Tobias, guided by the Archangel Raphael, marries Sarah and drives out the demon who has killed Sarah's husbands. Tobit regains his sight and lives into happy old age.

JUDITH

The story of the widow Judith. She gains the confidence of the Babylonian commander, Holofernes, who intends to punish the Israelites for not supporting his army. Waiting until he is drunk one evening, Judith cuts off Holofernes' head, thereby saving the Jewish people from their enemies.

1 AND 2 MACCABEES

Historical books detailing how the Maccabaeus family successfully resisted attempts to introduce Greek ideas into Jewish worship in the second century BCE.

THE BOOK OF WISDOM

This book describes the triumph of holiness over idolatry.

SIRACH

A reflection on the nature of wisdom and of proper behaviour to other people.

BARUCH

Baruch was Jeremiah's secretary. The book contains prayers, and includes themes of sin and repentance.

The New Testament

The Gospels

These four books are accounts of the life and ministry of Jesus and are the key texts for Christians. The word 'gospel' means 'good news' and at the heart of all four books is the triumphant story of Christ's death and resurrection. All the Gospels are thought to have been written a generation or more after Jesus' death, incorporating earlier accounts that are now lost. The actual authors of the Gospels are unknown.

MATTHEW

The first book of the New Testament. Matthew emphasizes the role of Jesus the teacher. It contains the largest collection of Jesus' sayings, centred on the Sermon on the Mount.

MARK

This is the shortest Gospel, and probably the first to have been written. It is a likely influence on the Gospels of Matthew and Luke. It has no information on Jesus' birth or childhood, but begins with his baptism. It emphasizes Jesus as the Messiah, who must suffer before he triumphs.

LUKE

This Gospel was traditionally attributed to the doctor Luke, a friend of Paul. It was almost certainly written by the same person who wrote Acts. Luke's Gospel portrays Jesus as a friend to everyone, including the outcasts of society, and emphasizes the message of hope for Gentiles as well as for Jews.

JOHN

The fourth Gospel is very different from the other three. It emphasizes Jesus' role as the living embodiment of God's Word. Jesus is seen less as a teacher – the Gospel contains no parables – and more as the Messiah, whose whole life, death and resurrection are part of the divine plan. Because of its seemingly more complex theology, John's Gospel is thought by many scholars to have been written later than the other three, towards the end of the first century CE, when Christianity was more developed.

Acts

The Acts of the Apostles was probably written by the author of Luke's Gospel. It describes the effect that Jesus' life, death and resurrection had on his followers. Under the influence of the Holy Spirit, they became committed to spreading the message of Christ to the whole world. The first seven chapters concentrate on the disciples' work in and around Jerusalem. Acts 8 introduces Saul, who is the main character of the second half of the book. After his conversion, Paul's career carries the good news throughout the Empire, finally reaching the capital, Rome.

THE SYNOPTIC GOSPELS

The Gospels of Matthew, Mark and Luke have many similarities. They often tell the same stories of Jesus in very similar language. For this reason, they are called the 'Synoptic' Gospels, from the Greek word 'synopsis' meaning, 'similar point of view'. Most scholars think that the first Gospel written was that of Mark and that Matthew and Luke used material from it. However, on occasions they tell a slightly different story from Mark and include details not contained in his account. This suggests that they may both have had access to another writer (whose work is now lost), referred to as Q. John's Gospel is written in a completely different style from the other Gospels, and tries not just to describe the events of Jesus' ministry but also to explain their meaning.

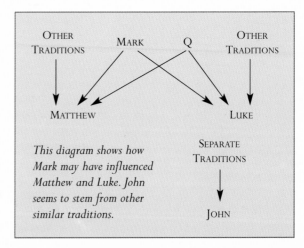

This diagram shows how Mark may have influenced Matthew and Luke. John seems to stem from other similar traditions.

The Epistles

The New Testament contains twenty-one epistles, or letters, sent by Paul and other Church leaders to different Christian communities around the Roman Empire.

ROMANS

The letter of Paul to the Christian groups in Rome was written after he had finished his mission in the eastern Mediterranean around 56CE. He describes how God's grace (God's unconditional love) has power greater than Jewish Law for those who believe in Jesus. Salvation is offered to all, Jews and Gentiles alike, if they believe in Christ.

1 AND 2 CORINTHIANS

Paul's first and second letters to the people of Corinth attempt to heal some divisions in the church there. The letters speak of sexual morality and proper behaviour, and stress the importance of Christian love.

GALATIANS

The letter to the church in Galatia (in modern Turkey) underlines the belief that faith in God through Jesus is more important than mere adherence to the Law. It argues that, by accepting Christ, Christians are the true descendants of Abraham.

EPHESIANS

Paul's letter to the believers in Ephesus paints a picture of the ideal Christian community.

PHILIPPIANS

The letter to the people of Philippi was written while Paul was in prison. He encouraged his church to face hardship and persecution for the sake of their faith.

COLOSSIANS

This was written to the church at Colossae, a town in Asia Minor near Ephesus, where false teachers had

Some of Jesus' disciples were fishermen and the everyday life of ordinary people in Galilee provides a constant backdrop to his teaching. His parables deliberately use familiar things to illustrate truths about the kingdom of God.

been preaching that circumcision and special dietary laws were necessary for salvation. Paul opposes this, saying that salvation comes through faith in Jesus Christ alone, not through the empty rituals of the Law.

1 AND 2 THESSALONIANS

These two letters by Paul were probably written in about 50CE, and are some of the earliest existing Christian writings. They encourage the church in Thessalonica to keep the faith in the face of persecution.

TITUS AND 1 & 2 TIMOTHY

These letters are written to named church leaders. They deal with the pastoral care of believers and administrative issues of church life.

PHILEMON

A letter to a Christian slave owner, Philemon, persuading him to see everyone, including slaves, as equal under Christ.

HEBREWS

This letter is directed at Jewish Christians who have been tempted to return to Jewish customs at the expense of faithfulness to Jesus, who is seen as salvation once and for all.

JAMES

The letter of James talks about the demands of the Christian life and says that salvation comes not through faith alone, but finds its expression in good deeds as well.

1 AND 2 PETER

Peter's letters encourage believers to stay true to Christ's teaching and to let their behaviour be a practical example to others.

1, 2 AND 3 JOHN

John's three letters warn believers to be wary of false teaching and to love one another as Jesus loved them.

JUDE

Jude's letter is a warning against false teachers.

REVELATION

The final book of the New Testament is said to have been written around 95CE. It is a dramatic and highly complex vision, which is often difficult to interpret. It closes with a glimpse of the end of time when a new Heaven and a new earth will appear and the Risen Lord, the Lamb of God, will usher in an eternity of peace and harmony.

WHO'S WHO

AARON
The elder brother of Moses and the
first anointed high priest. He acted as
his spokesman with Egypt's Pharaoh.
Exodus, Numbers

ABEDNEGO
A friend of Daniel, thrown into the
fiery furnace with his companions
Shadrach and Meshach on the orders
of Nebuchadnezzar. They were all
protected by God and survived.
Daniel

ABEL
The second son of Adam and Eve,
murdered by his brother, Cain.
Genesis

ABRAM/ABRAHAM
The Father of the Nation of Israel
and the Hebrew Patriarch from
whom all Jews trace their descent.
His name was changed by God as a
mark of the covenant.
Genesis

ABSALOM
The favourite son of David, who led
a rebellion against his father. Despite
orders to spare him, Absalom was
killed by Joab.
2 Samuel

ACHAN
An Israelite who looted from the
conquered city of Jericho, taking gold
and possessions in defiance of God's
instructions. His actions resulted in
the Israelites' failure to take the city
of Ai in their first attack. He was
stoned to death.
Joshua

ADAM
The first person to be created by God.
Genesis

AHAB
A king of Israel, who married Jezebel
and was condemned by Elijah for his
worship of the pagan god Baal.
1 Kings

AHIMELECH
A priest killed for helping David and
his followers escape from King Saul.
1 Samuel

ANANIAS
A Christian from Damascus whom
God sent to Saul after he had been
blinded.
Acts

ANDREW
A fisherman and the first of the
apostles to be called by Jesus.
The Four Gospels

AQUILA AND PRISCILLA
A Christian couple of Jewish origin
whom Paul met in Corinth.
Acts, Timothy

ASHER
One of Jacob's twelve sons.
Genesis, Joshua

ATHALIAH
A daughter of Ahab and Jezebel, who
seized the throne of Judah after the
death of her son, Ahaziah. She was
succeeded by the boy king, Joash, who
survived her attempt to massacre all
her opponents.
2 Kings, 1 Chronicles

BARABBAS
The robber freed by Pontius Pilate in
preference to Jesus.
The Four Gospels

BARAK
Deborah's commander who defeated
Sisera.
Judges

BAR-JESUS
A Jewish magician and a false prophet,
whom Paul met on the island of Cyprus.
Acts

BARNABAS
A fellow missionary who travelled
with Paul.
Acts, Corinthians, Galatians

BARTHOLOMEW
One of Jesus' twelve apostles.
Matthew, Acts

BATHSHEBA
David committed adultery with her,
had her husband, Uriah, killed, and
subsequently married her. She was
the mother of Solomon.
2 Samuel, 1 Kings

BELSHAZZAR
A Babylonian ruler warned of his
forthcoming death by a ghostly
apparition at a banquet.
Daniel

BENJAMIN
The youngest son of Jacob and Rachel.
Genesis

BOAZ
A farmer and landowner from
Bethlehem who married Ruth.
Ruth

CAIAPHAS
The Jewish high priest who carried out
the interrogation of Jesus before he
was handed over to Pontius Pilate.
Matthew, Luke, John, Acts

CAIN
The first son of Adam and Eve, who
killed his brother, Abel.
Genesis

CYRUS
A king of Persia, who conquered the
Babylonians and allowed the Israelites
to return home from exile.
2 Chronicles, Ezra

DAN
One of Jacob's twelve sons.
Genesis

DANIEL
A Jew who rose to prominence in the
Babylonian court, where he interpreted
dreams for King Nebuchadnezzar. He
became King Darius' chief minister.
Daniel

DAVID
A shepherd boy from Bethlehem who defeated the Philistine giant, Goliath. He became Israel's second king.
1 and 2 Samuel, 1 Kings

DEBORAH
A prophet and judge who, together with Barak, defeated Sisera, the Canaanite warlord.
Judges

DELILAH
The mistress of Samson, who discovered the secret of his strength and betrayed him to the Philistines.
Judges

DEMETRIUS
A silversmith at Ephesus, who stirred up a riot against Paul.
Acts

ELI
A priest at Shiloh and the guardian of the young Samuel.
Samuel

ELIJAH
A prophet of Israel who criticized Ahab and Jezebel's idol worship.
1 and 2 Kings

ELIMELECH
The husband of Naomi.
Ruth

ELISHA
A prophet. The successor to Elijah.
1 and 2 Kings

ELIZABETH
The wife of Zechariah and mother of John the Baptist. Mary's cousin.
Luke

ESAU
The son of Isaac and Rebecca, and twin brother of Jacob.
Genesis

ESTHER
A Jew who became the Persian queen and saved her people.
Esther

EVE
The first woman created by God.
Genesis

EZEKIEL
A prophet living in Babylon during the exile.
Ezekiel

GABRIEL
An archangel sent to interpret Daniel's vision and, later, to announce to Mary the birth of Jesus Christ.
Daniel, Luke

GAD
One of Jacob's twelve sons.
Genesis

GAMALIEL
A prominent Pharisee and teacher who was against mistreating those who taught about Jesus.
Acts

GEHAZI
Elisha's servant, who was punished with leprosy for his greed.
2 Kings

GIDEON
A soldier and judge of Israel who defeated the Midianites.
Judges

GOLIATH
The Philistine giant defeated by David.
1 Samuel

HAGAR
Abraham's concubine and the mother of Ishmael. Later sent away from the tribe after the birth of Isaac.
Genesis

HAMAN
The enemy of Mordecai whose plot against the Jews was foiled by Esther.
Esther

HANNAH
The mother of Samuel.
1 Samuel

HEROD ANTIPAS
The son of Herod the Great, he ordered the beheading of John the Baptist.
The Four Gospels

HEROD THE GREAT
A ruler of Judea under the Roman occupation.
Mark, John

HERODIAS
The wife of Herod Antipas, she asked for the head of John the Baptist.
Matthew, Mark, Luke

HEZEKIAH
The king of Judah at the time of Isaiah.
2 Kings, 2 Chronicles

HUSHAI
David's friend and trusted counsellor.
2 Samuel

ISAAC
Abraham's son by Sarah and the father of Jacob and Esau.
Genesis

ISAIAH
A major prophet of Judea.
Isaiah

ISHMAEL
The son of Abraham and Hagar.
Genesis

ISRAEL
The name given to Jacob after his encounter with the angel. Also the name given to his descendants.
Genesis

ISSACHAR
One of Jacob's twelve sons.
Genesis

JACOB
The son of Isaac and Rebecca.
Genesis

JAIRUS
The administrator of the synagogue at Capernaum whose daughter was raised from the dead.
Mark

JAMES
The name of two of the twelve disciples.
The Four Gospels

JEHU
The king of Israel, anointed by Elisha. He cleansed the kingdom of the worship of Baal.
2 Kings

JEREMIAH
A major prophet of Judah.
Jeremiah

JEROBOAM
The first king of the northern
kingdom of Israel.
1 Kings

JESSE
The father of David.
1 Samuel

JESUS CHRIST
A Jewish healer and teacher from
Nazareth. The person believed by
Christians to be the Son of God and
the promised Messiah.
The Four Gospels, Acts

JETHRO
A Midianite priest and the father-in-law
of Moses.
Exodus

JEZEBEL
The wife of King Ahab. She introduced
the worship of Baal, and was killed
by Jehu.
1 and 2 Kings

JOAB
A commander in David's army.
2 Samuel

JOASH
Made king of Judah at the age of seven.
2 Kings

JOB
A good man forced to suffer. His faith
is tested and is proved.
Job

JOHN
One of Jesus' twelve apostles.
The Four Gospels

JOHN THE BAPTIST
Sent by God to announce the coming
of Jesus.
The Four Gospels

JONAH
A reluctant prophet sent by God to
Nineveh.
Jonah

JONATHAN
The son of Saul and friend of David.
Killed, with his father, by the
Philistines.
1 and 2 Samuel

JOSEPH
1. One of Jacob's twelve sons.
Genesis
2. A carpenter in Nazareth, he was the
husband of Mary, the mother of Jesus.
The Four Gospels

JOSHUA
A brilliant military commander who
succeeded Moses as leader of the
Israelites and led them into the
Promised Land.
Exodus, Numbers, Joshua

JOSIAH
A king of Judah, who tried to return
the kingdom to pure forms of worship.
2 Kings, 1 Chronicles

JUDAH
One of Jacob's twelve sons after whom
the southern kingdom was named.
Genesis

JUDAS ISCARIOT
The apostle who betrayed Jesus.
The Four Gospels, Acts

LABAN
Jacob's uncle.
Genesis

LAZARUS
The brother of Mary and Martha, he
was raised from the dead by Jesus.
John

LEAH
The elder daughter of Laban and
Jacob's first wife.
Genesis

LEVI
One of Jacob's twelve sons.
Genesis

LOT
Abraham's nephew. He left Abraham
to live in Sodom.
Genesis

LYDIA
The silk merchant converted to Christ
at Philippi.
Acts

MANASSEH
One of Joseph's twelve sons.
Genesis

MARTHA
Sister of Mary and Lazarus.
Luke, John

MARY
1. Mother of Jesus, wife of Joseph.
2. Sister of Martha and Lazarus.
3. Mary Magdalene. A follower of Jesus
and the first to see him after the
resurrection.
The Four Gospels

MATTHEW
One of Jesus' twelve disciples
The Four Gospels

MATTHIAS
Chosen to replace Judas Iscariot as the
twelfth disciple after Judas' suicide.
Acts

MESHACH
One of Daniel's three companions,
who emerged from the fiery furnace
unharmed.
Daniel

MIRIAM
The sister of Moses and Aaron.
Exodus, Numbers

MORDECAI
The cousin of Esther. He helped her
outwit the evil Haman.
Esther

MOSES
Law-giver and towering leader of the
Jewish people at the time of the Exodus.
Exodus, Numbers, Deuteronomy

NAAMAN
A Syrian commander healed of a skin
disease by Elisha.
2 Kings

NABOTH
The owner of a vineyard that Ahab
coveted. He was killed by Ahab and
Jezebel.
1 Kings

NAOMI
Ruth's mother-in-law.
Ruth

NAPTHALI
One of Jacob's twelve sons.
Genesis

NATHAN
A prophet critical of David's adultery with Bathsheba.
2 Samuel, 1 Kings, 1 Chronicles

NEBUCHADNEZZAR
The king of Babylon at the time of the exile.
2 Kings

NEHEMIAH
A Hebrew advisor to the Persian king, he organised the rebuilding of Jerusalem's city walls.
Nehemiah

NICODEMUS
A Pharisee who visited Jesus in secret.
John

NOAH
A good man saved by God from the flood sent to wipe out humanity.
Genesis

PAUL
A follower of Christ and a gifted missionary. *(See also Saul)*
Acts, Letters

PETER
Also known as Simon Peter. One of the twelve apostles and a leader of the early church. *(See also Simon Peter.)*
The Four Gospels, Acts

PHILIP
One of Jesus' twelve apostles.
The Four Gospels

PONTIUS PILATE
The Roman procurator of Judea at the time of Jesus. He presided over Jesus' trial and consented to his execution.
The Four Gospels

POTIPHAR
An Egyptian officer whose wife falsely accused Joseph.
Genesis

RACHEL
Laban's daughter and Jacob's second wife. The mother of Joseph.
Genesis

RAHAB
A prostitute from Jericho who helped Joshua's spies.
Joshua

REBECCA
The wife of Isaac.
Genesis

REHOBOAM
Solomon's son and leader of the southern kingdom of Judah.
1 Kings, 2 Chronicles

REUBEN
The eldest of Jacob's sons.
Genesis

RUTH
A Moabite woman whose faithfulness to her Jewish mother-in-law, Naomi, was rewarded.
Ruth

SALOME
Daughter of Herodias whose dance before Herod led to the death of John the Baptist. She is not named in the Bible texts.
Matthew, Mark, Luke

SAMSON
An Israelite famed for his great strength and his opposition to the Philistines.
Judges

SAMUEL
A priest who advised against the introduction of a monarchy but who anointed Israel's first two kings, Saul and David.
1 Samuel

SARAH
The wife of Abraham. Mother of Isaac.
Genesis

SAUL
1. The first king of Israel. *1 Samuel*
2. A persecutor of Christians who became converted to Christ. Renamed Paul. *(See also Paul.) Acts*

SENNACHERIB
A king of Assyria. He beseiged Jerusalem, but failed to take it.
2 Kings, 2 Chronicles, Isaiah

SHADRACH
One of Daniel's three companions thrown into the fiery furnace, where he was protected by God.
Daniel

SIMEON
One of Jacob's twelve sons.
Genesis

SIMON
1. Simon Peter. One of the apostles. *(See also Peter.) The Four Gospels*
2. Simon the Zealot. One of the apostles. *Luke*
3. A Pharisee, at whose house the woman dried Jesus' feet with her hair. *Luke*

SOLOMON
Israel's third king, famed for his wisdom and his construction of the Temple in Jerusalem.
1 Kings

STEPHEN
The first Christian to be executed for his obedience to Jesus Christ.
Acts

THADDAEUS
One of Jesus' twelve apostles.
The Four Gospels

THOMAS
One of the twelve apostles, who wanted to see evidence of Jesus' resurrection with his own eyes. The risen Christ showed him marks on his body and the wound in his side.
The Four Gospels, Acts

ZADOK
The high priest at the time of King Solomon.
1 Kings

ZEBULUN
One of Jacob's twelve sons.
Genesis

ZECHARIAH
The father of John the Baptist.
Luke

ZEDEKIAH
The last King of Judah before the Babylonian exile. He was blinded by Nebuchadnezzar and taken to Babylon.
2 Kings, 2 Chronicles, Jeremiah

ZIPPORAH
Jethro's daughter and the wife of Moses.
Exodus

GLOSSARY

ALTAR
A table or block, often made of stone or wood, on which offerings or sacrifices are made to God.

AMEN
From the Hebrew meaning 'So be it', the word spoken at the end of prayers.

ANGEL
A messenger from God. In the Bible, the angels can take the form of winged creatures or of mysterious strangers who resemble human beings.

ANNUNCIATION
The announcement by the Archangel Gabriel to Mary that she was to give birth to Jesus, the Son of God.

ANOINT
To pour oil on a person's head as a sign of priesthood or kingship.

APOSTLE
One of the twelve principal followers of Christ. In Greek it means 'one who is sent'.

ARK OF THE COVENANT
A wooden box covered in gold containing the stone tablets of the Law, which were given to Moses by God on Mount Sinai. Solomon constructed the Temple in Jerusalem to house it permanently.

ASCENSION
Jesus' return to Heaven after he had been raised from the dead.

ATONEMENT
The putting right of a wrong done. Also, reconciliation between God and humanity. Christians believe that Christ's death on the cross is the final atonement for human sin.

BAAL
A male fertility god of the Canaanite religion. According to the Bible, Baal worship was one of the greatest threats to the worship of God for much of the history of Israel.

BAPTISM
A Christian religious rite involving the sprinkling of water over the forehead or total immersion in water. It signifies the washing away of sins and a new birth into the Christian life.

BEATITUDES
The blessings spoken by Jesus, especially during the Sermon on the Mount.

BLASPHEMY
Words or behaviour insulting to God.

CANAAN
The land, later known as Palestine, between the River Jordan and the Mediterranean Sea. This was the land promised by God to Abraham and his descendants.

CHRIST
A Greek word, meaning 'the anointed one'.

CHURCH
A community of Christian believers. Later used to describe the building in which Christian worship is held.

CIRCUMCISION
Removal of the foreskin of a male. In the Hebrew Bible (the Old Testament) it is a sign of God's covenant with the Israelites.

CODEX
A collection of manuscripts in single sheets, as opposed to a rolled scroll. The forerunner of the book.

COMMUNION
A deep and close relationship with a person or with God. Holy Communion is the Christian celebration of the events of the last supper, and is also known as the Eucharist.

CONVERSION
The change that happens when a

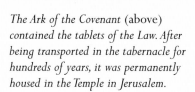

The Ark of the Covenant (above) contained the tablets of the Law. After being transported in the tabernacle for hundreds of years, it was permanently housed in the Temple in Jerusalem.

person begins to follow a particular religion, having previously followed a different religion or no religion at all.

COVENANT
A binding agreement, especially between God and humanity.

DEMON
Also refered to as an evil spirit. In Biblical times demons were thought to possess individuals, causing them to do strange and destructive things. Demons could be driven out by the power of God.

DEVIL
In the New Testament, the prime figure of evil and enemy of God.

ELDER
An older or more experienced member of a community entrusted with a leadership role.

EPISTLE
A letter, especially one contained in the New Testament.

ETERNAL LIFE
The life, after death on earth, spent in the eternal presence of God. The Life Everlasting.

EUCHARIST
The Christian ceremony commemorating the last supper. Also known as Holy Communion.

EXILE
The state of being unwillingly separated from one's homeland. In Jewish history, the enforced detention of the Israelite people in Babylon from 587 to 537BCE.

EXODUS
The departure of the people of Israel from Egypt. Their journey out of slavery into freedom.

FAITH
In the Bible, seen as personal trust in God or Jesus.

THE FALL
Humanity's rebellion against God and wilful descent into sin, having been given the free choice between good or evil.

GENTILE
A non-Jewish person.

GOSPEL
One of the first four books of the New Testament. Also the 'good news' of Christ.

GRACE
The undeserved and unearned love that God gives to humanity.

HEAVEN
The realm where God resides. The place to which people will go after death as a reward for their faithfulness to God.

HELL
In Christian theology, the subterranean realm reserved, after death, for sinners as a punishment for their wickedness.

HOLY OF HOLIES
The most sacred part of the Temple in Jerusalem, which housed the Ark of the Covenant.

HOLY SPIRIT
The invisible spirit of God active in the world. It is the third person of the Christian Trinity: Father, Son and Holy Spirit (or Holy Ghost).

IDOL
An image or statue worshipped as a god.

INCARNATION
The belief that God fully lived in the humanity of Jesus.

JUDGES
In the Bible, the tribal leaders who ruled over the people of Israel from the time of Joshua to the first of the kings, Saul.

KINGDOM OF GOD
The eternal realm inhabited by God here on earth and in eternity. Christians believe that sinners who have repented will be welcomed there after death.

LAW
The elements of Law and right and wrong laid down in the first five books of the Hebrew Bible, which are known collectively as the Torah in Hebrew.

MANNA
The bread-like food miraculously provided by God to the Israelites as they wandered through the desert, making their way from Egypt to the Promised Land of Canaan.

MARTYR
Someone who is prepared to suffer and die for his or her faith. It is the Greek word for 'witness'.

MESSIAH
The Hebrew word for the 'anointed one'. The Jews looked to a future saviour to set Israel free. He would be someone anointed to be king, from the house (or descendants) of David. In the New Testament, Jesus of Nazareth, also of David's line, is presented as the Messiah foretold by the prophets.

MINISTRY
Spiritual work, especially that done by an ordained person.

MIRACLE
A dramatic and surprising supernatural event, which is a sign of God's action in the world.

ORAL TRADITION
The technique of story-telling or religious interpretation that relies on the spoken word as opposed to the written text.

PARABLE
A story drawn from everyday life that is told to illustrate a spiritual truth.

PARADISE
Often used as a word for Heaven. Deriving from the Sanskrit word for a park, paradise is often imagined as a garden, filled with flowers and fed by cooling streams.

PASSION
The suffering of Christ leading up to his crucifixion.

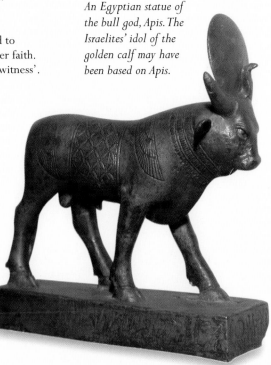

An Egyptian statue of the bull god, Apis. The Israelites' idol of the golden calf may have been based on Apis.

PASSOVER
The Jewish festival commemorating the Exodus from Egypt.

PATRIARCH
The male head of a family, particularly Abraham, Isaac and Jacob – the fathers of the Jewish people.

PENTATEUCH (THE TORAH)
The first five books of the Hebrew Bible: Genesis, Exodus, Leviticus, Numbers and Deuteronomy.

PENTECOST
A Jewish harvest festival, which celebrates the giving of the Law. The New Testament says that on the day of Pentecost the Holy Spirit descended on the disciples after Christ's death and resurrection.

PERSECUTION
Oppression, especially the cruel or unfair treatment of people because of their religion.

PHARISEES
Members of an ancient Jewish sect that interpreted the Law of Moses in a way which made it relevant

The festival of Passover (above) celebrates the escape of the Israelites from Egypt. Jewish families celebrate it every year, with meals of roast lamb, unleavened bread and bitter herbs.

to the times. They developed an oral tradition of Law in which the Torah was debated, interpreted and explained.

PRAYER
Direct communication with God – often to express thanks or to ask for something.

PRIEST
A person specially trained and prepared to supervise formal worship of God.

PROMISED LAND
The land of Canaan promised by God to Abraham and his descendants in exchange for complete obedience to God's laws.

PROPHET
Someone who receives messages from God and shares them with other people. Prophets often criticize the sins of the people and foretell the consequences if their sins continue.

PSALMS
Sacred songs or poems expressing the deepest of emotions. Many of the psalms of the Hebrew Bible are attributed to King David.

PURIM
The Jewish festival celebrating the events described in the book of Esther.

RABBI
A teacher of Jewish Law.

RECONCILIATION
The restoration of harmonious relations between two or more people, especially relations between God and sinful men and women.

REDEMPTION
The act of buying something back. In Christian thinking it is the payment of the ultimate price (the death of God's only Son) in order to deliver the world from sin and damnation.

REPENTANCE
The expression of genuine sorrow for one's sin.

RESURRECTION
Christ's return from the dead – not in another earthly body that would have to die again, but in a new body that would live forever.

REVELATION
The disclosure of God's plan.

SABBATH
The seventh day of the week, set aside for worship, prayer and rest. It commemorates the completion of Creation (as described in Genesis). Jews observe Saturday as the Sabbath.

SACRIFICE
An offering made to God. In ancient times this was usually the offering of an animal such as an ox or a lamb. In Christian thinking, the ultimate sacrifice took place at the crucifixion when Jesus, 'the Lamb of God', died to save the world.

SADDUCEES
The priestly class of religious leaders who controlled the affairs of the Temple in Jesus' day. They interpreted the Law literally and, unlike the Pharisees, rejected the oral tradition. They did not believe that anyone could come back from the dead.

SALVATION
The action of being saved, especially from sin and the torment of separation from God.

SAMARITAN
A person from Samaria in Palestine, who followed only the teaching of the five books of the Pentateuch.

SANCTUARY
The Holy of Holies in the Temple in Jerusalem.

SANHEDRIN
The Jewish council or court that arbitrated on religious matters.

SATAN
Derived from the Hebrew word meaning 'adversary', the Satan of the Hebrew Bible is an angelic being given the authority to test the righteousness of Job. In Christian

thinking, Satan is thought of
as the equivalent of the devil.

SCRIPTURE
Sacred writings.

SEPTUAGINT
The Greek translation of
the Hebrew Bible made
by Greek-speaking Jewish
scholars in the second century
BCE. To this, the books of the
New Testament were later added
to make up the Bible as recognized
by all Christians today.

SIN
An offence against God and
God's laws.

SON OF MAN
A phrase used by Jesus to describe
himself as someone who, fully human,
would have to die, but who would
also usher in the Kingdom of God.

SOUL
In Christian thinking, the non-physical
part of a person believed to survive
after death.

SPEAKING IN TONGUES
The ability, under the influence of
the Holy Spirit, to speak in foreign
languages. It was first given to Jesus'
disciples at Pentecost.

SPIRIT
Another word to describe the soul.
But also, as in Holy Spirit, the third
person of the Trinity.

SYNAGOGUE
A Jewish place of worship, study
and meeting.

SYNOPTIC
Seen from the same general point
of view. The Gospels of Matthew,
Mark and Luke are known as the
Synoptic Gospels. They share much
of the same information and describe
events from the same broad
perspective.

TABERNACLE
The tent which housed the Ark of the
Covenant on the Israelites' journey
from Egypt to the Promised Land.

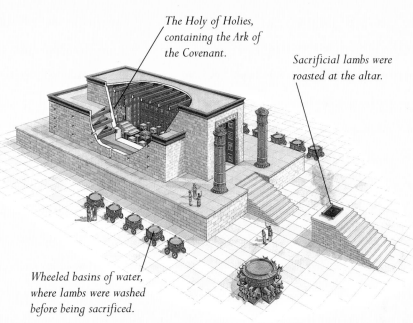

*The Holy of Holies,
containing the Ark of
the Covenant.*

*Sacrificial lambs were
roasted at the altar.*

*Wheeled basins of water,
where lambs were washed
before being sacrificed.*

*Solomon's Temple (above) was the spiritual heart of Jerusalem and the kingdom of
Israel. It was surrounded by a series of buildings and courtyards. The inner
courtyards were open only to Jews, and only the High Priest could enter the most
sacred place of all, the Holy of Holies, where the Ark of the Covenant was kept.*

TEMPLE
A building where people worship
God or gods. The Temple in Jerusalem
was constructed by King David's son,
Solomon, which became the focus of
worship for the entire nation. It was
destroyed by the Babylonians and
rebuilt after the Exile. This was
extended by Herod the Great and
destroyed by the Romans in 70 CE.

TEMPTATION
The inclination to do wrong.
Temptation is not a sin (Jesus himself
was tempted in the desert), but giving
in to it is (Jesus resisted all the devil's
offers).

THEOLOGY
Thinking about religious matters and
the study of religious ideas.

TORAH
Jewish Law, especially that derived
from the first five books of the
Hebrew Bible.

TRANSFIGURATION
The transformation in appearance that
came over Jesus on a mountain, where
Moses and Elijah appeared to him.

TRINITY
God in three persons: the Father,
the Son and the Holy Spirit.

WILDERNESS
The desert. In both the Hebrew Bible
and the New Testament it is seen as a
place of testing and preparation. The
Israelites were made to wander in the
wilderness for forty years to prepare
themselves for the freedom of the
Promised Land. Jesus spent forty
days in the wilderness, resisting the
temptations of the devil and preparing
himself for public ministry.

WISDOM LITERATURE
Books which deal with the deeper
meaning of life. They include the
Psalms, Proverbs, Ecclesiastes, the
Song of Songs and the Book of Job.

ZEALOTS
Groups of Jews who planned rebellion
against the Romans in the time of Jesus.

ZION
The fortified hilltop near Jerusalem
that lent its name to Jerusalem itself
and became the symbolic name of the
heavenly Kingdom of God.

covenant 17, 22, 45, 54, 57, 104, 117, 195, 226, 227, 237
creation 12, 54, 220, 226, 237, 239
Crete 211, 219, 229,235
crop 78, 175
cross 184, 202, 203
crucifixion 202, 233, 234
Cyprus 216, 235
Cyrus 136, 231

D

Dagon 71, 77
Damascus 104, 214, 215, 234, 235
Dan 31
Daniel 128, 130, 131, 132, 133, 231
Daniel, book of 238
Darius 131, 132, 133
David 73, 80, 81, 82, 84, 85, 86, 87, 88, 89, 90, 91, 92, 93, 94, 113, 119, 146, 147, 148, 167, 228, 229, 230, 233, 237
Dead Sea 228, 232
Dead Sea Scrolls 236
Deborah 66, 229
Delilah 71
Demetrius 218
demons 163, 178, 218
desert 32, 44, 53, 56, 59, 76, 104, 153, 154, 155, 156, 177, 237
deutero-canonical 236, 239
Deuteronomy 237
devil 155, 173, 216, 222
Diana 218
disciples 157, 158, 160, 162, 163,165, 167, 168, 169, 172,

175, 178, 180, 181, 182, 184, 185, 186, 188, 189, 190, 193, 194, 195, 196, 197, 200, 204, 205, 206, 207, 208, 209, 212, 215, 232, 234, 240
doctor 240
donkey 24, 47, 65, 69, 78, 87, 174, 189
dove 18, 154
dream 29, 32, 35, 36, 37, 147, 151, 211

E

earth 12
earthquake 104, 193, 217
Ecclesiastes 238
Eden 14, 15, 16
Egypt 21, 32, 33, 34, 37, 38, 39, 40, 42, 44, 45, 46, 47, 48, 49, 51, 53, 54, 56, 59, 65, 78, 95, 99,116, 124, 125, 151, 211, 226, 227, 237
Egyptians 40, 41, 42, 44, 45, 46, 47, 48, 49, 51, 56, 76, 122, 124, 125, 227, 237
Eli 74, 75, 77
Elijah 100, 101, 102, 103, 104, 105, 106, 107, 184, 185, 228, 229, 230, 231
Elimelech 72
Elisha 104, 107, 108, 109, 111
Elizabeth 146, 147
Elkanah 74
Emmaus 206, 232
Ephesians, book of 241

Ephesus 218, 222, 235, 241
Ephraim 66
epistles 241
Esau 27, 28, 31
Esther 134, 135
Esther, book of 238
Ethiopia 134
Europe 217
Eve 14, 15, 16
exile 124, 127, 231, 237, 238,239
Exodus, book of 237
Exodus, the 51, 226, 227, 228, 237
Ezekiel 127, 231, 238
Ezekiel, book of 238
Ezra 136, 137
Ezra, book of 238

F

faith 227, 231, 234, 235, 238, 241
famine 21, 37, 38, 39, 72, 171, 193, 227
farmer 16, 172
fiery furnace 128
fig leaves 15
fire 24, 47, 102, 104, 117, 199, 208, 211, 222, 223
first-born 27, 44, 48
fish 13, 46, 120, 156, 157, 180, 181, 207, 208, 235
fleece 67
flood 18, 63, 66, 227, 235
flour 101
food 17, 24, 38, 39, 46, 63, 65, 68, 73, 81, 90, 100, 125, 128, 136,153, 160, 176, 179, 180, 181, 219, 237
forbidden fruit 15
Fortress of Zion 88
frankincense 151

fruit 12, 14, 15, 140, 153, 223

G

Gabriel 146, 147
Gad 31
Galatia 241
Galatians, the 221
Galatians, book of 241
Galilee 147, 154, 156, 158, 159, 165, 168, 172, 177, 179, 196, 199, 200, 203, 209, 211, 215, 232, 233
Gamaliel 212
Garden of Gethsemane 196
Garden Tomb 233
Gaza 69, 71
Gehazi 108, 109
Genesis 237
Gennesaret 232
Gentiles 215, 218, 220, 234, 240, 241
giant 82
Gibeon 65
Gibeonites 65
Gideon 67
Gilead 32
goats 47, 49, 69, 119
goatskins 28
gold 22, 26, 37, 56, 58, 64, 96, 98, 111, 123, 125, 130, 131, 136, 151, 178, 222
golden calf 56, 57
Golgotha 202
Goliath 82, 84, 86
Gomer 238
Gomorrah 23, 118, 178
Goshen 39, 47
Gospels 240
grace 241
Greece 235

H

Habbakuk, book of 239
Hagar 22, 24
Haggai 136
Haggai, book of 239
Haman 134, 135
Hannah 74
Haran 226
harp 80, 81, 84, 141
harvest 37, 72, 73,
  108,172, 173, 176
Heaven 12, 20, 29,
  47, 53, 107, 154,
  160, 161, 164, 173,
  181, 186, 205, 209,
  213, 222, 223, 241
Heber 66
Hebrews 241
Hebron 22, 92
Herod Antipas 177,
  179, 192
Herod the Great 146,
  151, 177, 190, 232
Herodias 177, 179
Hezekiah 114, 116
high priest 197, 198,
  218, 233
Hilkiah 116
Historical Books 236,
  237
Hittite 90
Holofernes 239
Holy of Holies 58
Holy Spirit 146, 147,
  150, 153, 154, 155,
  164, 207, 209, 211,
  213, 215, 216, 222,
  234, 240, 253
Hosea 239
Hosea, book of 239
Huldah 116
Hushai 92

I

idol 56, 59, 102, 112,
  130, 229

idolatry 239
Idumea 232
India 134
insect 17
Isaac 23, 24, 25, 26,
  27, 28, 29, 42, 45,
  56, 102,212, 227,
  228, 237
Isaachar 30
Isaiah 114, 118, 119,
  156, 229, 231, 238
Isaiah, book of 238
Ishmael 22, 23, 24
Ishmaelites 32, 33
Israel 31, 39, 44, 52,
  64, 69, 72, 73, 75,
  76, 78, 79, 81, 88,
  91, 92, 95, 96, 98,
  99, 100, 102, 104,
  106, 107, 111, 112,
  113, 114, 116, 118,
  119, 122, 127, 134,
  137, 140, 142, 146,
  150, 151, 178, 206,
  209, 226, 227, 228,
  229, 230, 231, 237,
  238, 239
Israelites 34, 39, 40,
  41, 42, 44, 45, 46,
  47, 48, 49, 51, 52,
  53, 54, 56, 58, 59,
  60, 63, 64, 65, 66,
  67, 68, 76, 77, 82,
  90, 107, 110, 116,
  119,`127, 128, 136,
  211, 213, 215, 226,
  227, 228, 229, 230,
  237, 238, 239
Italy 235

J

Jabin 66
Jacob 27, 28, 29, 30,
  31, 32, 33, 38, 39,
  42, 45, 56, 102, 119,
  212, 227, 228, 237
Jael 66

jail 34, 38, 177, 212,
  214, 217, 218, 235
Jairus 168, 169
James, book of 241
James, brother of John
  157, 169, 178, 185,
  196
James, disciple 178
Jehoiakim 123
Jehu 112, 113
Jeremiah 122, 123,
  124, 125, 136, 231,
  238, 239
Jeremiah, book of 238
Jericho 60, 61, 63, 64,
  107, 125, 174, 188,
  228, 232
Jeroboam 99, 100,
  230
Jerusalem 74, 88, 90,
  92, 94, 95, 96, 98,
  113, 114, 116, 117,
  119, 124, 125, 128,
  130, 132, 136, 137,
  150, 151, 152, 165,
  166, 174, 184, 188,
  189, 190, 193, 206,
  209, 211, 214, 215,
  218, 223, 229, 230,
  231, 232, 233, 234,
  235, 237, 238, 239,
  240
Jesse 80, 81, 82
Jethro 42, 44, 53
jewels 58, 127
Jews 134, 135, 136,
  137, 160, 165, 174,
  200, 211, 215, 216,
  218, 220, 231, 232,
  233, 234, 235, 238,
  240, 241
Jezebel 100, 104, 105,
  106, 112, 113
Jezreel 105, 112
Joab 90, 93
Joash 112, 113, 116
Job 138, 139
Job, book of 238
Joel 211

Joel, book of 239
John, book of 240
John, first letter 241
John, second letter
  241
John, the apostle 157,
  169, 178, 185, 196,
  205, 208, 212, 222,
  223, 241
John the Baptist 146,
  153, 154, 177, 179,
  180, 184, 185, 192,
  209, 232
John, third letter 241
Jonah 120, 121
Jonah, book of 239
Jonathan 84, 85, 86,
  88
Joram 112
Joseph, Jacob's son
  31, 32, 33, 34, 35,
  36, 37, 38, 39, 40,
  49, 227, 237
Joseph, Mary's
  husband
  147, 148, 150, 151,
  152, 156
Joseph of Arimathea
  204
Joshua 53, 57, 60, 61,
  63, 64, 65, 66, 228
Joshua, book of 237
Josiah 99, 116, 117,
  122, 123
Judah 30, 33, 39, 91,
  95, 99, 112, 113,
  114, 116, 117, 119,
  122, 123, 124, 127,
  128, 130, 131, 132,
  134, 137, 228, 229,
  230, 231, 238, 239
Judas Iscariot 178,
  193, 194, 195, 197,
  199, 209
Jude 241
Judea 151, 153, 165,
  187, 200, 209, 215,
  232, 233
Judges, book of 237

ACKNOWLEDGMENTS

The publishers would like to thank the following artists
for their contributions to this book:

MAIN ILLUSTRATIONS:

Vanessa Card; Gino D'Achille *(Artist Partners Ltd)*;
Richard Garland *(Advocate)*; Michael Langham Rowe;
Massimiliano Longo *(Milan Illustrations Agency)*;
Chris Molan; Nick Spender *(Advocate)*

ADDITIONAL ILLUSTRATIONS:

Harry Bishop; Rob Hefferan *(Advocate)*;
David Kearney *(Artist Partners Ltd)*; John Keay;
Kevin Maddison; Rob Perry *(Advocate)*;
Francis Phillipps; Martin Reiner;
Timothy Slade; John Woodcock

The publishers would also like to thank the following
for supplying photographs for this book:

226 *tr* AKG London/Erich Lessing; **227** *tl* Robert Harding Picture Library/Michael Short,
c AKG London/Erich Lessing, *br* AKG London/Erich Lessing;
228 *cl* Robert Harding Picture Library/E. Simanor; **229** *tr* AKG London/Erich Lessing,
c AKG London/Erich Lessing; **230** *tr* Radu & Dinu Mendrea,
br AKG London/Erich Lessing; **231** TL AKG London,
bl Zev Radovan, Jerusalem; **232** *cr* Robert Harding Picture Library,
bl Ancient Art & Architecture/Ronald Sheridan; **233** *tl* Radu & Dinu Mendrea,
cr Radu & Dinu Mendrea; **234** *tr* Radu & Dinu Mendrea,
cl Robert Harding Picture Library/Tony Gervis, *c* Sonia Halliday Photographs,
br Robert Harding Picture Library; **235** BR Radu & Dinu Mendrea;
236 *tr* Ancient Art & Architecture, *cl* AKG London/Jean-Louis Nou,
bl Sonia Halliday Photographs, *br* Radu & Dinu Mendrea;
238 *bl* AKG London/Erich Lessing; **239** T Peter Sanders;
241 *cr* Sonia Halliday Photographs; **247** *br* Ancient Art & Architecture,
248 *bl* Robert Harding Picture Library/Photri

Every effort has been made to trace the copyright holders of the photographs.
The publishers apologize for any inconvenience caused.

The publishers also wish to thank Jennie Morris and Hannah Wilson
for their editorial assistance.